WRITING JOYCE

Advances in Semiotics

Thomas A. Sebeok, General Editor

WRITING JOYCE

A Semiotics of the Joyce System

LORRAINE WEIR

INDIANA UNIVERSITY PRESS
Bloomington and Indianapolis

Manufactured in the United States of America

Library of Congress Cataloging-in-Publication Data
Weir, Lorraine
Writing Joyce.

(Advances in semiotics)
Bibliography: p.
Includes index.
1. Joyce, James, 1882-1941—Criticism and inter-
pretation.   2. Semiotics and literature.   I. Title.
II. Title: Semiotics of the Joyce system.   III. Series.
PR6019.09Z94   1989   823'.912   88-45501
ISBN 0-253-36432-9
1 2 3 4 5 93 92 91 90 89

Lucan magister
(1977–1985)

"The work of art is a system of systems."

—Eco, *Theory of Semiotics*

"We have a duty towards music, namely, to invent it."

—Stravinsky, *Poetics of Music*

"The task is to see the riddle."
—Heidegger, Epilogue, "The Origin of
the Work of Art"

CONTENTS

FIGURES

ACKNOWLEDGMENTS

For detailed readings of the manuscript at various stages of production, I am indebted to Bernard Benstock, Robert M. Jordan, and Lorna Weir. For travel grants which made it possible for me to read early formulations of some of the material on Vico and *Finnegans Wake* in Venice (1985) and on catechism and catachresis in Copenhagen (1986), I am indebted to the Social Sciences and Humanities Research Council of Canada. Without a Leave Fellowship from the same agency in 1984–85 and a year's leave from the English Department of the University of British Columbia, this project would have been impossible. Without Paul Bouissac's invitation to give a version of the manuscript as a course on "Semiotics of the Joyce System" at the Ninth International Summer Institute for Semiotic and Structural Studies in Toronto in 1987, *Writing Joyce* might have gone on forever. Thanks to Thomas A. Sebeok, its end became a new beginning.

Portions of this book have appeared in earlier forms in *Texte*, the *Canadian Journal of Irish Studies*, and *Coping with Joyce*, ed. M. Beja and S. Benstock (Ohio Univ. Press, forthcoming).

I want also to thank my students in Vancouver and Toronto who have made theorizing in the classroom a joyous activity, often at times when its prospects otherwise in Canadian universities seemed bleakest; my research assistant, Cindy Flanders, who found footnotes and remained patient through an epic summer; Peter Quartermain, my teacher in all things Zukofskian; Mieke Bal and Wladimir Krysinski for support and encouragement; and, last and first, Peig McTague.

Extracts from *The New Science of Giambattista Vico* are reprinted from the Un-
abridged Translation of the Third Edition (1744) with the addition of "Practic of
the New Science," translated by Thomas Goddard Bergin and Max Harold Fisch.
Copyright 1948 by Cornell University. Used by permission of the publisher, Cornell
University Press.

Extracts from *"A"*, *Bottom: On Shakespeare* and *Prepositions* by Louis Zukofsky
are reprinted by permission of the University of California Press.

Diagram from *Semiotics and the Philosophy of Language* by Umberto Eco is used
by permission of Indiana University Press.

ABBREVIATIONS

"A" Zukofsky, Louis. *"A."* Berkeley: Univ. of California Press, 1978.

B Barthes, Roland. "Loyola." In *Sade/Fourier/Loyola*, trans. Richard Miller. New York: Hill and Wang, 1976.

E Joyce, James. *Exiles*. New York: Viking Press, 1951.

FW Joyce, James. *Finnegans Wake*. New York: Viking Press, 1958. Page and line numbers are cited parenthetically.

JJII Ellmann, Richard. *James Joyce*. Rev. ed. New York: Oxford Univ. Press, 1982.

NS Vico, Giambattista. *The New Science*. Trans. from the 3d ed. by Thomas Goddard Bergin and Max Harold Fisch. Ithaca: Cornell Univ. Press, 1948.

P Joyce, James. *A Portrait of the Artist as a Young Man*. The definitive text corrected from the Dublin holograph by Chester G. Anderson and edited by Richard Ellmann. New York: Viking Press, 1964.

SH Joyce, James. *Stephen Hero*, ed. John J. Slocum and Herbert Cahoon. New York: New Directions, 1963.

U Joyce, James. *Ulysses. The Corrected Text*, ed. Hans Walter Gabler with Wolfhard Steppe and Claus Melchior. New York: Random House, 1986. Episode and line numbers are cited parenthetically.

WRITING JOYCE

I

CONFIGURING THE SYSTEM
AN INTRODUCTION

> "To deconstruct is to do memory work."
>
> —Derrida, *Memoires*

> "His writing is not *about* something;
> *it is that something itself.*"
>
> —Beckett, "Dante . . . Bruno.
> Vico . . Joyce"

> "*In illo tempore . . .* "

Joyce

Joyce? Surely not James Augustine Aloysius Joyce (1882–1941), now of "Aleph, alpha: nought, nought, one" (*U* 3.39), a number "out of order" as we say. No fingernail parings in sight.

Trademark, then. Sign denoting system, "the Joyce system." Sign? A light which, lovingly subjected to prolonged exegesis and the production of perfect texts, will finally reveal . . . what? whom? If light, in darkness? Where? Only "written words? Signs on a white field" (*U* 3.15) after all?

"Yes" and also "the": end-words leaving us without endings, happy or otherwise (will Molly make Poldy's breakfast or not? some readers ask themselves; does Anna Livia's last word run the salmon leap and, "riverrun," begin the narrative again?). "Here, weir, reach, island, bridge," the *Wake* counsels (*FW* 626.07). Well then, I will.

System

Meeting that performative injunction demands competence in the working of "Once upon a time" and "Stately, plump Buck Mulligan" and "riverrun, past

Eve and Adam's,'' components of a system which is their aggregate and which, as linguists and cognitive scientists use the term, ''generates'' those components in their networks of interbranching subsystems. To write the system is both to invent and to perform it: ''invent'' in the medieval rhetorical sense of *inventio*, to come upon or discover what is already given and, working with the text, to ''draw out'' or foreground its modes of operation. In the process of acquiring competence in the working of the system, to write Joyce is to be written by the system which is ''Joyce,'' to submit to that ''order othered'' (*FW* 613.14) which is bracketed in *Finnegans Wake* by recursive markers of present and past, ''Fiatfuit'' (*FW* 17.32),''*Fuitfiat*'' (*FW* 613.14): performative injunctions once again.

''*Fiat*'': ''Let it be done unto me according to thy word'' (Luke 1:38): the doubly performative contract known as the Annunciation or response by Mary to the angel Gabriel, the announcing of her willingness to conceive Christ the word. Her strategy becomes a techne[1]: giving birth to the Word, she inaugurates both gestation and extratextuality as signs of writing or, to put it differently, she becomes what Umberto Eco calls a ''Model Reader'' or ''textually established set of felicity conditions . . . to be met in order to have a macro-speech act (such as a text is) fully actualized.''[2] But the referent comes eventually to dominate discourse, claiming ''truth-conditionality'' and ''sincerity'' (those Austinian signs of ''Presence'') as requisites necessary to the enactment of the performative. And by the time of Luther, the sacred text's revelatory capacity, its *kerygma* or proclamation of the divine referent, becomes a sign of the referentiality of the world. This is the proclamation of a truth made manifest to all believers, the beginning of a hermeneutic which— like its contemporary successors in the tradition of Austin and Searle, on the one hand, and Gadamer and Iser, on the other—would exact the democratic norm of felicity conditions from utterance and/as text, proclaim a truth manifest to all believers, and eventually become complicit in the proclamation of the humanist hegemony of Enlightenment. The encyclopedia is but a step away.[3]

''*Fuit*.'' Existing in other times, modernity closes the gap opened by the Enlightenment's Cartesian rupture of word and world and by its privileging of referential mimesis as both aesthetic and ontological techne. So the speculary ''Realism'' of nineteenth-century fiction, that literary reflection of the mercantile codes of emergent high capitalism, gives way to the *specula*/tive forms characteristic of modernity, whether medieval or twentieth-century, spanning the gap of humanism. With its encyclopedic claims and speculary ontology,[4] the book gives way once again to writing and to ''processual mimesis,''[5] thus performative discourse.

To write Joyce is to trace these ontotheological transformations; to account for the many technai of the system in terms of its own codes, directives and operations; to explore the conditions of competence designated by the system, this vast ''event created by language.''[6] In writing Joyce, we encounter the system as a teaching machine whose purpose is to teach us itself, leading us through the five-finger exercises of *Portrait* to the sequence of learning programs, ever increasing in complexity and mnemonic challenge, which is *Ulysses*, and into the dream narrative of *Finnegans Wake*, where dream sanction operates not a counter-narrative folded inside a referential-mimetic one but an *elaboratio*, an *inventio*, on the theme of the problematic of post-Cartesian narrative. And so back to *Portrait* with its Ignatian mnemonics and the "roturn" (*FW* 18.05) of the memory wheel.

In writing Joyce, we configure modernity as suture across the gap of the Enlightenment and, in following this vast performance system's[7] text directives, its instructions for processing and operating itself, we (re-)invent that "applied grammatology"[8] which stands in metonymic relation to modernity in all its forms, whether architectural or theoretical, whether musical or mathematical. Using the lexicon and some of the logical operations of Derridean deconstruction and Ecoian semiotics, we enter a system which generates them as it continues with every turn of the wheel to generate Vico and Ignatius Loyola, Quinet, Michelet and Zukofsky. In this vast ricorsive memory theater, "Nought is nulled" (*FW* 613.14) and the othering of order is an exercise in recombinant semes structuring, in Eco's phrase, a "semiosic web"[9] which is productive of its own noesis, thereby attempting—like Vico's *Scienza Nuova*—to heal the wound which is humanism.

Writing

"To control," writes Susan Oyama, "is not to stand outside the causal world; it is to rearrange oneself in it."[10] The condition of its *integritas*—that form of control demanded by a performance system—requires not passive submission on our part but, rather, engagement in its processing. Thus not a conversion, a permanent transcoding operation, but the demand placed on the listener by complex music, the willingness to be programmed, to enter into processually governed expectation, anticipation, and resolution. Our task, to rearrange ourselves "in" the system, is initially a theological one. But where is "inside"? If to process the system is not to stand "outside" its semantic claims, then how do we approach the task of standing "inside" it?

The challenge posed by this task *seems* to be a hermeneutic one; *Writing Joyce* responds using semiotics within a Derridean-deconstructive paradigm. Consider an ancient analogy: we are rebuilding a ship at sea, replacing one plank at a time. The structure, the system, is already given. Wiping our glosses with what we know, as the *Wake* instructs (*FW* 304.F3), our invention will succeed only to the extent that—to mix metaphors—our planks are a good fit and, perhaps, that we prefer teak to balsa wood. Further, we must operate in accordance with the design of the whole structure, and not simply of the particular instance. This analogy obviously has its limits, however, and we may still easily sink, not only because our materials may be inadequate to the task but also because we have missed connections in the system and our invention loses its theme.

It is a chance every textual analyst must take. In apprenticing ourselves to a cognitive architecture governed by performative injunction, we are "always already" bound by systemic codes. And since our boat is of the sort beloved of logicians, we are dealing with a nonreferential structure, a vast *Gedankenexperiment* or Borgesian aleph which, as fiction, lays no claims to truth-conditionality.[11] "Felicity,'' then—if such there be sans Marian "fiat"—consists only in our readerly willingness to learn the system or, refusing the task, to leave it to its own devices. The Joyce system, in other words, exists in a state of bounded implicature, knowing only itself, a feedback loop possessed of the materials necessary to its own invention. Fortunately, our analytic effort is also a community one, and we learn from each others' cognitive gaps and from our own "hides and hints and misses in prints" (*FW* 20.11) as well as our failures at appropriate operation of, for example, culinary codes which enjoin against the use of forks as weapons (*FW* 124.09).

Writing Joyce is, then, *a* semiotics of *the* Joyce system, and it assumes that the system stands in spite of the imperfections and idiosyncracies of any analysis, and thus that the analysis is, in logical terms, a second-order activity since systemic data are taken to preexist each particular writing of the system. However, in order to write the system, a metasystem must be created such that the demands of the system can be thought within the expanded frame of a deconstructive *inventio*. One of the results of this operation for the writing of the system is the production of a series of embedded texts which are slowly brought into alignment with systemic text-directives. This way of writing the system in itself produces a memory theater or teaching machine with its lexicon assembled in two ways: first, according to systemic text-directive, and second, according to systemic logic determining the outcome of linking operations. Thus in chapter 2, *Portrait* directs us to Ignatius Loyola's *Spiritual Exercises*, within which is embedded the catechetical "technic" foregrounded in *Ulysses* along with numerous extensions of mnemonic procedures operant in *Portrait* and expanded under the heading of *mnemotechnic* to meet the epic demands of mnemonic processing later in the system.

Those demands are epitomized in the development of a "technic" which synthesizes pun, riddle, allegorical trope, mirror language of the Jabberwocky sort, and epiphany as defined in *Stephen Hero*. At the metasystemic level, then, catechism bridges into catachresis which encompasses the semantic demands made by all of the terms in the preceding list. At this point, the introduction of Derrida on catachresis in *Glas* not only enables us to think the transformation from catechism to catachresis but also in a sense is already determined by the system insofar as Derrida's project is, in part, a Joycean deconstruction of modernity. Similarly, the transcoding of Joycean "technic" to techne and the embedding of Paul Ricoeur's reading of techne and of processual mimesis within the system enable us to begin the project of thinking the meaning of the Joyce system's performative operations. The same is the case with the introduction of Kenneth Burke's dramatistic theory of enactment with its embedding of the Thomist concept of form as act, an operation which brings a neo-Thomist theory of the performative into alignment with semiotic theories of gesture and of theatrical performance.[12]

In order to enable the reader to orient him- or herself quickly to this at times necessarily convoluted argument, I have preferred throughout *Writing Joyce* to choose textual examples from among a range of frequently cited and, for the most part, familiar Joyce passages. And, as we have already seen, terms as fundamental to Joycean critical practice as *epiphany, catechism* and *techne/technic* are reconsidered here although my quest is for neither of the typical contexts in which these concepts have traditionally been discussed, that is, in terms of the historical Joyce and of the Realist mode. That rejection of referential mimesis as operant strategy is a crucial determinant not only of the development of the Joyce system itself but, inevitably, of the writing of the system as well. One of the results of that challenge is the rejection of the custom, dating back to Stuart Gilbert's *James Joyce's "Ulysses,"* of referring to the chapters of *Ulysses* by their Homeric titles. This does not, of course, foreclose on Homeric transcodings of *Ulysses* since, as many commentators have shown, the requisite materials are embedded within the Joyce system. But it does help to break the habit of Realist domestication of the text, a habit which is surprisingly hard to break for anyone who has worked with the system as usually construed and has developed a form of nostalgia presently much encouraged by the fetishization of Joyce *in propria persona.*[13]

Perhaps, however, it is more difficult to become nostalgic about *Finnegans Wake,* and the shift from character names to sigla here may be the occasion of fewer problems for some readers, particularly as Roland McHugh has already paved the way for such a transition.[14] Finally, it should be noted that in its rejection of an implicit theology of the hermeneutic sort in favor of an explicit one which may be logologized, *Writing Joyce* is, despite its emphasis on performative discourse, concerned neither with the so-called oscillating perspectives of the subject nor with the apparently ever-receding horizons of Iserian theories of performance.[15]

Logology

If it is not the Protestant-humanist theology of phenomenological hermeneutics which motivates this writing, then, as Eco says, what theology does "legitimize" it?[16] In *The Rhetoric of Religion,* Kenneth Burke provides a response:

> If we defined "theology" as "words about God," then by "logology" we should mean "words about words." Whereupon, thoughts on the necessarily verbal nature of religious doctrines suggest a further possibility: that there might be fruitful analogies between the two realms. Thus statements that great theologians have made about the nature of "God" might be adapted *mutatis mutandis* for use as purely secular observations on the nature of *words.*
>
> [. . .]
>
> Hence, it should be possible to analyze remarks about the "nature of 'God,' " like remarks about the "nature of 'Reason,' " in their sheer formality as observations about the nature of language. And such a correspondence between the theological and the "logological" realms should be there, whether or not "God" actually *exists.* For regardless of whether the entity named "God" exists outside his nature sheerly as key term in a system of terms, words "about him" must reveal their nature as words.[17]

That key term or "summarizing word," Burke concludes, "is functionally a 'god-term,' "[18] and its language-making operations are, to use Roland Barthes' term in

Sade/Fourier/Loyola, "logothesis" (*B* 5), which is synonymous with the process of *inventio*.

Burke's trope opens the possibility of working *with* the grain of an explicitly theological system without falling back into the humanist substitution and commodification of psyche (old style) or subject (new style) as telos, and without writing theology. It is a version of a practice which Burke himself refers to as "joycing."[19] The construction of a materialist semiotics within a deconstructive paradigm thus requires a willingness to accept the Joyce system's explicit rejection of that mode of referential mimesis which may in part be summarized under the heading of psychologism in its various forms, and a willingness to jettison that teleological drive toward "aboutness" which the "Realist" tradition took as its speculary focus and which Western capitalist ontotheologies perpetuate through the dualist fetishization of "subjectivity." The drive to produce character and plot out of the materials of the Joyce system is, then, on this view, a reading *against* the system, a reading involved in the inevitable replaying of the narrative of the dominant ideology which is overlayered upon the system by, and becomes invisible to, those who choose this cognitive frame.

Taking a variety of forms, the drive toward reification of the components of the Joyce system includes the perpetuation of Realist readings of the texts, the recent search for the Holy Grail in the form of the pure text as fetish—a stage in Joycean critical practice which threatens to impose the entropy of a hermeneutic/exegetical method for decades to come—and, of course, the possibilities for reification associated with Greimassian semiotics with its emphasis upon geometric fixity of grids and paradigms. Which is not to argue against the use of the second and third of these textual strategies (though certainly against the first) but, rather, to indicate caution precisely with respect to the framing of the resultant data and the selection of semiotic modality required by the focal system.

Toward what Jurij Lotman classifies as a "dynamic model of a semiotic system," then[20]; toward a materialist semiotics which can accommodate processual mimesis and which can work with a textual system as a network of semiosis—a "semiosic web." In processing the system, in following its encoded programs according to text-directives, we acquire competence in its operation/s. This process is what I call "working the system," a cognitive activity impossible without the prior acquisition of a considerable degree of fluency in working its components. To the extent that we acquire such competence, we are "inside" the system and free to "rearrange" ourselves in its cognitive architecture (in the sense in which computer designers speak of the machine's architecture or modes of configuration of data), in terms of which we learn to configure the system by achieving facility in its maneuvers. We are, to use another computer cliché, "formatted" by the system as we process it, and we therefore become capable of knowing or experiencing it.

Like any pedagogical system grounded in sequential processing of increasingly complex data and logical operations, the Joyce system initiates us (as chapter 2 argues) in *A Portrait of the Artist as a Young Man* into the practice of what Barthes refers to as the "exercising of the *Exercises*" (*B* 42), an operation basic to the processing of the system as a whole, that is, to *Portrait*, *Ulysses*, and *Finnegans Wake* considered as one vast system.[21] At the same time, *Portrait* inducts us into the elementary use of catechetical paradigms and of epiphany as processual strategy, both operations which will become much more complex in *Ulysses* and *Finnegans Wake*. Later, as catechism branches into catachresis in *Ulysses* and the requirements of "postcreation" (*U* 14.294) incline the system toward an increasingly complex memory theater, the system's performative injunctions become more and more frequent and its encoding of logological modes of transsubstantiation and anastomosis more evident.

In part, this sacramental trope is the process which Joseph Frank identified as "Spatial Form in Modern Literature" in his classic essay,[22] but Frank's attempt to use what Kenneth Burke would call the dominantly visual "terministic screen"[23] of Lessing's *Laocoön* in order to resolve the telos of *Ulysses* into a static moment of all-comprehending noesis results in a reification of Frank's logological point. Deconstructing Frank's concept of "spatial form" in chapter 3 becomes a sustained exercise in memory work with the help of the "high semiotics"[24] of Augustine, Aquinas, and the inheritors of this tradition in contemporary sacramental theology. As both Zukofsky's "*A*" and *Finnegans Wake* teach, before we can forget, we must remember, and remembering back through some fundamental principles of sacramental theology, we encounter a rhetoric which is already well accommodated to its subject and which, if approached logologically, may enable us to formulate a theory of performative enactment of the Joyce system.

In his list of the "Ten Little Middle Ages" in *Travels in Hyperreality*, Eco has characterized this practice in terms of the persistence of the *philosophia perennis* in many contemporary kinds of "formal and logical thinking."[25] As he remarks, "the perennial vigor of the Middle Ages is not derived necessarily from religious assumptions, and there is a lot of hidden medievalism in some speculative and systematic approaches of our time, such as structuralism."[26] By foregrounding some of these materials in *Writing Joyce* we do, however, run the risk of slipping into that form of neo-Thomism which Eco sees looming behind "the pastoral and dogmatic views of Pius XII or John Paul II . . . ,"[27] the negative side of the *philosophia perennis*.

We can, of course, avoid the risk by refusing to deal with the theological aspect of the Joyce system, or we can adopt Burke's strategy of logologizing while retaining awareness of the drive of the Joyce system toward all-inclusiveness (though certainly not toward the doctrinal stances of Eco's looming figures). For many readers, this will still seem to be an enormous risk but it is one which the Joyce system requires us to take if we wish to work (with) it. Until we have undergone this Classical exercise in discipline in the guise of mnemotechnic, we are not free to re-member the system for we must already know the function of each of its members within the semiosic web from which it derives its meaning. Having deduced form, we define function.

It is essential to note again, however, that where the visualist analogies characteristic of Iserian-phenomenological approaches to performative discourse (as well as of Frank's concept of "spatial form") would logically lead us to individualist interpretations based on shifting horizons or Riquelmian "oscillating perspectives" experienced uniquely by each perceiver, semiotic analysis of this sort is not concerned with focalizing the viewer's position (whether horizon or perspective) and determining how that stance affects individual apprehension of the text. Such a subjectivist approach inevitably produces, as Georges Poulet has argued, a description of the interpreter who contains the text and without whom the text has no meaning.[28] Materialist semiotics by definition can have little or nothing to do with such Platonizing moves.

Modernity

"The word 'modern,' " writes Ernst Curtius in his great compendium, *European Literature and the Latin Middle Ages*, "is one of the last legacies of late Latin to the modern world."[29] First appearing in the sixth century, *modernus*, derived from *modo* ("now"), rendered possible for the first time the comparison of ancients and moderns, *antiqui* and *moderni*, an antithesis perpetuated in battles of books ever since. One twelfth-century variation on this theme, the skirmish between *artes* and *auctores*, forced the *moderni* of 1170 onto the defensive, as Curtius notes. Roger Bacon (d. 1294) summarizes the main issues as follows:

> For the past forty years certain men have risen up in the disciplines and have made themselves masters and doctors of theology and philosophy, although they had learned nothing worth knowing. . . . They are boys who know nothing of themselves or of the world or of the learned tongues—Greek and Hebrew. . . . These are the boys of the two university orders, such as Albert [Albertus Magnus] and Thomas [Aquinas] and others, who in many cases enter [holy] orders at twenty or even younger. . . . Thousands enter who can read neither the Psalms or Donatus, yet who as soon as they have taken their vows are set to study theology. . . . Hence endless error rules amongst them.[30]

Similarly, the insistence upon brevity and the castigation of the ancients for their superfluity of expression, charges made by the first rhetorician to identify himself as a modern, Matthew of Vendôme, could only have resulted in the further alienation of anyone aligned, like Bacon, with the ancients. Consider, for example, Matthew's typically modern way of condemning the ancients for their erring ways. "Hoc autem modernis non licet," he declares;[31] such habits are not permitted by modern practice.

Not only is the term *modern* not a recent invention but modes of text production typical of modernism have much in common with their medieval antecedents, as such medievalists as Eugène Vinaver, Paul Zumthor, and Eugene Vance have been pointing out for many years.[32] Mikhail Bakhtin's concern with the polyglossia and "interinanimation of languages" characteristic of the "prehistory of novelistic discourse" is an aspect of the same study, as is his analysis of the relation between epic and novel.[33] My point is, however, not that medieval and twentieth-century versions of the modern are identical in theory and/or practice but, rather, that in following the Joyce system's text-directives which draw the two together, we undertake a Joycean version of thinking an expanded concept of modernity. More than an importation of "modernité," then, modernity in *Writing Joyce* designates a complex heritage, which is summed up in chapter 3 under the heading of "Gothic pedagogy."[34]

One of the agents in this process is Kristeva's concept of intertextuality,[35] a concept thoroughly familiar to medieval writers engaged in the grafting of one text onto another and producing layered intradiegetic as well as marginal commentaries. Characteristic of a period of roughly fifteen hundred years during which history consisted of the palimpsesting through constant "retranslation and reuse"[36] of past and present "auctoritees," this medieval version of postmodernist "historiography" was grounded in an apprehension of history as a continuous, present-tense process, a performative enactment of contrafacted[37] time as text. In the Joyce system's version of this process, the systems of Aquinas, Ignatius Loyola, and Giambattista Vico, among others, function as intertexts, components not of the encyclopedic mode, as is often maintained, but of the tradition of the *speculum* and of what I refer to as *specula*/tive allegory. As is paradigmatically the case with *Finnegans Wake*'s privileging of the "Tunc" page of the Book of Kells (*FW* 122.23), the Joyce system rhymes *then* and *now, tunc* and *nunc,* in a grammatology which inscribes Vico's Derridean theory of writing into a Gothic pedagogy of the *speculum.*

Logologically considered, contrafacted history, with its vast systems of rhetoric governing all of the arts, is the continuous revolutionary *now* of modernity across Western culture. In terms of Gothic architecture, it is the geometric *manifestatio* of world-order, a visual performative.[38] So conceived, modernity has dominated Western thought for many more centuries than post-Cartesian reconstructions of world-order which we continue to think of as characteristically modern in spite of all evidence to the contrary in the arts, as well as in philosophy and the physical sciences. However, it cannot be denied that there are severe ideological constraints upon this reading of modernity, for to accept the bracketing of humanism as a transient phenomenon is an event fraught with consequences unacceptable to many of us. Nonetheless, this is the direction which the Joyce system as an "archeology of our thought" takes, a direction precisely described in Foucault's conclusion to his great study of this historical othering process, *The Order of Things.* "Man," Foucault writes,

> is an invention of recent date. And one perhaps nearing its end.
> If those arrangements [of thought] were to disappear as they appeared, if some event of which we can at the moment do no more than sense the possibility [. . .] were to cause them to crumble, as the ground of Classical thought once did, at the end of the eighteenth century, then one can certainly wager that man would be erased, like a face drawn in sand at the edge of the sea.[39]

In tracing the disappearance of that face, modernity in the twentieth century has sought, through the disruption of the cognitive architecture of humanism, to set in place a network of logical conduits which may mend the gap opened by the En-lightenment.

Taking modernity as historical paradigm, *Writing Joyce* considers an array of relations between medieval and twentieth-century semiotics relevant to the Joyce system. Our purpose is not a comparison between medieval and twentieth-century sign theories, however, but a writing of the Joyce system—that "immense work of bricolage, balanced among nostalgia, hope, and despair," as Eco describes medieval modes of preservation of the past[40]—within the "continuous present tense integument" (*FW* 186.01) which it designates as its own field of enactment.

To be distinguished from postmodernism's dream of a limited modernism—a dream which forgets, for example, that Pound's making it new required study of Arnaut Daniel and Eliot's of Dante—this Joycean discursive network rejects the notion that modernity may be confined to, say, Paris in the twenties or inscribed within a referential-subjectivist paradigm. And where, as Andreas Huyssen has argued, American poststructuralism has allied itself with the " 'anything goes' variety"[41] of postmodernism in its commodity fetishization of the subject, *Writing Joyce* works the Joyce system within the paradigm of modernity which it shares with Derridean deconstruction.

This attempt to avoid the flicker or "moiré"[42] effect caused by theorizing the Joyce system within postmodernism's paradigm of a limited modernism seeks also to align the Joyce system with a theoretical practice grounded in the system's own operations. An othering operation performed upon "order," the Joyce system is an "applied grammatology," a carefully programmed deconstruction of precisely those concepts which postmodernism associates with modernism and which—as is paradigmatically the case with the Gothic pedagogy of modernity—cannot be ex-perienced in any other way than through textual production leading to performative enactment.

Envoi

My "auctoritees" are many, and I am happy not to claim neo-Romantic "origi-nality" for *Writing Joyce*. Where Burke's logology makes it possible to work with sacramental theology without theologizing, Derrida's grammatology makes it pos-sible to think the results of the first operation into the second, of logology into the writing of the system itself. These are two of the core moves or macro-operations of this enterprise. In turn, a series of "terministic screens" has been used in the analysis of various aspects of the system, in each case designated by it. Thus Ignatius Loyola's *Spiritual Exercises*, Vico's *Scienza Nuova*, and various theories of *musica speculativa*, filtered through aspects of another analysis: Barthes' *Loyola*, Donald Phillip Verene's *Vico's Science of the Imagination*, Louis Zukofsky's "*A.*"

Other core materials for *Writing Joyce* have come from Vincent Descombes on the encyclopedia, John Freccero on Augustinian speech act theory, Emile Benven-iste's and Barbara Johnson's recastings of Austin's theory of the performative, and Paul Ricoeur on the theory of mimesis in *The Rule of Metaphor*. Among Joyce scholars, Umberto Eco has been the pioneer in medieval/modern studies with his *Aesthetics of Chaosmos*. That *Writing Joyce* would have been impossible without Eco's development of materialist semiotics will be obvious, and although I sometimes disagree with his conclusions (for example, in my reworking in chapter 4 of Eco on the encyclopedia and on Deleuze and Guattari's theory of the rhizome), I am happy to acknowledge my particular indebtedness to Eco's masterpiece, *Semiotics and the Philosophy of Language*. Gregory Ulmer's study of Derrida, *Applied Grammatology*, has also been crucial to my understanding of the Joyce system as a pedagogy.

It is a pleasure to see that the works of two of the finest readers of the Joyce system, Jacques Derrida and Umberto Eco, can be brought together in the analysis of the system and that, contrary to the dogma of some theory-commentators, materialist semiotics and Derridean deconstruction need not be seen as fundamentally opposed. Although this is not the place to develop this argument, I hope it will also be clear that, again *pace* some commentators, it is not because both modes are, to use that singularly vague and unhelpful term, "poststructuralist" that they can be harmonized. Despite the fact that both semiotics and deconstruction are characteristic of modernity, neither has its roots exclusively or even primarily in the twentieth century. The impact of medieval sign theory, of Scholastic methodology, and of C. S. Peirce's neo-Scholastic semiotics on Eco, and of Rabbinical traditions of exegesis of Torah and Talmud on Derrida,[43] are further indications of modernity's *specula*/tive development across the gap of the Enlightenment.

Like all memory theaters, *Writing Joyce* is a product of a community of mind/brains,[44] and I hope that it will prove useful to those interested in semiotics and theory in general as well as to those primarily concerned with Joyce. The Joyce system teaches a mode of semiotic configuration which, if it is meaningful to say that this system is paradigmatic of modernity, ought to be widely applicable as a *model* (though certainly not in all of its specifics) to other modern texts, whether pre- or post-Enlightenment. Although I do not claim that all modern texts work as the Joyce system does, it would be interesting to see to what extent, for example, Gertrude Stein's production does. The model should also be applicable to the tradition of what I have called *specula*/tive allegory, a genre which persists as a strategy of resistance across the rupture of the Enlightenment, as is evident in such examples as Sterne's *Tristram Shandy*, Melville's *Moby Dick* and William Blake's *Jerusalem* and *The Four Zoas*.[45]

As for the predictive capacity of descriptive semiotics, it must also be said that there are those who regard this analytic mode as being in itself so powerful that any text, once fed into the hopper of semiotics, will emerge not only dis- (rather than re-) membered but uniformly sausage-shaped as well. However, given both the complexity of the Joyce system and the processual nature of the "dynamic model of semiotics" employed in this book, I hope I have been unsuccessful in producing such results. Our aim is the exploration and description of the workings of a system governed by performative injunction. Mourning the departure of plot and character, however, there will likely still be some readers who will perceive the antihumanist force of the Joyce system as in some way personally dehumanizing (so fragile is our sense of our own hegemony, after all) or who will believe semiotics in itself to be a mode destructive of the "life" of texts. Those for whom their own existence is an insufficient sign of "life" will likely never be happy with either semiotics or the Joyce system.

Of course, a descriptive semiotics is only as "good"—logical, thorough, detailed, conceptually rigorous—as the system it takes as focus. In the case of the Joyce system, no single example of a descriptive-semiotic analysis can ever be inclusive enough, but not, I would argue, because of limitations inherent in the methodology (though different methods logically produce different results, the specifics of the data base, so to speak, should not be significantly altered from one analysis of the same factors to another). Rather, it is because of the limitations of time, patience, knowledge, and inventive capacity of the analyst. It is a truism of Joyce criticism that no one ever knows enough to know the whole system thoroughly, and this is no less the case where the analysis is a semiotic one.

Finally, it should be noted that, in spite of the claims of many commentators to the contrary, neither Derridean deconstruction nor Ecoian semiotics is "neutral" or "value-free" or claims ideological "purity." Neither does the Joyce system. All are involved in thinking/configuring/inventing—and resisting—an array of the constituents of Western culture. That this process in *Writing Joyce* is also, as is the case with Luciano Berio's analysis of tone and register in *Ulysses*, an *Omaggio a Joyce* is a crucial aspect of its inscription.

II

BARTHES' *LOYOLA*/JOYCE'S *PORTRAIT*

TAXONOMY AND PARADIGM

"Now, patience; and remember patience is the
great thing, and above all things else we
must avoid anything like being or becoming
out of patience."

—*FW* 108.08

"Yet is no body present here which was not
there before. Only is order othered."

—*FW* 613.13

Finnegans Wake is a text preoccupied with its own condition of being, its own
textuality and performance system. Again and again the *Wake* interrogates its readers, inscribing them within its own pedagogical injunctions, deconstructing its own
system ("His producers are they not his consumers?" [*FW* 497.01]), foregrounding
its own "stolentelling" (*FW* 424.35). The same could be said of *Ulysses* and *A
Portrait of the Artist as a Young Man*: in the case of the former, most obviously
in III.2 with its catechetical techne or mode of processing and production; in the
case of the latter, in the third or retreat chapter with its Ignatian *Spiritual Exercises*
as pedagogical modeling system. Each of these texts has, in Borges' words, created
its own precursors.[1] Each functions within the Joyce system as a whole while
fulfilling its pedagogical function in the traditional, sequential manner, proceeding
from least to most complex. *Portrait*, then, is the beginning of this induction process.

In *The Archeology of Knowledge*, Michel Foucault has argued that "The frontiers
of a book are never clear-cut: [. . .] it is caught up in a system of references to
other books, other texts, other sentences: it is a node within a network."[2] Ignatius
Loyola's schema for the production of what Barthes refers to as "semiophany" (*B*
53) is one node within the semiotic network of the *Portrait*, one "precursor"
inscribed across the discourse system which is the text. But Loyola's priority is a
matter not of chronology or biography but of textual necessity and performative

injunction. Barthes' analysis of the *Spiritual Exercises* is an implicit archeology, an intertextual mapping, of Ignatian calisthenics in their relation to *Portrait*. By constituting this Barthesian reading as one node within the network of the Joyce system, we begin the work of articulating *Portrait*'s pedagogical strategies and of inscribing its third chapter as a model for the production of the text as a whole.[3] This bifocalized reading acknowledges the impossibility not only of unmediated access to the novelistic text but also, as it were, of the Mercator projection of this textual mapping, for the precision of the grid has nothing to do with externally derived truth or referentiality. As Derrida puts it, "We must begin *wherever we are* and the thought of the trace, which cannot take the scent into account, has already taught us that it was impossible to justify a point of departure absolutely."[4]

Barthes/Loyola

Classification, structure, visible character, tabulation: these are the foci of the Ignatian system as it is presented in the *Spiritual Exercises*, the formulaic guide to the administration of the Jesuit retreat. A multiple text, the *Exercises* operates on four levels in Barthes' analysis. The first is the literal text or the "proper level of the discourse" (*B* 41), addressed to the retreat director. The second level is the semantic text or the argument of the discourse which the director addresses to the exercitant. It is the "contents" of the first level. The two texts have a common actor, the director, who is in the first instance the receiver of the *Exercises*, and in the second their donor (insofar as the relationship between director and exercitant is one of donation—the director gives the *Exercises* "virtually, as one *gives* food" [*B* 41]). At the level of the semantic text, the exercitant is also the receiver who, having accomplished this task, will proceed to "send" the message, writing with the second text a third. This third level is, then, the "acted" or allegorical text— the "exercising of the *Exercises*" (*B* 42), as Barthes puts it. Consisting of the meditations, gestures and practices given to the exercitant by the director, the allegorical text is, in turn, addressed to God as receiver. Thus the fourth text is the anagogic one in which God responds to the message, and the sign (the gesture of the first three texts operating in harmony) is "liberated." Clearly, then, it is incumbent upon the exercitant to become a "logo-technician" (*B* 44) or constructor of language just as Loyola in the giving of the *Exercises* became a "Logothete" (*B* 3) or the founder of a language.

Logothesis is "semiophany" (*B* 53), not a language of communication outside itself but a "new language, traversed by (or traversing) natural language, [and] . . . open only to the semiological definition of Text" (*B* 3). If Loyola had wanted to say *something*, Barthes writes, "linguistic language" would have sufficed. Loyola could be summarized if this were the case (*B* 16). But Loyola's language exists to provide a code for deciphering (rather than, as Barthes writes, a code to be deciphered [*B* 48]), to "provide the means for capturing the sign of Divinity" (*B* 45). Four operations are central to this language. The first, self-isolation, refers to the fact that the new language must arise from a "material vacuum" (*B* 4), the product of the physical conditions of the retreat. The second,

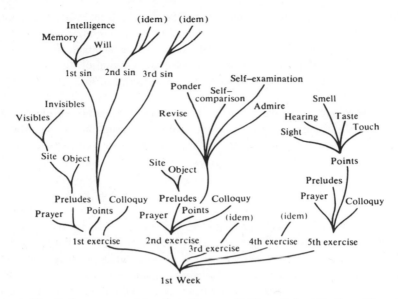

Figure 1. The "arborescence of Ignatian discourse." (From Roland Barthes, "Loyola")

articulation, refers to the endless production of rules of assemblage (*B* 60) of the data resulting from the logothete's segmentation of (in Loyola's case) the body and the Christian narrative. Thus the Ignatian rhetorical technique of composition of place is substituted for "creation" (*B* 4). The third operation, ordering, involves the "mystical sequence to a higher order" (*B* 5) as the Ignatian retreat director operates the exercises in replicating sequences in the service of the new discourse. Finally, the fourth operation, "theatricalization" (*B* 5), involves the production of a "writing [that] . . . only recognizes 'instances' " or the "unlimiting of the [conventional, 'linguistic'] language" (*B* 6). This "unlimiting" process sees Loyola as scenographer dispersed across the framework he has produced, arranging topoi, cases, data *ad infinitum* (*B* 6).

In the beginning, both retreat director and exercitant "flounder" in profound aphasia (*B* 45). Reaching out for the system before them, they grasp through this language of interrogation (*B* 45) the code which will enable them to discover the will of God in each instance of intersection of topos and case. The binary structure of the retreat (*before* the Election of the exercitant's choice of conduct about which he has previously been uncertain, and *after* the Election, facing its consequences [*B* 47]) pivots upon the moment of freedom which is the moment of nothingness. Between this moment and the conclusion of the *Exercises* in the *Lectio divina* stretches the articulation of the Images[5] and topoi, governed by the "protocols" of the retreat situation. These "protocols" or physical conditions of the retreat constitute the circumstances of the logothete's self-isolation, the conditions necessary to the creation of a "linguistic vacuum" (*B* 49) in the exercitant—an articulated aphasia—out of which will come the elaboration and eventual triumph of the new language, logothesis. The elimination of both worldly, physical language and worldly, physical comforts results in the exercitant's sole focusing upon the unique language he must speak (the creation of the allegorical text) and whose code Loyola is attempting to establish. Its analog is the initiation ceremony in which, having followed the ritual procedures under the guidance of the shaman, the novice must finally retreat into isolation in order to wait for the coming of his own song, his voice—precisely a semiophany rather than a theophany (*B* 53), a response which is language itself.

Vehicle of semiophany, the Ignatian technique of composition of place consists for Barthes of the collocation of Images or units of imitation (*B* 54). These are visual units, "views" framing tastes, odors, and so on as well as data processed through the optical system (*B* 55). Composition of place is articulated imitation, deictic in that it designates but does not define (*B* 62). It is the Ignatian linking of the medieval rhetorical mode of topography with the Classical art of memory (*B* 55)[6] but, differing from the art of memory in this, it "attempts to found meaning on matter and not on concept" (*B* 62) where the Classical memory tradition fused them, seeing matter as cue to concept. Thus, in the example which Barthes uses, the exercitant places himself before the Cross and "attempts to go beyond the signified of the image (the Christian, universally meditated meaning) to its referent, the material Cross, this crossed wood whose circumstantial attributes he attempts, through the imagining sense, to perceive" (*B* 63). The Image is reabsorbed within the system, having transcended its signified—or operated nonreferentially in the first place—and returned to the code.

The same process is apparent in the Ignatian version of the *Lectio divina* or meditation on the (divine) name, the working of a series of variations upon all the signifieds of a single noun in order to arrive at an apprehension of the whole. Wresting from the form of the noun the whole gamut of its meanings, this process of reading meaning through permutation extenuates the Subject or topos of meditation, conforming to the same modes of repetition within the allegorical text (*B* 59). The retreat director's articulation of the code (the semantic text) thus leads to this third level of controlled (re-)assemblage performed by the exercitant. In turn, the exercitant's task of assemblage falls under two headings, repetition and narrative. Repetition—or "exhausting the 'pertinences' of a subject" (*B* 60)—takes three forms: rumination or the complete redoing of an Exercise by the exercitant, recapitulation (*summatio*), and varied repetition or the systematic variation of the viewpoint of a selected subject (*B* 60). These traditional rhetorical techniques are in turn brought to bear upon the exercitant's dealings with the topoi of meditation as he undertakes a "weaving of meditation," working methodically with the set topos and then its cases, point by point, in order to evoke the Images with which the Ignatian language is being composed as the exercitant weaves (*B* 58–59). Thus "the imagining of Hell consists in perceiving it five consecutive times in the mode of each of the five senses: seeing the incandescent bodies, hearing the screams of the damned, smelling the stink of the abyss, tasting the bitterness of tears, touching the fire" (*B* 59). Finally, the exercitant must live out "scenes" (*B* 61) from the life of Christ (thus fulfilling his task of narrative), himself experiencing through the use of articulated Images reaching out across their visuality to the referent, the stages of, for example, the Crucifixion. Relentlessly the coded programs of the system fall into place in the exercise of logothesis.

(Barthes/)Loyola/Joyce

In the Joyce system, the most elementary form of the Ignatian code invented for deciphering is to be found in Stephen Dedalus's definition of the "epiphany," found in the fragmentary draft manuscript known as *Stephen Hero*:

> By an epiphany he meant a sudden spiritual manifestation, whether in the vulgarity of speech or of gesture or in a memorable phase of the mind itself. He believed that it was for the man of letters to record these epiphanies with extreme care, seeing that they themselves are the most delicate and evanescent of moments. (*SH* 211)

But the application of this concept (*epiphaneia*: appearance)[7] is entirely visual as Stephen Dedalus tells his companion Cranly that the Ballast Office clock is "capable of an epiphany":

> I will pass it time after time, allude to it, refer to it, catch a glimpse of it. It is only an item in the catalogue of Dublin's street furniture. Then all at once I see it and I know at once what it is: epiphany. . . . Imagine my glimpses at that clock as the gropings of a spiritual eye which seeks to adjust its vision to an exact focus. The moment the focus is reached the object is epiphanised. (*SH* 211)

Thus topography and the Ignatian Image are linked as Stephen Dedalus manifests his striving to "draw out a line of order, to reduce the abysses of the past to order by a diagram" (*SH* 33). In Joyce's notes to his play *Exiles*, the system is presented even more explicitly. First we are given two lists of Images relevant to the situation of Bertha and Richard Rowan:

> Snow:
>   frost, moon, pictures, holly and ivy,
>   currant-cake, lemonade, Emily Lyons,
>   piano, window sill.
> tears:
>   ship, sunshine, garden, sadness, pinafore,
>   buttoned boots, bread and butter, a
>   big fire. (*E* 121)

Then, having provided topoi and cases (incipient Images stripped of literal text), Joyce proceeds to catalogue them:

> A persistent and delicate sensuality (visual: pictures, adorned with holly and ivy; gustatious: currant cake, bread and butter, lemonade; tactual: sunshine in the garden, a big fire, the kisses of her friend and grandmother) runs through both series of images. (*E* 122)

establishing again the requisites of the Ignatian Image which "frames" data from all sensory systems, resolving them into the (epiphanic) "view" which is articulated fully in the *Portrait* in terms of Ignatian composition of place.

Framing that system is the multiple text structure of Barthes' Ignatius. Clearly, the literal text of the *Portrait* is again the artifact itself, the literal level of the book addressed to the reader (who thus becomes surrogate retreat director). The director or donor of the *Exercises* proceeds to give them to the exercitant at the level of the semantic text as the reader exercises the narrative, giving it to him- or herself in the process of critical comprehension and exercising it in perpetual apprenticeship. If literal and semantic texts are regarded as unified in the *Portrait*, the position of the allegorical text becomes immediately apparent. Written with the semantic text, the allegorical level (the exercitant's assigned meditations, practices, and so on) is the reader's learning of the gestures and practices—the metalanguage—of the narrative or literal text. Completing the hermeneutic circle, the anagogic text makes manifest through exercise the logothesis or code for deciphering which is, like Ignatian language, "the means for capturing the sign of Divinity"—in Joyce, the operations of semiosis. That which can be summarized (and which does not occur in Ignatius) is the narrative, the literal/semantic text, existing only in service of the arrangement, the articulation, which finally enables the reader to become, as it were, his or her own retreat director, no longer a novice exercitant but a thoroughly competent one, capable of working the code in polyphonic bliss.

Not a reconstitution of the literal/semantic text, articulation uses repetition (rumination, recapitulation, varied repetition) as rhetorical strategy both within the text and in terms of the reader/exercitant's procedures for recovery of its coded messages. Like his Ignatian counterpart, the Joycean exercitant must become a logo-technician. This is Stephen Dedalus's task as well. His growth in terms of Image competence mimes the growth of the system as a whole within this text. The following sequence is typical of this development:

1. *O, the green wothe botheth.* (*P* 7)

Fusion of two elements from the overheard adult version of the song "O, the wild rose blossoms / On the little green place" (*P* 7), the child's version transforms material Images of items from the topoi "rose" and "green" into "conceptual" cases (to use Barthes' dichotomy), constituting an element in the semiophany of the visual through language, the allegorical level of these elements in full articulation throughout *Portrait*.

2. He stood still and gazed up at the sombre porch of the morgue and from that to the dark cobbled lane-

The narrator here presents Stephen Dedalus in the act of defining the causes of his olfactory sensation occasioned by

way at its side. He saw the word *Lotts* on the wall of the lane and breathed slowly the rank heavy air.

—That is horse piss and straw, he thought. It is a good odour to breathe. (*P* 89)

data focused intradiegetically. Through the narrator's cataloguing of topographical data framed by the word *Lotts* (a good example of a minor Subject and its cases), the encoded perceptions of Stephen Dedalus are, as it were, focused for the reader. Stephen Dedalus's conclusion completes the framing of visual/olfactory data in an Ignatian operation of mortification of the senses through sensory experience, an anticipation within the literal text of the foregrounding at the beginning of chapter 4 of such penances after the retreat (thus Stephen Dedalus's exercising of the allegorical text of the retreat).

3. And under the deepened dusk he felt the thoughts and desires of the race to which he belonged flitting like bats, across the dark country lanes, under trees by the edges of streams and near the poolmottled bogs. A woman had waited in the doorway as Davin had passed by at night and, offering him a cup of milk, had all but wooed him to her bed; for Davin had the mild eyes of one who could be secret. But him no woman's eyes had wooed. (*P* 242)

The complexity of this passage's contrapuntal structure indicates immediately the encoding of a more complex form of perception. The topos "woman" and one of its major cases, bats, have here been elaborated far beyond their initial entries in the novel and become absorbed (again, visual data—matter—being appropriated by concept) into a complex topography of Davin (peasant Ireland) and the environs and incident which he described to Stephen Dedalus earlier in the narrative, here absorbed through the narrator into Stephen Dedalus's memory theater, memory loci representative of Ireland and sexual desire.

In this last example, the narrator presents Stephen Dedalus in the act of reassemblage as, articulating and repeating the system to him- or herself, the reader/exercitant recovers the elements of the code, acquiring the skills of the logo-technician.

Functioning as Barthesian logothete, Stephen Dedalus undertakes the four operations productive of language in Loyola's system. Self-isolation, the first operation, is an obvious aspect of Stephen Dedalus at the literal level—the growth of the Byronic artist-exile seen very much in the act of "founding" his own language from the first page of the *Portrait* (as shown in the first example above). That process, in terms of both Stephen Dedalus and the text, is the articulation of sensory data through Ignatian Images, the "cutting up" of the body at both first- and third-person levels of the literal text. "Scenarios" are articulated through Ignatian composition of place, producing a series of evolving systems of assemblage programmed according to the codes governing Joycean topoi. The result is not an Ignatian mystical sequence to a higher order but nonetheless a progress of sorts toward the ironic higher order of Stephen Dedalus's artistic aspirations. Emerging from the retreat exercises, Stephen Dedalus's new language of Thomist aesthetic as well as foregrounded composition of place and what Barthes calls "image-reservoir perception" (*B* 55) involves an ironic but Ignatian "theatricalization" of self. More important, this operation is seen as a device in the service of the "unlimiting [of] the language" of mimetic discourse, producing a writing upon which the compositor arranges (in Ignatian repetition) his codes. Thus the seeming fragmentation of the literal text at the end of the novel resolves itself into a typographic (visual/framing) foregrounding of Image and coded utterance ("Item: he eats chiefly belly bacon and dried figs. Read locusts and wild honey" [*P* 252]). Composed of a set order of entries and elaborations, these subcodes replicate in sequence according to textual program rather than *ad infinitum* like their Ignatian counterparts.

The elaboration of the topos water provides an example of this process in its movement from an early experience of Stephen Dedalus on the Subject of "the white look of the lavatory" with its cases:

> There were two cocks that you turned and water came out: cold and hot. He felt cold and then a little hot: and he could see the names printed on the cocks. (*P* 11)

to the meditation on his patronymic during which Stephen Dedalus

> seemed to hear the noise of dim waves and to see a winged form flying above the waves and slowly climbing the air. What did it mean? Was it a book of prophecies and symbols, a hawklike man flying sunward above the sea, a prophecy of the end he had been born to serve. . . . (*P* 173)

and finally to the epiphany of the birdlike girl:

> A girl stood before him midstream, alone and still, gazing out to sea. She seemed like one whom magic had changed into the likeness of a strange and beautiful seabird. Her long slender bare legs were delicate as a crane's and pure save where an emerald trail of seaweed had fashioned itself as a sign upon the flesh. Her thighs, fuller and softhued as ivory, were bared almost to the hips, where the white fringes of her drawers were like feathering of soft white down. Her slateblue skirts were kilted boldly about her waist and dovetailed behind her. Her bosom was as a bird's, soft and slight, slight and soft as the breast of some darkplumaged dove. But her long fair hair was girlish: and girlish, and touched with the wonder of mortal beauty, her face. (*P* 175)

Gazing out to sea, she "suffers" his gaze, "gently stirring the water with her foot hither and thither" (*P* 176). Twice repeated in the same paragraph after this entry, the phrase "hither and thither" encodes the sound of the river Liffey, eponym of ▲ in *Finnegans Wake* "hitherandthithering" along her course (*FW* 216.04).[8]

The traditional association of water and woman in these passages (obviously anticipated in the emphasis upon "cocks" in the first excerpt) moves to the assimilation of Dedalus (rather than of his true exemplar, Icarus) with the birdlike girl— birds auguring Stephen Dedalus's artistic calling as does the subsequent reference to ibis-headed Thoth, god of writing (*P* 229). Writing, or more specifically words, have functioned as a Subject of this topos from the beginning, as the first passage demonstrates. The sequence makes equally clear Stephen Dedalus's visual perception of a named world ("Signatures of all things I am here to read," as *Ulysses* has it [3.2]), in fact of a world in which sensory experience and linguistic denotation of it are equivalent. Shivering, thinking of the watercocks, Stephen Dedalus's attention is drawn not to an Image of cold and then hot water but rather to one of the "names printed on the cocks."

A movement toward a Bachelardian semiophany of water, the passage focuses all of the major elements in the second excerpt given, presenting printed names alongside the "quaint device" in a medieval book whose Image is conjured by the "winged form" who, in turn, issues from the imagined perception of "the noise of dim waves" (note the auditory Image supplanted by the visualism of "dim"). As hawklike man branches into birdlike girl, so the emphasis upon the elaboration of the girl's birdlike attributes branches into repetition (of the Subject and thus of the topos) with variations. In addition, repetition within each passage (of "cocks," "waves," "girlish"), rumination in the puzzling-out process central to the first passage, and repetition with variation of the topos water across all three passages, and of the Subject "bird" with an assortment of its cases in the second and third passages: all fulfill Ignatian categories. And, finally, Ignatian recapitulation occurs obviously at allegorical and anagogic levels as well as, within the literal text, after a passage like the third one above.

First summarizing the import of this experience, Stephen Dedalus once again resolves to "recreate life out of life" (*P* 176). Recapitulating on the level of the Image, we have: "Glimmering and trembling, trembling and unfolding, a breaking light, an opening flower, it spread in endless succession to itself, breaking in full crimson and unfolding and fading to palest rose . . . " (*P* 177). And recapitulating on the level of synchronic Joycean discourse, we have Stephen Dedalus falling asleep on the beach at North Bull Island across Dublin Bay from Sandymount Strand, site of LB's sleep at the end of *U* II.10. When Stephen Dedalus awakens, the Image is of

> A rim of the young moon . . . [cleaving] the pale waste of sky like the rim of a silver hoop embedded in grey sand; and the tide was flowing in fast to the land with a low whisper of her waves, islanding a few last figures in distant pools. (*P* 177)

Before he sleeps, LB studies his reflection in the Cock Lake[9] on Sandymount Strand:

> Tide comes here. Saw a pool near her foot. Bend, see my face there, dark mirror, breathe on it, stirs. All these rocks with lines and scars and letters. . . . What is the meaning of that other world. (*U* 13.1259)

So the topos of water branches to include both birdlike girl and Gerty MacDowell
(Ignatian Images correlated within the system, Dedalus and LB aligned as voyeurs,
the irony of Stephen Dedalus's Byronic phase spotlighted); the topographical al-
location of water and word expands to include word and world[10] (the Flood and
the birth of language in Vichian *Finnegans Wake*); the mirror code introduced in
aqueous surroundings links Stephen Dedalus and LB, and *U* I.3 is assimilated into
U II.10, crowned by the resolution of the same Subjects and cases in *U* II.12. And
the "green wothe" of *Portrait*'s first page is repeated with variation in the roseate
recapitulation of the birdlike girl Image transformed into a memory locus, topography made emblematic and immobilized within the system, awaiting the next turn
of the memory wheel of Joycean discourse.

Approached from another direction, however, the central topos of *Portrait*'s
Ignatian meditation becomes neither water nor birds but Stephen Dedalus himself.
Just as in the *Spiritual Exercises* the Subject is methodically confronted with the
items or cases on a list of more general headings in order to evoke the Images with
which Ignatius is composing his language, so in *Portrait* Stephen Dedalus is methodically confronted with those items or cases of sensory and linguistic data which
will evoke the Ignatian Images, as we have already seen. In full articulation at the
level of the allegorical text, these Images constitute the predominantly visual/spatial
code of this stage of Joycean logothesis. The "spatialization" of name which occurs
throughout the literal text, especially in its first two chapters, is an aspect of this
code. From Stephen Dedalus's early situation of himself as an Image in the composition of the universal place, the apotheosis of topography—

> *Stephen Dedalus*
> *Class of Elements*
> *Clongowes Wood College*
> *Sallins*
> *County Kildare*
> *Ireland*
> *Europe*
> *The World*
> *The Universe*   (*P* 15–6)

we move to

> —I am Stephen Dedalus. I am walking beside my father whose name is Simon
> Dedalus. We are in Cork, in Ireland. Cork is a city. Our room is in the Victoria
> Hotel. Victoria and Stephen and Simon. Simon and Stephen and Victoria. Names.
> (*P* 95)

As the Ignatian meditation upon the physical sufferings of Christ leads inevitably
past Christ the signified to the Cross (the signifier which guides the exercitant into
the allegorical text), so Stephen's construction of himself as a memory locus within

the theater of discourse moves beyond the narrative deixis of these names and out into the realm of signs as reversible modules governed only by the syntactic structures of logothesis.

Where the reader/exercitant performs Joycean *nembutsu*[11] in the articulation of the discourse, the literal text's Stephen Dedalus performs his equivalent in the course of the retreat. Halfway through the retreat (the "still point" at the core of the central chapter of the book),[12] Stephen Dedalus's "soul sank back deeper into depths of contrite peace, no longer able to suffer the pain of dread, and sending forth, as he sank, a faint prayer" (*P* 129). At the moment of the prayer's exhalation, the period of freedom in nothingness which immediately precedes it has passed; he has begun the process of Election. As the retreat director articulates the Ignatian exercises, creating their semantic text before the exercitants, that overheard text is embedded within the novel's literal one. Focusing Stephen Dedalus's attention upon the operations of logothesis, the retreat sermons and their aftermath for the exercitant focus the reader's attention upon the novel's operations. Stephen Dedalus, who has been formed until this pivotal point according to the procedures of composition of place, Ignatian Images and their repetition and articulation, and whose given phenomenology has been one of Ignatian "views" both sensory and linguistic, now learns those operations directly.

Beginning with a caution to "*remember only the last things and thou shalt not sin for ever*" (*P* 112), the retreat moves to an elementary exercise in semiophany focused by a semantic interrogation ("Now what is the meaning of this word *retreat* and why is it allowed on all hands to be a most salutary practice . . . ?" [*P* 113]) and its response: "A retreat, my dear boys, signifies a withdrawal for a while from the cares of our life, the cares of this workaday world, in order to examine the state of our conscience, to reflect on the mysteries of holy religion and to understand better why we are here in this world" (*P* 113). Repeating with elaborate variation the call to memory, the Joycean catechetical techne employs both the rhythm and the repetition of question/answer mnemonic learning of the Catechism (its transformation, as we see in Stephen Dedalus's case, into the allegorical text of a life both chosen and abandoned). Its efficiency in the case of the focal exercitant is perfect: "His soul, as these memories [of Clongowes associated with his old teacher now retreat director—another marker of this chapter's arc of recapitulation] came back to him, became again a child's soul" (*P* 112). Topoi are then announced (death, judgment, hell, heaven) and an exhortation to correct conduct is given— basic components of the system established from the beginning. As Image and topography had earlier fused around names as visualized loci, so the initial impact of this first retreat sermon stresses these elements once again: "The letters of the name of Dublin lay heavily upon his mind, pushing one another surlily hither and thither with slow boorish insistence" (*P* 115), the repeated phrase "hither and thither" operating synchronically, foregrounding the logothetic movement of the literal text for the reader/exercitant as, diachronically, it foregrounds the approaching Ignatian training of subject/exercitant.

The next day of the retreat brings not only "death and judgement" but also a narrative that shifts slowly from the familiar narrative voice miming the perceptual

processes of Stephen Dedalus as it deals with them to the retreat director's voice
with its exercises in composition of place, not labeled by him until the fourth
sermon.[13] First: exercise, sensory cataloguing; then: definition, verbal cataloguing.
Gestures as deliberate, formulaic, programmed as those of the Noh define the
director's semantic text (rendered allegorical through the semiotics of gesture): "The
preacher took a chainless watch from a pocket within his soutane and, having
considered its dial for a moment in silence, placed it silently before him on the
table" (*P* 120–21)—a vocabulary of visual excess (*chainless* watch, *within* his
soutane, *before him* on the table, *in silence/silently*), a deixis of the absent, the
invisible, the linguistically replete. Sensory cataloguing begins: "Hell is a strait
and dark and foul-smelling prison, an abode of demons and lost souls, filled with
fire and smoke" (*P* 123)—the setting of Subjects, to be followed by their cases in
sensory order beginning with the elaboration of the visual. Hell is "a neverending
storm of darkness, dark flames and dark smoke of burning brimstone, amid which
the bodies are heaped one upon another without even a glimpse of air" (*P* 123),
and proceeding through smell and touch to a statement which mimes the cataloguing
practices of the medieval *speculum*:

> Every sense of the flesh is tortured and every faculty of the soul therewith: the eyes
> with impenetrable utter darkness, the nose with noisome odours, the ears with yells
> and howls and execrations, the taste with foul matter, leprous corruption, nameless
> suffocating filth, the touch with redhot goads and spikes, with cruel tongues of flame.
> (*P* 125)

Filth, most suffocating in its namelessness, anticipates the aural agony of the
damned, forced to suffer again the words which induced them to sin. The sins of
the ear are language sins, as through the ear comes the exercise of purgation,
language wounds healed by logothesis. Election, transcending language, is the next
step.

From the invocation to memory which commenced these exercises, the retreat
moves in its fourth and final sermon to the topography of the eyes, its Subject, "*I
am cast away from the sight of Thine eyes . . .*" (*P* 130). And in a sermon which
is a virtuoso invention on Ignatian Images, the retreat director first defines his
technique:

> —This morning we endeavoured, in our reflection upon hell, to make what our holy
> founder calls in his book of spiritual exercises, the composition of place. We en-
> deavoured, that is, to imagine with the senses of the mind, in our imagination, the
> material character of that awful place and of the physical torments which all who
> are in hell endure. (*P* 130)

Consistently shifting from the literal to the allegorical within the exercise itself, the
director begins the consideration of the "spiritual torments of hell" with a rumination upon the psychological pain of loss but soon returns to putrefaction, blood
and the violence of hell, working to his crescendo, a Baroque variation upon the

theme of eternal damnation in terms of grains of sand. Proceeding in a series of antitheses of presence and absence, the Image requires the exercitant to imagine such items as "an enormous mass of countless particles of sand multiplied as often as there are leaves in the forest, drops of water in the mighty ocean, feathers on birds, scales on fish, hairs on animals, atoms in the vast expanse of the air . . . " (*P* 135). How long would it take, the director asks, for a bird to carry that mountain of sand away grain by grain? The labor would scarcely have begun, comes the response, after "millions upon millions of centuries," but still that does not give us an Image of the span of eternity: "At the end of all those billions and trillions of years eternity would have scarcely begun" (*P* 135). Such is the "totalitarian economy" of the Ignatian system, as Barthes says (*B* 52).

After the retreat, Stephen Dedalus encounters his own guilt (his response to the Ignatian theses) figured in eyes and words. Waiting at the threshold of his room, he knows that "faces were there; eyes: they waited and watched" (*P* 139), and in a strong foregrounding of his allegorical dream-text, Stephen's response to the Images of hell is a vision ("He saw," as the narrator says) of "goatish creatures with human faces" in a field thick with excrement.

> Soft language issued from their spittleless lips as they swished in slow circles round and round the field, winding hither and thither through the weeds, dragging their long tails amid the rattling canisters. They moved in slow circles, circling closer and closer to enclose, to enclose, soft language issuing from their lips, their long swishing tails besmeared with stale shite, thrusting upwards their terrific faces. . . . (*P* 141)

The moment of Election was the spiritual half of this Ignatian binary structure; the moment of rejection of the past is a starkly physical one, the agony of guilt passing from the signified of hell to the referents of Stephen Dedalus's tormented imagination. Its logothetic end-product is the anagogic text of viscera's response (he is soon seized by convulsions of vomiting), followed not only by prayer but by Ignatian tears, for Barthes reminds us of the "veritable code of tears" (*B* 74) which is entered in Loyola's *Spiritual Journal* by means of a sign system denoting their intensity.

Guilt leads to confession but first Stephen Dedalus interrogates himself about the nature of mortal sin:

> Even once was a mortal sin. It could happen in an instant. But how so quickly? By seeing or by thinking of seeing. The eyes see the thing, without having wished first to see. Then in an instant it happens. But does that part of the body understand or what? (*P* 143)

The response to this Ignatian deficit financing of the visual (recapitulating the association of hot and cold water with printed names on watercocks) is the "ebbing back" to Stephen Dedalus of "Consciousness of place" (*P* 144) in the last six pages of the chapter as scenes begin to "compose" themselves around him. The structure is briefly in balance: methodical mortification of the senses coexists with

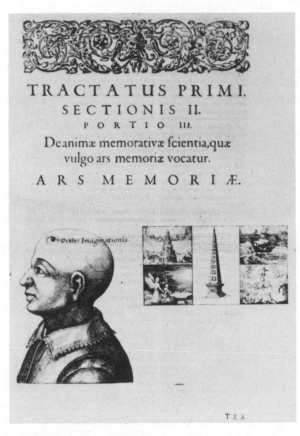

Figure 2. The "Oculus Imaginationis." (From Robert Fludd,
Utriusque Cosmi . . . Historia, Tomus secundus, 1619)

the newly conscious awareness of topography. There is even a certain satisfaction
in the economy for at times "he seemed to feel his soul in devotion pressing like
fingers the keyboard of a great cash register and to see the amount of his purchase
start forth immediately in heaven, not as a number but as a frail column of incense
or as a slender flower" (*P* 151). In this, Stephen Dedalus differs from Barthes'
Loyola, who would have favored the crisp perfection of the soul's number.

To the extent that Stephen Dedalus is capable of it in the *Portrait*, that sort of
perfection is seen most strongly in his use of composition of place in the service
of his neo-Thomist aesthetic presented in the last chapter of the novel. There the
"first phase of [aesthetic] apprehension is a bounding line drawn about the object
to be apprehended" (*P* 216), the Blakean allusion to the engraver's "bounding
line"[14] stressing the visual delineation of the Image being presented. Perhaps, too,
this process of apprehension is "luminous" (*P* 216) in tribute to the Classical
memory tradition's need to place the mnemonic object in a well-lit situation in
order that the *oculus imaginationis* might grasp it clearly on recall. The instant of

nothingness before Election is projected in Stephen Dedalus's notion of the moment of aesthetic pleasure as a "luminous silent stasis" which finds for its Image an Ignatian trope linking the spiritual to the physical in service of the conceptual, for aesthetic pleasure is "a spiritual state very like to that cardiac condition which the Italian physiologist Luigi Galvani . . . called the enchantment of the heart" (*P* 217). The material for "enchantment," the anagogic text of the viscera, is gathered from Stephen Dedalus's Dublin memory theater, Images deposited in literary loci to be used in the process of reassemblage which will be the text of logodaedalus:[15]

> His morning walk across the city had begun, and he foreknew that as he passed the sloblands of Fairview he would think of the cloistral silverveined prose of Newman; that as he walked along the North Strand Road, glancing idly at the windows of the provision shops, he would recall the dark humour of Guido Cavalcanti and smile. . . . (*P* 179)

Stephen Dedalus/SD

Like the great wheels within wheels of Giordano Bruno's memory system in *De umbris idearum*,[16] the texts of *Portrait* turn one upon the other, their center the moment of Election at the core of chapter 3. Before the retreat, it is the wheel of Stephen Dedalus's unknowing; after the retreat, the wheel of his deliberate composing. Moving as it were at different speeds, one wheel casts its Images upon another, Ignatian codes modifying the referential level of the text. Catching up with the verbal universe of which he is composed, Stephen Dedalus becomes cognizant of those techniques and operations which, through repetition and articulation, *are* Stephen Dedalus. Actively aware of his Dublin memory theater, using topography in the construction of memory loci, using loci in the deconstruction of topography's immediacy, creating a logothetic vacuum which—mirrored in the journal fragments of the book's conclusion—will be the occasion of "language tide" in *Ulysses*: Stephen Dedalus becomes SD, the paradigm of the codes of his articulation. But where the Ignatian code for deciphering is "the means for capturing the sign of Divinity," the Joycean—endlessly recursive—is the means for capturing only itself,[17] a semiophany in the service of language itself, programmed in the literal texts of Joycean discourse as an "arborescence" (*B* 57) of perceptual paradigms. First of those paradigms which we are taught to recover in the Joyce system, SD is (on the level of the literal text) the exposition of a dominantly visual semiotic, and then (on the level of the allegorical text or processual-mimetic level) the paradigmatic root of that branching complex of data, topographic and mnemonic, which begins in the *Portrait*. The same modal balancing in *Ulysses* eventually isolates the operations of logothesis in II.11 in which, equipped with the logo-technician's understanding of the basic perceptual paradigm SD, the reader/exercitant celebrates the reassemblage of language, of names triumphant in the extended moment of the "postcreation" (*U* 14.294) which is Joycean semiophany.

An invention on the theme of Ignatian *Lectio divina*, Stephen Dedalus, the exercitant of *Portrait*'s literal text, is discovered as the goal of its anagogic one. As the name of the deity is deconstructed into its signifieds—a process of reading—so the topos Stephen Dedalus is deconstructed into its Subjects and cases. Meditation on the name (and its codes) articulates and reassembles the allegorical text, the "portrait" emerging from the pointillism of its narrative—*re*-assembled, for the process unfolds in endless circularity, anagogic/paradigmatic generating allegorical/processual and so on until out of polyphony at last emerges the "unique language" which, like that of Barthes' Loyola, cannot be given in any other way. We move from the *Lectio divina* of Stephen Dedalus's name (which is the perceptual paradigm SD when the reading has moved along all topoi, all cases given) to its signifieds (Images, topography, loci) in order to arrive at a whole, to wrest—as Barthes says—from the form SD the whole gamut of its meanings (moving back along the axis of topoi), thereby to extenuate the Subject, Joycean discourse itself.

III

FROM CATECHISM
TO CATACHRESIS
ULYSSES AS GOTHIC PEDAGOGY

> "Narrating is an *act*."
>
> —Genette, *Narrative Discourse*

> "No one is speaking these words or thinking
> them: they are . . . printed sentences."
>
> —Jameson, "*Ulysses* in History"

Our progress as readers of the *Portrait* is SD's. First, acquisition of competence through the Ignatian strategies of repetition, recapitulation and the "weaving of meditation." Eventually, the achievement of performance of the discourse or of Barthesian semiophany. At the end of the *Portrait* SD must go into exile, in part because his level of competence exceeds the potential of the text which is a reading of him or of "SDness," as it were. SD as code has exceeded the bounds of the textual program which activates "him." In *U* I.3 we see the results of that semiotic predicament. Thus, as Joseph Frank remarked of *Ulysses*, SD "can only be reread"[1] and is presented in the act of exercising first one sensory code, then another, considering the code-switching maneuver of synesthesia and then back to *Lectio divina*, searching for the Ignatian Image which will contain polysemy, struggling to label the codes in order to define the subject, rerunning the program to try to find the gap—black hole or rabbit hole—into *nembutsu*, the experience of theophany remembered, semiophany glimpsed in *Portrait*. The program shifts, dreams its own integration into a larger system, and, encountering death in the corpse of a dog on the Strand, dreams of resolution in at/one/ment, transsignification, the longing toward "all" (*U* 3.452).

    —a dangerous longing even if this form of dreaming is simply the repetition of codes, subcodes and cases of the semantic grid of the text; a longing which the strategies of *Portrait* alone will not satisfy. In the immense work of elaboration which is *Ulysses*, SD's incipient neoplatonism must be tempered by similarly extended logological controls. Diverted from SD's temptation toward transcendence as solution, the reader/exercitant must be trained in procedures which are extensions of the earlier repertoire. "Exercising the *Exercises*" (*B* 42) becomes a more demanding business as codes and programs multiply and acquire complexity of both number and *signifiance*, and a major new perceptual paradigm is added: LB (Leopold Bloom). Through realignment and expansion, the whole system shifts and with it the exercitant's task. In turn, the system's pedagogical directives become more complex and are characterized by a performative operation which we shall call gestural enactment. Its ancestors are Joseph Frank's "spatial form" and Gérard Genette's "spatialité sémantique du discours littéraire."[2]

"Spatial form": *ex cathedra*

Frank begins his classic essay "Spatial Form in Modern Literature" (1945) with a discussion of Lessing's *Laocoön*, a work which he sees as having developed "a new approach to aesthetic form"[3] which is crucial to the understanding of modernist texts. In Frank's reading, Lessing presents "aesthetic form" as "the relation between the sensuous nature of the art medium and the conditions of human perception," thus breaking with concepts of form as "an external arrangement provided by a set of traditional rules."[4] Taking from the *Laocoön* a sense of the complex interrelationships between time and space in the plastic arts in particular, Frank turns to modernist classics from the *Cantos* to *The Waste Land*, from *Nightwood* to *Ulysses*, in an effort to define that central operation which he calls "spatial form."

In itself a figural resolution of the problem, this phrase encapsulates the "internal conflict" in classic modernist texts "between the time-logic of language and the space-logic implicit in the modern conception of poetry."[5] This tension is the result, for Frank, of the introduction of nonsequential modes of order into these texts and of the consequent requirement that readers "read reflexively" in order to apprehend "units of meaning . . . reflexively in an instant of time."[6] Finally, grounding his argument in authorial intention, Frank maintains that Joyce "proceeded on the assumption that a unified spatial apprehension of his work would ultimately be possible."[7] This apprehension he associates with the process of rereading which, as we have seen, is for Frank one of the defining processual characteristics of modernist texts and, in particular, of *Ulysses*.

In "La Littérature et l'espace," Gérard Genette explores this concept of space further:

> l'espace du livre, comme celui de la page, n'est pas soumis passivement au temps
> de la lecture successive, mais qu'en tout qu'il s'y révèle et s'y accomplit pleinement,
> il ne cesse de l'infléchir et de le retourner, et donc en un sens de l'abolir.[8]

For Genette, the semantic field transformed by Mallarmé's exploitation of the graphic resources of the printed page and by Proust's attempt to overthrow "la tyrannie du point de vue diachronique introduit par le XIXe siècle" is a space of simultaneity in which we learn to recognize "les effets de convergence et de rét-roaction."[9] Thus, Borges' library, Foucault's *theatrum philosophicum*, Joyce's system of systems.

In "Discours du récit," Genette extends these observations to confront a problem which has long concerned critics of Frank: the seeming obstacle which the temporality and sequentiality of language present to the theory of spatial form.

> Produced in time, like everything else, written narrative exists in space and as space, and the time needed for "consuming" it is the time needed for *crossing* or *traversing* it, like a road or a field. The narrative text, like every other text, has no other temporality than what it borrows, metonymically, from its own reading.[10]

Moving spatial form toward post-Einsteinian concepts of the space-time continuum, Genette not only stresses the fact that sequential processing of the text is bound up with the literal spatiality of the text as object but also poses the problem of the relationship between, on the one hand, the reading process and experience and, on the other, the text's mode of operation at the micro- and macrostructural levels.[11] For Genette, resolution is to be found in a theory of mimesis which is both "illusion" and "act"[12] and thus a mode of representation which is nonreferential, since, as Umberto Eco puts it, "the referential fallacy consists in assuming that the 'meaning' of a sign-vehicle has something to do with its corresponding object."[13] According to Genette,

> mimesis in words can only be mimesis of words. Other than that, all we have and can have is degrees of diegesis.[14]

The experience of spatial form becomes, then, a particularly sustained version of the "noematic phase"[15] of apprehension of a narrative, that is, the narrative *as* experienced, the totality of synchronic processing of the text which concludes the reading act. But Frank's term, far narrower and more limited than his admittedly sketchy definitions of it, still poses the problem of a seeming opposition between the concept of form and that of act, particularly when act is defined in Genette's sense. A partial resolution of this problem would seem to be found in Frank's reading of Lessing's concept of form: "Form issue[s] spontaneously from the organization of the art work as it present[s] itself to perception."[16] But this statement creates more complicated problems of its own as well, problems which center on the "noematic structure of action"[17] (whether spontaneous or organized) and upon the locus of the experience of the art work. To use Paul Ricoeur's Husserlian terminology again, Frank would seem to be arguing that *Ulysses* occasions a particular intensification and complication of the noematic phase of apprehension. Let us consider this problem further by approaching from another angle.

If we follow Kenneth Burke's strategy of "perspective by incongruity"[18] while working with spatial form, the Classical concept of *ekphrasis*, much adopted by Romantic poets, and the Pauline theory of recapitulation or *anakephalaiösis*—a term used by Paul (Ephesians 1:10) and borrowed by the early Greek fathers of the church—may prove useful.[19] Ekphrasis, "the concentration of action in a single moment of energy,"[20] finds some of its most familiar representations in the ekphrastic moments of Keats's Grecian urn or Eliot's Chinese jar in "Burnt Norton":

> Only by the form, the pattern,
> Can words or music reach
> The stillness, as a Chinese jar still
> Moves perpetually in its stillness.[21]

As in the *Laocoön*, the emphasis here is upon the art object rather than the perceiver's experience of it. As the jar moves in its stillness, it balances kinesis—the process of being—against stasis—the integrity of its own form—and thus within the poem the jar becomes an icon of a mode of resolution of time which is unattainable in the world of human action. But in the next six lines of "Burnt Norton," another approach to the problem of time is introduced:

> Not the stillness of the violin, while the note lasts,
> Not that only, but the co-existence,
> Or say that the end precedes the beginning,
> And the end and the beginning were always there
> Before the beginning and after the end.
> And all is always now.

While the ekphrastic topos continues to resonate in the last line of this passage, the explicit rejection of ekphrasis as a solution to time's effects ("Not the stillness . . . , / Not that only . . . ") carries us to the topos of recapitulation or *anakephalaiösis*. It is defined by theologian Hans Urs von Balthasar as "not just flowing backward to the beginning, but movement forward in time as the integration of the beginning in the end, . . . [which] is the significance of the movement forward itself, insofar as it is at once in time and above time."[22] Or, in John Freccero's elegant definition, the "gathering up in an epistrophic moment" which, he argues, is "the essence of thought for Augustine."[23] Augustine's concept of history is an extension of the same topos: "at once linear and circular, a syntax that moves toward its own beginning."[24] Thus what Wendy Steiner has termed "Cubist historiography"—an understanding of history moving "not as a plotted narrative toward a resolution, but as a cubist painting whose elements maintain their heterogeneity . . . in an aestheticized structure of interrelations"[25]—may more accurately be seen as a theory of history which in the Western tradition has its origins in Augustine. As Freccero argues, Augustine marks the beginning of a turning away from the exclusive privileging of the spoken word in Christian theology and the onset of "the reverse process, where the visual and spatial perception of the word as *read* becomes an emblem of a simultaneity that is preferable to sound and the fall into time."[26] In its rejection of pure sound as analog, Eliot's variation on this theme approaches the Augustinian emphasis upon the association of spatiality with simultaneity, a collapsing of the categories of time and space which will eventually result, in *The Four Quartets*, in resolution into Christ as word, thus ending where Augustine himself did. Through the appeal to recapitulation, the pressure of the ekphrastic moment in the *Quartets* is relieved.

Augustine's emblem of simultaneity, Christ the word, serves to balance a system which otherwise threatens to suffer an instability similar to that exhibited by Frank's spatial form (or Eliot's *Quartets* if we can imagine them without the god-term), but it is a balance which is sustained only as long as we accept the insertion of transcendental signified as telos. Viewed logologically, Pauline recapitulation becomes a kind of animated and centered ekphrastic moment in the dual sense of kinetic animation and of inspiriting process, an infusion of anima in its Aristotelian sense of essence. In this context, then, spatial form may be seen as a "maxim" in Grice's sense[27]—a maxim which attempts to stand in symbolic relation to modernist texts in their attempts to encode Verbum, and to the reading response patterns enjoined upon readers who undertake the works of, for example, Joyce. But if the noema has become the discourse system in performance, the text itself becomes more than "a game whose rules must be established in the process of play."[28] So we return to logologized theophany, Barthes' semiophany.

Spatial form appears, then, to be the kernel of a dramatistic theory which encodes the relationship between form and act at both textual and metatextual levels and which, in focusing on the dialogic structure of the interchange between text and programmed reader, seeks to articulate the ekphrastic leap beyond the restrictions of sequential time which characterizes modernist discourse. But we must now, following Freccero, include Augustine in this schema as well and, as Frank did in a later essay, also cite Erich Auerbach's figural schema and its models in Scholastic thought and Gothic art.[29] In his attempt to articulate the demands placed by such works as *Ulysses* and *Nightwood* on readers, Frank began the long process of writing the semiotics of the Joyce system but he chose what Genette calls an "architextural" mode, a mode which privileges the noematic or essentialist at the expense of the noetic or processual-mimetic level of apprehension of the text.[30] Not "Proust palimpseste," then, this textual space is *ex cathedra*, beyond "scholasticism in stone" (*JJII* 515) as jest or cliché to the absolute literality of it: Gothic pedagogy in text and gesture.[31]

Gothic pedagogy: processual mimesis

In *The Rule of Metaphor*, Paul Ricoeur is concerned with, among other things, the rereading of the concept of mimesis to its origins in Aristotle's *Rhetoric* and *Poetics*. In contrast to the euhemerized, naively referential versions of mimesis which have long dominated and still do control a number of areas of literary criticism (including, alas, Joyce studies), Ricoeur stresses the processual foundation of Aristotle's concept of *mimêsis phuseôs*.[32] Usually rendered as the "imitation of nature," this phrase—as Ricoeur, Foucault and Derrida[33] have variously argued— has been inscribed within an ideology which has taken as its central concern the formation of an antagonistic relation between "nature" and "man" concomitant with the inscription of the human as divinely ordained conqueror of all other life forms and of the earth itself. Mimesis has become a mode of ownership rather than a means of production.

Returning to an understanding of mimesis as process, which has both analog and origin in the Thomist concept of the act, Ricoeur maintains that mimesis

> does not signify only that all discourse *is* of the world; it does not embody just the *referential* function of poetic discourse. Being *mimêsis phuseôs*, it connects this referential function to the revelation of the Real as Act. [. . .] To present men "*as acting*" and all things "*as an act*"—such could well be the *ontological* function of metaphorical discourse. . . . [34]

Reading the "Real as Act" logologically, we can discern both the Augustinian concept of the text as "nascent speech act"[35] and the Thomist concept of form as act,[36] both rooted in the Aristotelian understanding of mimesis as techne which Ricoeur glosses from the *Ethics* as

> something more refined than a routine or an empirical practice and [which] in spite of its focus on production, . . . contains a speculative element, namely a theoretical enquiry into the means applied to production. It is a method; and this feature brings it closer to theoretical knowledge than to routine.[37]

A mode of articulation as both utterance and motion, mimesis as techne is a method of enactment "which composes and constructs the very thing it imitates" and is the "structure of plot."[38] Or, in Augustinian terms, the human response to the originary speech act of creation.[39]

Like Roman Jakobson's definition of the "poetic function" as an accentuation of the message at the expense of the referential function, human utterance within the Augustinian speech paradigm is referential in a purely semiotic sense.[40] "The medium is the message,"[41] as Marshall McLuhan's instant decompression says, but in the Christological tradition, human message as sign vehicle can never fully capture the divine *signans* which activates it, nor can it re-present that originary act except in its own embodiment of the gesture of creation. The essence of that mime—verbal and kinesthetic—is, in the Christian tradition, the ritual drama of the liturgy.

A trope founded on a pun, the liturgy is, like all tropes, an event since "the figures of signification 'occur through a new signification of the word.' "[42] As an "act-event,"[43] the central drama of the Catholic liturgy, the Mass, may be classified as both an act of rememoration (*memoria passionis*)[44] and one of performative utterance in the sense in which Émile Benveniste uses J. L. Austin's term. Thus, "an utterance is performative insofar as it *names* the act performed. . . . The utterance *is* the act; the utterer performs the act by naming it."[45] In the Thomist sense of the word, "form" is an utterance: an act which is performative in time and, if encoded in the spatiotemporal continuum of liturgy, in space as well. Thus

Joseph Frank's concept of "spatial form" becomes liturgical enactment if liturgy is defined as a fixed, processual system encoding prescribed gestures and words, enacted and concelebrated by priest and people, and centered on the enunciation of the Word in time, the conversion of utterance into flesh. Noesis and noema are here bound into enactment.

Grounding his observations in the medieval theologian Amalarius's expositions of the Mass as highly allegorized sacred drama, O. B. Hardison writes that there were "two concurrently developing patterns" in that celebration:

> The first is the ritual, which, in spite of its highly stylized form, is a true and visible sequence of actions and texts. The ritual is timeless. It always occurs in the present and its central features are unchanging. It is not a representation but a re-creation. It is linked indissolubly with a second order of events which occurred in chronological time and which must therefore be re-created in the present by meditation—by an effort of the memory heightened through contact with the ritual. The two elements cannot be separated.[46]

Until the period of reform which commenced with the efforts of Pope Pius X in the 1890s, the Roman Mass was essentially a processual system having both an ekphrastic center (the consecration or ritual transformation of immanent product into transcendent process) and a recapitulative movement guided by a set program both printed (the Roman *Ritual*, the missals in common use by lay participants until the 1960s) and mnemonic (the trained memories of lay participants who—perhaps without any comprehension of the semantic field of the Latin Mass—nevertheless knew the responses and recognized all the familiar verbal and kinesthetic gestures of the celebrant).

The experience of the Tridentine Mass for many lay people in fact bore a striking resemblance to that of the members of the audience at the performance of an oral narrative. Harold Scheub writes of the "process of patterning"[47]—or what we will refer to here as programming—which is experienced by the audience at the performance of an oral narrative in which both verbal and kinesthetic expression by the performer serves to unite the group in a sort of performative communion. Against the "grid" of highly formalized gestures the performer sets the verbal narrative. When fully used, the gestural grid creates its own patterning which "is not reflected in the words of the narrative, a patterning evoked by the words."[48] It is a literal "embodiment" of the semantic grid of the narrative. Contemporary Catholic theologians refer to this form of processual mimesis in the context of the sacrament of the Eucharist at the center of the Mass as "transsignification."[49]

An amplification of the Augustinian concept of transsubstantiation, transsignification refers to the association of "the substance of bread and the substance of the body of Christ" as operant within the context of a "sign-act" which is the Eucharistic transformation.[50] Logologically speaking, the process is one of transcoding which is motivated (in Kenneth Burke's sense: moved to act/ion) by the enactment of performative utterance. Which is to say that through the synesthetic performance of strictly encoded gestures, the discourse system enacts itself insofar as the components of that system are operant (that is: celebrant, lay participants, the various texts of encoded verbal and kinesthetic gesture; logologically speaking: text characterized by that form of processual mimesis and logothetic programming which has been encapsulated as "spatial form," and competent readers willing not to "suspend disbelief"—since belief is never in question here—but first to submit to textual programming and then, achieving familiarity with the maneuvers of the system, to enact the text as performative discourse insofar as these components share fully in the enactment or "exercising" of it).

In this sense of "liturgy," then, the demands of those texts characterized by "spatial form" are demands of liturgical enactment. Logothesis, in other words, is no longer sufficient in itself to meet the text-directives of the Joyce system by the time of *Ulysses*. The reader/exercitant must now function not only as logo-technician (as s/he did of *Portrait*) but also as performer of a very particular kind. As Scheub notes, "Decoding occurs not [only] through analysis but [also] through participation."[51] Our emendation needs to be taken a stage further, however, since in performative discourse of the sort we are concerned with, analysis and partici-pation are utterly entwined. Like the Romantic version of the ekphrastic moment, the noetic moment for these texts is a synesthetic one.

We have come a long way toward the description of both Roman Catholic liturgy and its logological analog, the act-event of transsignification which is both process and product in a text like *Ulysses*, as formulations of what Walter Ong has called "oral noetics." In *Orality and Literacy: The Technologizing of the Word*, Ong has synthesized three decades of his research into oral and mnemonic paradigms and presented a description of the main features of primary oral culture and its expression in oral performance. Going beyond the generic restrictions imposed by Albert B. Lord and his school, Ong—like Jeff Opland, the fine scholar of Anglo-Saxon and African oral traditions—has extended the concept of "formulaic expression" to include all forms of language activity within a primary oral culture. As Ong puts it, "primary orality is radically formulary."[52] Further,

> Oral noetics, as manifested in poetry and narration of primary oral cultures, organizes thought largely around a controlled set of themes, more or less central to the human lifeworld: birth, marriage, death, celebration, struggle (ceremonial or ludic, and polemic or martial), initiation rites, dance and other ceremonies, arrivals and de-partures, descriptions or manipulations of implements [. . .], and so on.[53]

Both the thought and the poetic expression of such cultures have a "mnemonic base"[54] which has its major expression in "formulary devices" (a term which Ong uses with reference to a variety of forms, including proverbs, adages, "program-matically mnemonic verses" including Homeric phrases of the "rosy-fingered dawn" sort, "cumulative commonplaces" or "prefabricated purple patches" on a standard topos, and "standardized verbal expressions"). The "mnemonic base," however, extends beyond these devices to include a number of rhetorical charac-teristics of "orally based thought and expression."[55] Among these features are additive style, aggregative structures featuring epithet clusters and heavily adjectival phrases, and what medieval rhetoricians referred to as *copia* or redundancy, including such forms as *amplificatio* and *elaboratio*.[56] In this linguistic conserver-economy, not novelty but integration into existing styles and structures is valued. So is what Ong refers to as "agonistic tone" or the privileging of flyting, vituperation and praise ritualized in performance.

Oral noetic economies are characterized in oral performance and in everyday activities as what Ong calls "homeostatic" in the sense that they "live very much in a present which keeps itself in equilibrium or homeostasis by sloughing off memories which no longer have present relevance,"[57] a process which requires a constant reintegration of a renewed, reshaped past into the present time of performance. The past is rewoven into the language of the present. Formulary devices serve in oral enactment as regulators of a system which contains within itself the linguistic and cultural checks and balances necessary to the stabilization of the whole. This process of balancing is facilitated, perhaps in part caused, by the prevalence of "situational" rather than "abstract" thinking in primary oral societies.[58] Thus—in examples which Ong cites from the fieldwork of A. R. Luria among predominantly oral people—geometrical figures, logical puzzles, syllogisms and the like, and requests for definitions are quickly discounted. "Try to explain to me what a tree is," Luria said to one young man. "Why should I? Everyone knows what a tree is"[59] was the reply, an exchange which is not as far from Gothic pedagogy as it may at first seem.

Luria's attempt at a sequentially structured dialogue is foiled from the beginning by his subject's recognition of and suspicion toward his own "kerygmatic assumption"[60] about "reality" and trees, not to mention his condescending tone. Refusing to play his part, the young man blocks the attempted exchange without revealing to his questioner the bias of the latter's expectations. In Luria's world, "tree" can be defined; in the young man's more literal and situation-bound world, the essence of tree ("what a tree *is*") cannot be "defined" but only performed. As for Aquinas, for Luria's informant "form is act." In refusing a travesty of diegesis, Luria's subject asserts with Gérard Genette that "mimesis in words can only be mimesis of words,"[61] and with Emile Benveniste that "the utterer performs the act by naming it."[62] By refusing to "name" the tree, the young man refuses to enter his questioner's world of logical categories in which words can be made to represent things. He rejects, in other words, what Genette calls *mimologie*[63] and opts instead for the processual, nonreferential bias of his oral noetic culture. It is this ontological model which is at the heart of the preecumenical Roman liturgy and of what Kenneth Burke calls "scholastic realism."[64]

"La Liturgie est fondamentalement une pédagogie," writes Marcel Jousse.[65] Those who come to this school to learn must apprentice themselves to the text and, in the act of memorizing it, begin to apprehend the teacher's message encoded in the text. Breaking through the shell of referential expectations and desire for instant and soon forgotten bits of information which is characteristic of cultures of "secondary orality" like our own, the student learns—as Jousse puts it—to eat the bread of the Eucharist, the book of the Gospels and the Teacher, Christ.[66] This is

Jousse's paradigm of knowledge or total apprehension which is emblematized and realized in the Eucharistic *Cum-unio* or at/one/ment of teacher with pupil.[67] For Jousse this is an interactive and completely balanced paradigm, a stable system, despite the seeming disparity, theologically speaking, between levels of divine and human knowledge. Like Aquinas's universe, Jousse's is an utterly knowable one in which human beings are, so to speak, synchronized with their world and capable of articulating even the far reaches of mystery since words exist to enact that which they name. It is the mode of enactment which is central to Jousse's inquiry into psychobiology and oral noetics, a study which begins with investigation of the gestural semiotics of the Gospels.

For Jousse a holistic concept, gesture has its roots in the "rhythmo-catechistic" milieu[68] of Palestine at the time of Christ. The narratives of this oral noetic economy are characterized, according to Jousse, by a heightened stress upon balanced formulaic utterance performed in such a way that verbal and kinesthetic gestures are and were in complete harmony. The products of gestures of the laryngo-buccal muscles of the mouth and throat, words were used in the Palestinian milieu of Christ and his disciples within the living context of holistic gestural interaction as body communicated with body. Utterance was a synesthetic act-event. Within this milieu, verbal knowledge could not be separated from other modes of corporeal apprehension. Activities involving the same sets of muscles—eating, speaking, reading aloud—became, as it were, thematized under the same heading and so the teacher's task was the transmission of gestural sets and paradigms, the kinesthetic "handing down" of embodied knowledge. As Jousse notes, every memory, every act of rememoration, is in itself a system of individual gestures which replays the encoded gestures of the past, handling them with full mastery in the process of re/call.[69]

So for Jousse the Gospels came to be "played" in particular ways known to Christ and crafted by him in such a way that the synesthetic gestural resources of his culture would be permanently "embodied" within the language later to be set down in writing. Precisely in order that the chirographic stage might in time be reached by the Gospels, the language had to have both a strong mnemonic base and an equally tenacious gestural encoding, thus employing human capacities which would be sustained across time, particularly as "anthropos acquires everything he knows in this way."[70] *Mime*, Jousse's term for this mode of synesthetic gestural enactment, is the means of apprehension and experience which is congruent with the operative mode of the Gospels and also with what Jousse viewed in orthodox terms as the inscription and enactment of the Gospels in the liturgy and particularly in its central celebration, the Mass. An "aide-mémoire,"[71] the Mass for Jousse is a mime which enacts not the referential but the processual paradigm which it co(m)[cum]-memorates. It is a gestural enactment of community rememoration at each level of synesthetic experience, its goal the performative discourse of transsignification. "De la page écrite [of the *Ritual* and the Gospels] va surgir le mimodrame."[72]

An exploded *Lectio divina*, the Joussean semiotic of gestural enactment takes gesture as techne in the production of Gospels, liturgy and catechism, the pedagogical modes of oral noetics. Like the Ignatian logothetic system, the Joussean proceeds on the basis of what Patrice Pavis refers to in the context of theater as the ''performance-text,''[73] the enacted, enunciated text. However, where the Ignatian performance-text (the allegorical or ''acted'' text of the *Spiritual Exercises*) is given by the retreat director to the exercitant and is thus already a transsignification of the Ignatian printed text into the oral noetic text of meditations, gestures and spiritual practices assigned to the exercitant, the Joussean analog is, in a sense, the point of intersection of the printed text of Gospels or *Ritual* and the reader/receiver/ participant. Similarly, the Ignatian ''anagogic text'' (the linguistic response generated by but transcending the system of its production) finds its Joussean analog in the formulaic gestural response encoded in the Gospels and in the celebration of the Mass. A significant difference is apparent here, however, since the Joussean response component of the gestural paradigm exceeds neither the paradigm nor the performance-text as a whole. As Ong comments, even syntax is mnemonic: every element of the performance-text is both congruent with and in metonymic relationship to the whole of which it is a part.[74] Once again, the knowable world. To construe this world is to enact its synesthetic gestures.

But *Ulysses* is not, in any strict sense, the product of primary oral transmission in either the Parry/Lord or the Jousse modes. Eminently the product of a technologized culture, in neither its corrupt nor its now virtually immaculate typographic incarnations does it body forth sage or spirit in holy fire or otherwise. *Ulysses* is a book but a book which, as Walton Litz has written, ''lives in our minds as both process and product.'' It is a narrative whose ''intrinsic genre,'' Litz continues, ''is our total image of the work, which is recreated and modified each time we reread it.''[75] Or, as Hugh Kenner puts it, *Ulysses* is ''a kind of hologram of language, creating a three-dimensional illusion out of the controlled interference between our experience of language and its arrangements of language.''[76] Holographic performative, then; gestural enactment. ''Form is act.''

''Beyond Z'': *da capo*

Like *Portrait* and *Finnegans Wake*, *Ulysses* repeatedly defines itself, instructs us in its semiotic operations, specifies its genre, provides models of the relationship between its micro- and macrostructures, gives us practice sessions in decoding. It is like them as well in its elaboration of the strategies of oral noetics within the modality of print, its usurping of the referential bias of print ontology and adaptation of that skew as a Burkean ''terministic screen.'' The noetic *Ulysses*, then—the product of performative discourse in its semiotically fixed and experientially transient enactment—is a ''place,'' a locus on a memory chain, where no *one* speaks or thinks,[77] where the ''postulate of depth''[78] (or the ''kerygmatic assumption'') reveals precisely nothing, where everything is given, specified—even M'Intosh, our token mystery. And it is a system in which supplements are unnecessary if we come to the reading with that level of competence which the text demands, a not

unreasonable requirement in a work which seeks in an expanded ekphrastic moment—better: hour or day—to *be* an "act" in the sense which we have been
pursuing in this chapter.

Not only unnecessary, supplements are in fact excluded from this "form" which
is an act, for *Ulysses*—taking what Michel Beaujour calls its "topo-logie"[79] (topology, topos/logic) from oral noetics rather than print ontology—may be classified
as a *speculum mundi* rather than as an encyclopedia. As Beaujour writes, medieval
specula or mirrors

> sont des groupements de *lieux* ordonnés selon une métaphore topique . . . qui (que)
> fournit une taxonomie; et chacun des *lieux* contient virtuellement le développement
> dialectique d'un discours descriptif ou conceptuel, qui peut accessoirement s'illustrer
> de micro-récits exemplaires. Le *miroir* ne vise donc pas à narrer, mais plutôt à
> deployer intelligiblement une représentation des choses, or du sujet qui les connaît,
> tout en ménageant la possibilité de la possibilité de renvois d'un lieu en un autre,
> et celle d'ajouts dans les lieux déjà parcourus.[80]

We have already encountered a version of this form in the Ignatian "arborescence"
of paradigms in *Portrait*. Contrast the encyclopedia, which strives to attain a sequentially structured perfection—from A to Z—and, in so doing, to enclose the
world and thus achieve "comprehensive coverage" of the "sum" of knowledge.[81]

What is centrally involved here is an epistemic shift from the Scholastic premise
of comprehensibility of the world and its mirror, "man," to the post-Enlightenment
"scientific" paradigm of mystery enacted in the epistemological battle between
darkness/ignorance and light/scientific knowledge.[82] The encyclopedia, disseminator of higher knowledge to the laity, may thus be seen paradoxically as the
battleground of the foes of "irrationality" typically equated with medieval modes
of knowing and, in particular, with Scholastic realism. Involved in a constant
struggle to "keep abreast" of the latest knowledge, as the cliché has it, the encyclopedia as form was and is caught in the drive toward the fullness of sequentiality
since only through the full saying of "knowledge" can mystery be vanquished.
This is the fruitless struggle to push back the boundaries of ever-encroaching darkness conceived as that which the light of science has not yet demystified. As Vincent
Descombes puts it:

> On the one hand, the name of Encyclopedia excludes the supplement, for this title
> announces that the book is meant to have a comprehensive coverage of its subject
> from A to Z. On the other hand, in order to be what it claims and means to be, the
> Encyclopedia must allow the possibility of a supplement, an exposition beyond Z:
> if the book lacks such a supplement . . . it will be unworthy of its name.[83]

But "it belongs to the *eidos* of an 'encyclopedic' Summation *not to be* 'encyclopedic,' not to be able to close itself in the circle A-Z, not even supposing that
the book is in fact perfect, i.e., encyclopaedic."[84] Defining itself in terms of the
closed system, the encyclopedia is thus condemned to openness and therefore to
the courting of mystery. In contrast, the *speculum*, by displacing the goal of achieved

perfection to the god-term, is free to catalogue according to the convention of *elaboratio* enacted upon the topoi of the age. Thus, among others, "les neuf sphères du ciel, les neuf ordres angélique, les quatre éléments, les quatres humeurs du corps et de l'âme, les quatre âges du monde, les sept âges de l'homme, les sept vertus et les sept péchés capitaux."[85] Or, following the taxonomy of the *Speculum Maius* of Vincent of Beauvais: *Speculum naturale*, *Speculum historiale*, *Speculum doctrinale*, and *Speculum morale*.

Grounded in the assumption of an interactive, mirroring relationship between the world and humankind, and specifically between the world and the word as performative utterance, the Scholastic ontology which structures the *speculum* asserts the existence of an always and already comprehensible universe. These are the roots of Gothic pedagogy—as Beaujour points out, a mode of knowing which has its "architectural isotope"[86] in the Gothic cathedral with its system of "*lieux* concrétisés" in stone and iconography, "système qui programme une multitude de renvois entre les images et les fonds qui s'évoquent et se désignent les uns les autres dans leur contexte symbolique."[87] In its Joycean variation, this system begins with the theory of the epiphany in *Stephen Hero* and is elaborated in *Ulysses* by way of the extratextual programming device of allusion, the intratextual programming devices of the motiv system and overdetermination, and the hybrid devices of the pun and the riddle, both of which we will classify under the heading of catachresis. In turn these devices give rise to particular textual operations or sequences of programmed implicature which are activated during the processing of the text or that stage which we have already referred to as the assemblage of the "performance-text." At this point the data called up by the reader's enacting of and, in a sense, being enacted by the textual programming devices begin to become memory events.

In both the Linati and the Gilbert schemas of *Ulysses*, these events are governed by the specific "technic" or techne of each chapter, a mode of enactment which orchestrates the various phases of programmed implicature across the chapter as well as across the whole system. Repeated gestural enactment of the performance-text leads finally to apprehension of *Ulysses* as what we have called performative discourse—like Ignatian "semiophany" in that this dialogic process can be produced in no other way. But let us begin again in an eminently traditional place, with the Joycean concept of the epiphany.

As has often been pointed out, the concept of the epiphany has its origin in the Biblical story of the Magi who "journied from afar" to worship the Christ-child and celebrate the coming of the Messiah into the world.[88] What has not been stressed about this sequence in its Joycean application is, however, an aspect of it which the seventeenth-century homilist Lancelot Andrewes delighted in emphasizing: that the Magi "saw before they came, came before they asked; asked before they found, and found before they worshipped."[89] Following the star which they interpreted as signifier of the long-awaited event, they moved toward the expected signified, whose incidental details remained to be experienced but whose meaning they had already apprehended in the context of the prophetic tradition within which the child would later situate himself. Using the language of that tradition, their greeting commenced the process of inscription of the Word within the words already given and thereby the extension and modification of that language. Accordingly, this act-event was a teleological rather than a supplementary one. Alpha and omega, the Messiah came in a moment both ekphrastic and recapitulative, expressing the essence of language and in every sense *being* its meaning. Epiphany is thus an occasion of inscription rather than of transsignification: meaning is situated within the world system which occasions and mirrors it (the god-term author/izing his/her own text) rather than being the resolution of a conjunction of disparate systems the fusion of which is the act-event (the Eucharistic moment at the center of the Roman Mass).

—an important distinction and one central to Joyce's dealings with the concept of epiphany, for in *Stephen Hero* it is the object of the perceptual process which "is epiphanised" (*SH* 216) and not the subject who is thereby transformed. "Imagine my glimpses at that clock," SD tells Cranly, "as the gropings of a spiritual eye which seeks to adjust its vision to an exact focus. The moment the focus is reached the object is epiphanised" (*SH* 216). Like his earlier rejection of referential mimesis in favor of a neo-Thomist concept of the "artistic process . . . [as] a natural process" (*SH* 175), SD's concern here is to stress that subject and object achieve not fusion or symbiosis but, rather, exchange between compatible systems, each comprehensible to the other.

The epiphanic moment is the product of a reading process producing an experience of simple cognition rather than of kerygmatic revelation. At first "only an item in the catalogue of Dublin's street furniture," the catalogued clock—inscribed within a written system whose purpose is that of the *speculum* rather than the encyclopedia—"is epiphanised" when "all at once I see it and I know at once what it is" (*SH* 211). But SD's knowledge remains *specula*/tive (rather than speculary, the moment being one of cognition rather than of Narcissistic introjection; the perceiving subject does not experience transformation as a result of or in the course of the exchange). Not an ekphrastic moment, the epiphany involves neither the "still moment" of insight called up in Eliot's image of the "Chinese jar" nor the transsignifying capacity of liturgical ekphrasis. What transpires is the conversion of one term (catalogued clock as signifier) to another (the subject's discourse), a performative utterance which enunciates the quiddity, the "whatness," of the object through the temporary vehicle of the subject. Or, as SD has it in *Ulysses* I.2, "It must be a movement then, an actuality of the possible as possible" (*U* 2.67). SD is situating the catalogued Ballast Office clock as potential performative the utterance of which will fulfill the "demands" of the clock just as, in its Biblical form, epiphany refers to the utterance of the Magi witnessing the Christ-child as divine performative. The act-event *was* the utterance or enunciation, the witness which in itself was neither—in terms of the Biblical epiphany—the coming of the god-term (which was already in evidence) nor the informing of the Magi (who already knew). This is the beginning of the Joyce system's adaptation of epiphany, by way of the locus parallax, to the more complex requirements of the performative discourse which is *Ulysses*.

One goal of that discourse is monist synthesis, the early stages of which we can also recognize in *Stephen Hero*'s stress upon the *integritas* of the Ballast Office clock and the decorum of respect involved in the epiphanizing of its icon. One of the forms which that decorum takes in *Ulysses* is a mode of processual mimesis which has usually been seen as characteristic only of the later, "experimental" chapters. In fact, the world enunciates itself repeatedly throughout the system. "Sllt" says the printing press at the *Freeman's Journal* in II.4:

> The nethermost deck of the first machine jogged forward its flyboard with sllt the first batch of quirefolded papers. Sllt. Almost human the way it sllt to call attention. Doing its level best to speak. That door too sllt creaking, asking to be shut. Everything speaks in its own way. Sllt. (*U* 7.174)

As with *Portrait*'s induction of the reader into *Lectio divina*, we are here programmed in the comprehension of this form. Both terms of the equation are given in repeating sequence (the movements of a specific kind of machine, the icon of the sound made by such a machine in action) and the emblematic resolution of these terms is clearly stated as a maxim of the type characteristic of LB ("Everything speaks in its own way") followed by a recapitulative statement of the code phrase "Sllt."

The famous example of the cat's meow at the beginning of II.1 provides another instance of this mode of processual mimesis as well as a term necessary to the assemblage of LB as perceptual paradigm. Here we move from the cat's initial "Mkgnao" to "Mrkgnao," "Mrkrgnao" (*U* 4.16, 4.25, 4.32) and, immediately preceding the transcoding move to MB's first statement, "Mn," we have the cat's happy response to a saucer of milk, "Gurrhr," a delighted switching of codes (*U* 4.57, 4.38). It is interesting to see MB's code phrase associated with the hungry, unsatisfied cat's utterance rather than with its later, more contented one as well as to observe that within the LB paradigm, Gothic pedagogy dictates that both animals and inanimate beings "speak." Later, in II.8, the door in the newspaper office will "speak" again, enabling LB to make a distinction which the whole discourse system calls into question ("There's music everywhere. Ruttledge's door. ee creaking. No, that's noise" [*U* 11.964]) and which is contradicted later on the same page when MB's "Tinkling" is punningly classified as "Chamber music."

Performative utterance grounded in processual mimesis takes on the properties of heightened iconicity across the text as well, begging the question of who speaks. For example, in II.6 the discussion of the father-son relationship in *Hamlet* mutates into a rhythmic *specula/*tion on Shakespeare's will:

> Leftherhis
> Secondbest
> Leftherhis
> Bestabed
> Secabest
> Leftabed   (*U* 9.701)

And in II.8 the techne of *fuga per canonem* arranges numerous examples of iconically stressed processual mimesis. Simon Dedalus's tenor voice "soared, a bird, it belled its flight . . . the endlessnessnessness . . . " (*U* 11.745); MB's "wavyavyeavyheavyeavyevyevy hair [is] un comb:'d'' (*U* 11.809); and LB's flatulent ''last words'' go through as many mutations as the cat's earlier in the day, from ''Prrprr'' to ''Fff! Oo. Rrpr'' to a triumphant crescendo, ''Pprrpffrrppffff'' (*U* 11.1293). In II.12 the Gong says ''Bang Bang Bla Bak Blud Blugg Bloo'' (*U* 15.189); and in this processual chiasmus, Plumtree becomes ''Peatmot. Trumplee. Moutpat. Plam-troo'' (*U* 17.604), a transformation no more dramatic than that undergone by LB's name, subject in his youth to the anagrammatic variations

> Ellpodbomool
> Molldopeloob
> Bollopedoom
> Old Ollebo, M. P.
>
> (*U* 17.405)

But the text's insistence that no one ''speaks'' any of these words except the reader is perhaps even more pointedly evident in its denomination of referential mimesis *in absentia*. MB, for example, holds her teacup ''by nothandle'' (*U* 4.333), while in II.8 ''Bloom sang dumb'' (*U* 11.776) and the blind stripling ''unsee-ing . . . stood in the door. He saw not bronze. He saw not gold'' (*U* 11.1281). In the same chapter is a list of phenomena associated with sound: ''snakes hisss'' but ''hens don't crow'' (*U* 11.964), and a lull in conversation is encoded as ''None nought said nothing. Yes'' (*U* 11.224). Here we begin to see a shift which goes beyond manipulation of double negatives and into the problem of the enunciation of the negative as a category meaningful in itself.

Unlike SD's composition of his name as place in the universe of *Portrait* (an act of ''topo-logie''), LB's inscription is fragmentary: ''I [. . .] AM A'' (*U* 13.1258). The sentence is open, its syntax incomplete as the course of the ''everchanging tracks'' which MB and LB follow as they sleep, journeying westward (like Gabriel Conroy, toward death) along earth's orbit in ''neverchanging space'' (*U* 17.2310). Infinity is a place in the system, space a neverchanging element in its topology. ''Nought is nulled'' (*FW* 613.14) in the gestural enactment of the performance-text. The inscription of absence, the specification of what was but is no more, the denomination alike of incapacity and category shift: these are the materials of the *speculum mundi* which requires performative iteration whose tracks are the synoptic paths of memory events.

No more solid than SD's words in II.3, memories in a dialogic economy demand full gestural enactment lest their syntax be broken forever. So, like the young SD of *Portrait*, LB is also given to an Ignatian weaving of categories:

> Mouth, south. Is the mouth south someway? Or the south a mouth? Must be some. South, pout, out, shout, drouth. Rhymes: two men dressed the same, looking the same, two by two. (*U* 7.714)

—a process which introduces both the locus parallax and the ancient topos *coincidentia oppositorum*,[90] the co/incidence of opposites. Cusa's formula is used in its strictest sense here: terms denominated as opposites which have their incidence in a shared or joint manner. They co/operate, in other words. In order to move from the condition of "rhymes" to the state which II.12 classifies as "Jewgreek is greekjew. Extremes unite" (*U* 15.2097), the epiphanic relation of enacted rhyme must be displaced within the system, supplanted by parallax and then, through a neo-Hegelian reduction of opposites, the transient state of co/incidence achieved briefly through the techne of III.2, the catechetical form of the processual mimetic mode.

"Timeball on the ballastoffice down" is our first indication of this shift within the syntax as are the terms introduced within the LB paradigm immediately after this statement:

> Fascinating little book that is of sir Robert Ball's. Parallax. I never exactly under-stood. There's a priest. Could ask him. Par it's Greek: parallel, parallax. Met him pike hoses she called it till I told her about the transmigration. O rocks! (*U* 8.110)

Between II.5 and II.12, LB enacts parallax without expressing it, thinks again of getting someone to define it for him, but does not solve the problem which it poses until Chris Callinan asks him "What is the parallax of the subsolar ecliptic of Aldebaran?" (*U* 15.1656) "Pleased to hear from you, Chris. K. 11" LB answers, thereby bringing into co/incidence the topos parallax and two of its loci, the number eleven and Kino's advertisement for trousers. Kino's ad, which LB sees just before his meditation on Sir Robert Ball's astronomical text (in which he hoped to find a definition of parallax as an astronomical term), is the immediate occasion of his association of parallax with MB, whose assignation with Boylan has placed her and LB in a more than usually parallactic relationship that day. Able to define me-tempsychosis for her as transmigration of souls, LB is later unable to satisfy his own curiosity or to switch codes to deflect parallax away from associations with male genitalia ("O rocks" [*U* 4.343]). Which brings us back to Kino's trousers, the legs of which obviously do not exist in a parallactic relationship to each other (as the ones of the number eleven do) any more than do train tracks ("*Rose of Castille*" / "Rows of cast steel" [*U* 7.591])—yet another locus on this memory chain—which inevitably meet at infinity, a transmigration of lines otherwise known as "Amiens St. Station" or, in the *Wake*, the geomater's "quincecunct" (*FW* 206.35).

Infinity is both part of the problem and an essential component of the system, for the repeating elevens of Kino's trousers bring us both to the system's formulation of motiv as synchronic process—the inscription of infinity within the text—and to LB's mnemonic act-event, the vision of Rudy which, at the end of II.12, emble-matizes the "hallucinatory" techne of the whole. As one of II.8's polysemous maxims puts it, "Symmetry under a cemetery wall" (*U* 11.833), the performative inscription of death within the symmetry of the body as both erotic and mnemonic locus. For an oral noetic *specula*/tive economy, looking back "in a retrospective arrangement" (*U* 14.1044) is the beginning of an epiphanic co/operation of re-membered past gathered into remembering present inscribed in performative time which, through gestural enactment of the performance-text, becomes the synchronic moment of performative discourse. The full textual sequence is a transformative one, beginning as we have already seen in the conversion process of the epiphany and ending, by way of liturgical transsignification grounded in a recapitulative mode of processing, in an ekphrastic experience of gestural enactment—''spatial form'' in all its erotic and textual dimensions.

   Thus the noetic *Ulysses*, a synchronic act-event which II.11 approaches by way of anastomosis (enacted *anakephalaiösis* or recapitulative reweaving) as a vehicle of ''postcreation'' (*U* 14.294). As language speaks its own changes in that chapter— passing from Anglo-Saxon to evangelical rhetoric, catching up the threads of literary as well as ''vulgar'' dialects in the production of the system's Vulgate—memory is woven into present creation. If ''form is act,'' gynecological formation and sexual act are necessary initial processes in the after-birth of the text, processes which must be iconically operative before the act-object, language, ''is epiphanised.'' Language's epiphany, then, is II.11 in itself (the enactment of conversion) just as its necessary consequence and co/incident is II.12, the reweaving of the text. As one instance of the ''looking back in a retrospective arrangement'' motiv has it, ''all seemed a kind of dream'' (*U* 16.1401).
   But dream is simply another techne in the system, though perhaps a more than usually sacramental one. As LB says, ''You call it a festivity. I call it a sacrament,'' to which Alexander Keyes responds, ''When will we have our own house of keys?'' (*U* 15.1681) We are reminded that in III.2, LB ''as a competent keyless citizen . . . had proceeded energetically from the unknown to the known through the incertitude of the void'' (*U* 17.1019), the known in this case being the kitchen door to which he had gained access, having forgotten his housekey in his other trousers' pocket, by climbing over the area railing and briefly experiencing the ''incertitude of the void'' before landing unscathed on the pavement below. Like the circle described around crossed keys in LB's variation on the papal emblem, the House of Keyes ad, the void is a closed system having a definite beginning and end and, in this case, even extending in a straight line. In parallel specification of absence, the failed parallax of trousers unworn meets the progress of astronomical time not yet experienced since the creation of the universe: ''nought nowhere was never reached'' (*U* 17.1068).
   Not only inscribed within the system, however, the ''void,'' the end-term of parallax, is the operative force of the sacramental syllogism. Two catechetical exchanges from III.2 will help us here:

   What visible luminous sign attracted Bloom's, who attracted Stephen's, gaze?

   In the second storey (rere) of his (Bloom's) house the light of a paraffin oil lamp with oblique shade projected on a screen of roller blind supplied by Frank O'Hara, window blind, curtain pole and revolving shutter manufacturer, 16 Aungier Street.

   How did he elucidate the mystery of an invisible attractive person, his wife Marion (Molly) Bloom, denoted by a visible splendid sign, a lamp?

> With indirect and direct verbal allusions or affirmations: with subdued affection and admiration: with description: with impediment: with suggestion. (*U* 17.1171)

This elaboration of the penny-Catechism definition of a sacrament as "an outward sign of inward grace"[91] moves carefully through the classic weaving of the memory loci of light and darkness associated with this topos: from "luminous sign" to source of light, from visible to invisible and back, from seemingly superfluous detail ("*oblique* shade," "blind *supplied by Frank O'Hara*," and so on) to the assimilation of *specula*/tive data to the source of *illumination*, MB mystified. And although the sacramental process of transformation here is not "violent and instantaneous, upon the utterance of the word" as it is in II.11 after the cloudburst (*U* 14.1389), it is nevertheless the fulfillment of "performed possibility" like Mina Purefoy's child (*U* 14.1413), performed (logologically speaking) by the system's drive toward performative enunciation of its own techne.

Nowhere more evident in *Ulysses* than in II.12, techne structures a text whose performance is the weaving of the certitude of the void into the incertitude of the present, the certitude of the diachronic into the incertitude of the synchronic. It is an epic elaboration of the text's speaking *in absentia*, culminating in one version of the trope toward which all of *Ulysses* moves, the resolution of epiphany into sacrament, the factoring of past by encoded present which is the motiv system here resolved for an instant in the figure of Rudy.

Troping the separation of dream-time from wake-time, Rudy foregrounds II.12's use of hyperbole in the service of processual mimesis. A "fairyboy . . . dressed in an Eton suit with glass shoes and a little bronze helmet," Rudy reads "from right to left inaudibly, smiling, kissing the page" (*U* 15.4959), an icon of gestural enactment. As Barbara Johnson says of all readers of performative discourse, Rudy is one of the "effects"[92] of the text which he reads—a text perhaps Hebrew, perhaps speculary—reminding us of the difficulties of all "secondary modelling systems."[93] Closed within the text, he is lodged in a kind of textual hypogram[94] from which LB is forever excluded. Like the object which "is epiphanised," Rudy exists only within the continuum of the reading act, a parallax which cannot be resolved into infinity except by the end of the text, the final turn of LB as perceptual paradigm. To use Johnson's terms again, Rudy's " 'truth' puts the status of the reader in question"—both LB's status as reader of the vision and our status as readers of the book—and " 'performs' . . . [the reader] as its 'address.' "[95]

Earlier in II.12, Shakespeare seems to be performed in a similar way but the moment in which he "is epiphanised," the product of co/incident gazes, is radically different from Rudy's. Briefly accessible to his producers SD and LB, Shakespeare is also easily dispensable as Rudy is not. "The mirror up to nature" (*U* 15.3820), the vision of the bard's face rigid in paralysis, emblematizes the relation between aesthetic and natural process presented in *Stephen Hero*. Gazing into the hall mirror, LB and SD are figures of nature, bound together not only by rhyme but by a co/incident search for meaning in performative utterance. "Tell me the word, mother, if you know now. The word known to all men" (*U* 15.4192), SD begs his mother in II.12. In II.6 he has already received his answer ("Love" [*U* 9.429]), but only after the game of naming the world, begun in *Portrait*, expands by way of LB to include the naming of variations on love, hate, and death, and ends with MB's "yes."

No more SD's answer than SD is his, LB is a co/incident term, not a solution. In this textual "topo-logie," perceptual paradigms must achieve a dialogic relation (seen in extended form in III.2) but that relation is bound into the interattractive force field of "neverchanging space" (*U* 17.2310) rather than into self-centered romantic attachment. Thus although Nicholas of Cusa's neoplatonic label for this attraction is "love,"[96] his reference is to the attraction of substance for substance, "love" driven by energy of enactment or Kenneth Burke's concept of "motivation" in the sense of the textual encapsulation of the activity of motiv systems. But before considering motiv/ation as a form of parallax (its elements co/inciding at points of semantic "infinity" across the text, its intratextual programmatic activity serving as a metonymic guide to the recovery of performative discourse), let us return to SD and LB as "reagent" and "reactor," respectively, and take another look at "substance."

In the midst of a catechetically structured recital of the ills to which life is subject, III.2's catechist asks,

> Did Stephen participate in his dejection?
>
> He affirmed his significance as a conscious rational animal proceeding syllogistically from the known to the unknown and a conscious rational reagent between a micro and a macrocosm ineluctably construed upon the incertitude of the void. (*U* 17.1012)

The unknown macrocosm, the void, is a place, a locus on a memory chain, a destination attainable through the exercise of the syllogism. Like the motiv "parallax" with its locus "metempsychosis" and subset "transmigration of souls," SD's syllogism is a vehicle of parallax (through the end-terms of SD's "Ineluctable modality of the visible" [*U* 3.01]) and of parallactic enactment whose root paradigm is that of the act of reading. "Signatures of all things I am here to read" says SD (*U* 3.02), like Bloom eroding any distinction between animate and inanimate in his quest for understanding of the substance, the mode of operation and being of all creation. "Seaspawn and seawrack, the nearing tide, that rusty boot. Snotgreen, bluesilver, rust: coloured signs . . . ": like the Ballast Office clock, already catalogued, *signifiant*, waiting to "be epiphanised," followed by a "dog's bark" (*U* 3.310) and a dead dog, by SD's lips which "lipped and mouthed fleshless lips of air: mouth to her moomb. Oomb, allwombing tomb" (*U* 3.401).

Because the syllogistic move—like the pun to which the *in absentia* code approaches via catachresis—is fundamentally a sacramental one, the point of intersection is the point of semantic infinity on this ever-triangulating grid. Logologically viewed, the transsignification process which is the defining characteristic of the Eucharist (considered in orthodox terms to be the sacrament defining all others, given its central position in the Roman liturgy) involves the transformation of material elements (here, bread and wine) into spiritual ones (body and blood of Christ), the latter so integrated into and transformative of the former that the reception of even a fragment of the consecrated bread or a sip of the consecrated wine is said to constitute the reception of Christ. In this sacramental sense logologized, then, SD is the reagent in the transsignifying, syllogistic process, LB the field of enactment, and MB the occasion of transformation. At the processual mimetic level, what is being enacted throughout 16 June 1904 is the void, the point of parallactic infinity, Rudy bound in speculary reading, the god-term, the *raison d'être* of Gothic pedagogy, the performative discourse of the sign in the world through the naming of all of its parts, "world without end." Joyce's *Commedia*.

To which LB's response in III.2 is equally significant for the system as a whole:

Was this affirmation apprehended by Bloom?

Not verbally. Substantially. (*U* 17.1016)

Not understanding, not cognition but *apprehension*, and apprehension which moves a stage beyond LB's inaudible speaking of Rudy's name. Here there are no words: apprehension has reached its ultimate form as substance. The very stuff of being, the wholeness and particularity of SD's statement, is consumed in sacramental fashion. So LB models the reception of the performance-text in his role as "conscious reactor against the void of incertitude" (*U* 17.2210). But in contrast to SD's emphasis on the void, LB's on incertitude characterizes the reader's primary analytic task in the Joyce system: to submit to textual programming, thereby reducing the incertitude occasioned by our acculturated bias toward referential mimesis and thus toward mystery and kerygmatic reading. Beginning to move beyond plot- and character-functions (to the extent that these devices are used in *Ulysses* as a means of orienting the novice reader), we approach competence in the procedures of the system's processual mimetic ontology. The diegetic microstructure, in other words, serves the primary purpose of situating the competent reader within the textual syllogism which requires the response demanded by all performative utterance: enactment in the weaving of the discourse system which is the textual macrostructure. When our sense of balance falters and the "terministic screen" of the microstructure dominates our reading, the system contains us within a complexity of semiosis for which the referential cannot begin to account. Like the equally facile rejection of medieval systems of thought, the rejection of *Ulysses* by critics whose ideological adherence is to unreflective "realism" has to do neither with the Gothic pedagogy of medieval and modern systems nor with their products.[97]

Motivation, then, or the intratextual factoring of the text by such elements as parallax (in the fundamental sense of motiv: a recurrent unit acquiring meaning beyond its basic semantic value as a result of repetition across the text or any portion of it)—or "looking back in a retrospective arrangement"—mimes the semiotic operations of the text as a whole. Through the co/incidence of units constituting the motiv, the text finds one vehicle of synchrony or the achievement of, as it were, the strengthening of its paradigmatic axis. This operation is what II.11 refers to as "retrogressive metamorphosis" (*U* 14.390) since such readerly cognitive processing must always be the consequence of rereading, reflection, analysis. *"Da capo,"* as II.8's instruction says (*U* 11.1245). In this mnemonic exercise, III.2 provides rhythmo-catechetic training, the response paradigms generated by its techne hypostatizing not character and plot but "topo-logie," troping the performative utterance of the text and modeling its most basic operation.

From catechism to catachresis

In the course of his study of the Gospels as "sémiotique narrative," Louis Marin reflects on the meaning of locus, *lieu*, in the context of the discovery of Christ's empty tomb:

> Que ce lieu soit un *tombeau* et que le fait de l'absence soit celui du *cadavre* disparu, cela introduit la transformation de la topographie en topique, de lieu de l'espace en lieu de parole, dans la dimension sémantique de l'histoire.[98]

Jousse's concept of the "rhythmo-catechizing" process inscribed across the Gospels intersects with Marin's theory at the point where catechism takes over from event and the *"cadavre* disparu," the corpse of authenticity, has its absence inscribed at semantic infinity. Thus the necessarily parallactic enactment of the catechetical techne mimes not the recovery of the author but the recovery of the topoi in the process of enactment of the performance-text. Like the holistic gestural enactment of the Gospels in the liturgy, the processing of Joycean performative discourse requires a training process in the recognition of what "is epiphanised" at the motivic level as well as at other levels of patterning across the system. The initial and most basic demand is for the skills nurtured in an oral noetic milieu, one in which texts (oral or written) carry the systemic requirement of synesthetic mnemonic processing as described by such scholars as Opland, Scheub and Ong.

Marin's conversion of "lieu de l'espace en lieu du parole" is, however, not that of the Joyce system for the Joycean accommodation of typography to topography (which is the figure of *topographia*, in Irish the more restricted form being *dinndsenchús* or the "lore of places") effects the system's attempt to erode the boundaries of spatial and temporal modalities. *Topographia*, then, is correlative of the space-time continuum in modern physics or, as we have seen, the logothetic dissolution of such boundaries in synesthetic enactment through Gothic pedagogy. Caught up in the recapitulative movement which is particularly strong in this chapter, the parallactic "topo-logie" of III.2 with its catechetical response paradigms becomes a massive review exercise, and we are put through our dramatistic paces.

What we learn is, however, not scientific, not encyclopedic but once again *specula*/tive. If III.2 is the great repository of responses required throughout *Ulysses*, it is also the text's best example of the *speculum* in action and of the thoroughly comprehensible world to which that form bears witness. Comprehensible not in the scientific sense but in the *specula*/tive one as evinced in the Catechism, where, as in this mode's great exemplar, Aquinas, responses exfoliate, repeatedly intersecting others within a wholly predetermined order, a Gothic architecture of congruent word and world. Never totally and seldom even partially "answers," these responses are co/incidents together with their questions, both question and response having the status of memory event, or what we have been referring to as response paradigms. Thus the emphasis in this techne is equally on question and response and on the dialogic structure of their joint enactment, a structure in which neither changes as a result of or is affected by the other even in the sense that responses are occasioned or generated by questions. In this the response paradigms of III.2 are typical of the progress of perceptual paradigms SD and LB across 16 June 1904.

Response paradigms are memory events in part because neither component is predictable within the paradigm or the sequence of which it is a part. The catechetical act is grounded in paradigmatic order and syntagmatic processing more particularly than is the act of reading in general precisely because so much of what we learn through this mode will strike us as being non/sense outside the system. Its sense, in other words, is defined by and within the system as is the case with all processual mimesis. Not referential function but mnemonic placing within the topography of the whole is the criterion for inscription of data. Consider LB's catechized conclusion about the nature of the heavens:

> That it was not a heaventree, not a heavengrot, not a heavenbeast, not a heavenman.
> That it was a Utopia, there being no known method from the known to the unknown. . . . (*U* 17.1139)

But, as we have seen, SD's syllogistic procedure used later by LB in the sacramental elucidation of MB, "invisible attractive person . . . denoted by a visible splendid sign" (*U* 17.1177), does accomplish the movement from known to unknown, from world to designated void. So the parallactic motiv of void and incertitude takes precedence as signaled in III.2's earlier response that "the heaventree of stars hung with humid nightblue fruit" (*U* 17.1039) was the "spectacle" which confronted SD and LB as they emerged into the garden. Tree, grot, beast and man may, however, not a heaven make or a utopia; they are among the materials of a *speculum mundi*, a knowable, cataloguable system of which "heaven" or semantic infinity is one component.

So is its co/incident term, necessarily enacted with it, for if love is the will to form in this system, then hate, or "aosch" as the *Wake* has it (*FW* 286.02), must be inscribed as well. This is one function of II.9 summed up in parallactic fashion by LB: "Hate. Love. Those are names. Rudy. Soon I am old" (*U* 11.1069): a present-tense naming which, fulfilling Benveniste's principle, performs the act it utters. What act? Only by spinning the dramatistic wheel of motiv/ation can we respond (not "answer": author/ity resides within the system) to that question; only by calling up the vision of Rudy and synthesizing it with the loci on the topos of age for LB. Only by remembering the *signifiance* of names in *Portrait* and noting the shift from Stephen Dedalus in the Universe to LB's and SD's association of language with gesture: "the structural rhythm" of enactment (*U* 15.107) in II.12, the gestural language of seduction in II.10 ("Still it was a kind of language between us," says LB thinking of Gerty MacDowell [*U* 13.944]). In its weaving of the loci and topoi of the system, the catechetical techne precipitates its own unweaving as well, a process co/incident with aggregative performance and necessary to it, for however ekphrastic the moment as continuum, however recapitulative the motiv/ation, the performance must end. And that end, ever insuperable, must be inscribed within the system as well, inscribed so fully that the moment of semantic infinity—the moment when parallax at last accepts the intersection of its lines—will also be part of the gestural repertoire.

This is the function of the pun, a form of catachresis or "misuse" which epitomizes the defiance of the ontological primacy of sequentiality in the act of reading. Where catechism is dialogic, catachresis in its punning form is syllogistic, its middle term dispersed from the immediate occasion into the system. A device of segregation and dissociation in the Joyce system,[99] catachresis mimes the Babel of all language, temporarily hazarding a creative aphasia. But used within a system characterized by a high degree of redundancy and motivic patterning, and itself inscribed within the text's motiv/ation, catachresis has the effect of ictus, a term whose neurological meaning is as useful here as its poetic one. In prosody ictus refers to the strong beat in a metric foot while in neurology it designates that brief pause which comes before the beginning of certain kinds of epileptic seizures, a pause which stands in double relation to the ensuing event for it is both a warning of a time of disruption to be suffered within the neurological system and a last brief space of clear, sometimes heightened, awareness before interruption of consciousness occurs. Ictus serves, then, both to stress its own inscription and to presage its own undoing.

Within a system characterized by processual mimesis, ictus mimes the moment of death. Like epiphany, catachresis serves to clear an opening in language, to interrupt the relentlessness of inscription and enact the absence of name. An extension of what we have called parallax *in absentia*, catachresis as a single event attempts to subvert the memory system built up through enactment of performative discourse while retaining that system's place within the semiosis of the system. Attempting to sustain the instant of transsignification by intensifying the polyvalence of that process, catachresis refuses to accede to the syntactic demands of conversion and remains grounded in the iterability of the word and in its status within the logothetic economy of performative utterance. Analogous to Freudian dreamwork, as we shall see in the next chapter, catachresis synthesizes question and response, past and future, manifest and latent, catalyzing dichotomies into polyvalent units within the memory system. But the analogy is a partial one at best for catachresis in the Joyce system works in triumphant defiance and rejection of mystery—or, in terms of Freud's ontotheology, of the "unconscious" with its claims to encyclopedic rather than *specula*/tive operation. Like parody, catachresis operates in this context as a vehicle of full saying, sometimes of homage, rather than of revelation or kerygma. And, like epiphany, catachresis epitomizes the system's defiance of the ontological primacy of sequentiality in the act of reading, attempting through the dissemination and re/collection of its terms to test the memory system built up in the course of its own enactment in performance. In all this the Gothic pedagogy of III.2 provides an extended initiation, a rigorous exercising of procedures in place in elementary form since the beginning of the *Portrait*. To see how the Joycean ''double gesture''[100] of catachresis as founding trope and deconstructive pedagogy functions at its most complex level, however, we must turn to *Finnegans Wake* and the principle of Vichian morphogenesis.

IV

PERFORMING THE DREAMWORK

FINNEGANS WAKE AS
VICHIAN MORPHOGENESIS

"He who meditates this science narrates to
himself this ideal eternal history so far as he
himself makes it for himself. . . . "

—*(NS* 349)

"Omnis mundi creatura
quasi liber et pictura
nobis est in speculum;
nostrae vitae, nostrae sortis,
nostrae status, nostrae mortis
fidele signaculum."

—Alanus de Insulis

In his *Isagoge*, Porphyry was the first in the Western tradition to adapt Aristotle's
theory of division in the *Posterior Analytics* to a tree diagram, a model from which
"every subsequent idea of a dictionary-like representation stems."[1] Developed by
medieval writers as a way of showing how "man" can be defined with reference
to the hierarchy of inanimate and animate creation with its end-point in God, the
Porphyrian tree appears to be a structure absolutely ordered in terms of fixed hier-
archies. Thus in one of Eco's examples, shown in figure 3, binary opposites appear
to be logically balanced, and such categories as rational/irrational and living being/
nonliving being proceed systematically through the terms of a fixed hierarchy from
the general category of substances to the specific cases of man, god, horse and cat.
However, as Eco has shown, Porphyrian trees often give the impression of order
while, on closer examination, displaying a much more random mode of organization
in which, for example, the category of two-footedness is applied to disparate beings.
As Eco puts the problem, "Is 'two-footed' as referred to man the same as 'two-
footed' as referred to a bird? Is 'rational' as applied to man the same as 'rational'
as applied to God?"[2] Or, in the case of figure 3, is incorporeal substance necessarily
both nonliving and vegetal? Are horses and cats necessarily both irrational and
vegetal?

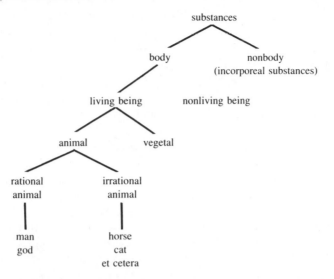

Figure 3. A Porphyrian tree. (From Umberto Eco, *Semiotics and the Philosophy of Language*)

In SD's Porphyrian tree of naming in *Portrait*, similar confusions occur. Having situated his name firmly amid the finite *differentiae* of "The Universe," he must consider the main branch of his tree, the god-term:

> God was God's name just as his name was Stephen. *Dieu* was the French for God and that was God's name too; and when anyone prayed to God and said *Dieu* then God knew at once that it was a French person praying. But though there were different names for God in all the different languages in the world and God understood what all the people who prayed said in their different languages still God remained always the same God and God's real name was God. (*P* 16)

Not surprisingly, "It made him very tired to think that way" (*P* 16). Unequal to the metaphysical task at hand, Porphyrian mnemonics quickly collapse into tautology as "The tree of genera and species, the tree of substances [and here the tree of specific languages and the principle of Christological language, the Word], blows up in a dust of *differentiae*, in a turmoil of infinite accidents, in a nonhierarchical network of *qualia*."[3] A rebound effect of the deconstructed tree diagram, this aleatory order grounded in the dense soil of catechetical response paradigms—Joussean "rhythmo-catechizing" applied to every other aspect of pedagogy—is evident in its simplest form in a passage several pages later in *Portrait*. In the infirmary after being pushed into the squareditch, SD's codes begin to shift:

> The fire rose and fell on the wall. It was like waves. Someone had put coal on and he heard voices. They were talking. It was the noise of the waves. Or the waves were talking among themselves as they rose and fell. (*P* 27)

The waves have lost their figurative place. No longer bounded within the confines of simile, they burst through metaphor into a radical reclassification analogous to the recasting of Porphyrian tree from dictionary or catalogue of fixed elements to encyclopedia or catalogue of elements no longer absolutely bound to their points of origin. But, as Eco writes, "The encyclopedia is a pseudotree, which assumes the aspect of a local map, in order to represent, always transitorily and locally, what in fact is not representable because it is a rhizome—an inconceivable globality"[4] bound into the scientific episteme with its inscription of kerygma.

The *speculum*, on the other hand, is a conceivable globality whose components exist in a state of self-correcting perpetuity immune to post-Enlightenment myths of scientific origination. Joussean "rhythmo-catechizing" or "eating the book and the teacher" becomes, then, an internally dictated survival strategy within the rhizome, a strategy which takes catachresis—as we have seen—as its epitome, as founding trope and deconstructive pedagogy. Troping the performative enactment of the Joyce system, catachresis models the text's operations in synecdochic fashion by mirroring the dialogic structure of the response paradigm but setting its resolution into bounded implicature. Catachresis is thus a way in which the Joycean memory system controls both what is and what is not explicitly given, by creating riddling situations, pun situations, in which the suspended term is heard like an overtone sounding within the given harmonics of the system. "Scribings scrawled on eggs" (*FW* 615.10) in other words, the syllogistic resolution waiting to be "eaten" when and as enacted. The operations of catachresis mime the processing of the whole system.

Parody here functions in much the same way. Not a kerygmatic strategy but a deconstructive one, parody is a mode of homage, inscribing (often ironically) one text into the semantic environment of another. An inevitable consequence of processual mimesis in a dialogic environment, parody "sings another's song," inscribing that song beyond "copyright," beyond ownership, in the ongoing narrative of the culture. Taking the production of such a narrative as one of its tasks, *Finnegans Wake* finds itself in precisely the position of Eco's Porphyrian tree. For as its roots struggle to set the textual rhizome more deeply into the earth of oral poetics (whether Irish, Homeric or Vichian), its flower becomes the heliotrope of another order, a "botanical calligram"[5] whose principles of morphogenesis inform Vichian new science. In the process, Porphyry—as we shall see in the next chapter—meets John McCarthy, and one tree becomes another.

"A tree story": *The New Science*

Among the meanings ascribed to morphogenesis by René Thom in his book *Structural Stability and Morphogenesis*, the one we need here is "decomposition of natural process,"[6] a phrase whose coincidence with SD's assertion in *Stephen Hero* of the "artistic process . . . [as] a natural process" (*SH* 175) helps to focus one of the major shifts in the system between *Stephen Hero* and *A Portrait of the*

Artist as a Young Man, a shift which anticipates the mutation from chapter III.2 of *Ulysses* to chapter II.2 of *Finnegans Wake*. In many ways the midpoint of this transformation, the stories of *Dubliners* are the product of a *translatio* or code-heightening by which the referential mimesis and author/itative discourse of *Stephen Hero* become the processual mimesis and performative discourse of *Portrait*. In other words, the "natural process" of nineteenth-century modes of rendering Presence as "consciousness" firmly in control of God the father-narrator mutates under the pressure of the morphogenetic principle within the system into the decomposition of that process through a deconstructive analysis of "composition," "nature," "process," and their supposed interaction. The recombinant semes[7] of the father-narrative undergo an Ignatian weaving of categories, a massive exercise of *ana-kephalaiösis* or recapitulative reweaving which, in the sense of the term which Bach preserves, *invents* Joycean discourse as memory wheel. Control is transferred from the "father," the patriarchally authoritative narrator of/in the text, to the programmed interaction of text and reader, in itself a no less absolute structure of power than the first but a differently constituted one, determining a different mode of reception.

Morphogenesis is thus a mode of invention, a techne, a principle of code-generation, whose motiv/ation is recursive or, in Vichian terms, ricorsive. "Ordovico or viricordo," as the *Wake* has it. "Anna was, Livia is, Plurabelle's to be" (*FW* 215.23). Defined by Vico in terms of the "virile heart," the motivs of strife, insurrection and siege on both personal and political levels delineate an order of male succession and design. But the way of order in Vico is also that of peace and inner balance, and the new science itself is a memory theater, a hall of topoi which mirror, often anamorphically, the condition of the human world. *Vi ricordo* (Ital.: "I remember you") as much as *viri cordo* (Lat.: "the heart of man"). As Donald Phillip Verene puts it:

> When we enter Vico's [memory] theater, we enter the *sensus communis* of the human race. The objects of Vico's frontispiece and his explanation of the significance of each place us immediately in the center, in the clearing he makes for us around which the oppositions of humanity can be arranged. Each of Vico's axioms is a recollective universal, a production of the bonding of the philological with the philosophical which can concretely affect the memory. His 114 axioms circulate before us, leading our memory to the "inner writing" of the human world, to its inner form.[8]

Ignatian *Lectio divina* has become Vichian *Lectio humana*, both systems of "topologie" characterized by *translatio* or intrasystemic transcoding, but proceeding in seemingly opposite directions: the Ignatian away from man toward God, the Vichian away from God toward man. In both cases, opposites coincide on the memory wheel.

Like Ignatian calisthenics, Vichian mnemonics serve a primarily pedagogical purpose. They are an "applied grammatology" grounded in the principle that human history is the product of human action rather than of divine intervention: "That

which did all this was mind, for men did it with intelligence; it was not fate, for
they did it by choice; not chance, for the results of their always so acting are
perpetually the same" (*NS* 383). Flux and reflux, peace and war, exist in an ongoing
condition of vital interrelationship, of "corso" and "ricorso" bound together in
the "setdown secular phoenish" (*FW* 4.17) of human life. Lacking the elegant
simplicity of Phoenix cycles, history is a muddled and muddied inscription of
recursively recirculating ups and downs, middles and beginnings and endings deconstructing each other "down all the ages" like Anna Livia's "mamafesta" alias
the letter scratched up in the midden by Biddy Doran, whose mixed identity (both
hen and old woman) reflects another version of ricorsivity, the motiv of ecosystemic
balance which we saw at work in *Ulysses* as well.

One of the Joyce system's major transformations of *The New Science*, this ecosystemic motiv filters what is known as the "*verum factum* principle" in Vico
through Ignatian *Lectio divina* to produce a manifold troping of "natural process,"
an *ars combinatoria* of mnemonic inventions. For Vico,

> Human knowledge arises . . . from a defect of our mind, i.e., from its extremely
> limited character as a result of which, being external to everything and not containing
> what it strives to know, it does not produce the truths which are its aim. The most
> certain things are those which, redressing the defects of their origin, resemble divine
> knowledge in their operation, inasmuch as in them the true is convertible with what
> is made.[9]

Because the human mind is, for Vico, "external to everything" and does not contain
the objects of its desire to know, it must attempt in its human intellectual operation
to imitate divine knowledge. In modern terms this is a kind of synaptic mime, a
processual mimesis at the highest level of abstraction and one which by definition
cannot of itself "produce the truths which are its aim."[10] Since for Vico the
production of truth is a theologically restricted activity, the human production of
imitative process comes to have value in and of itself in his system. This is epitomized in the "dipintura" which was designed under Vico's direction and engraved
to serve as frontispiece to the second edition of *The New Science*.[11]

Exhibiting the familiar Gothic pedagogical goals of synchrony and space-time
resolution, Vico's "dipintura" is an iconic *speculum mundi* which compresses
human history into an emblem and human knowledge into a *scienza* (*scientia*), a
mode of knowing.[12] Further, the "dipintura" serves as a rhetorical caution in
graphic form, a warning to readers who would interpret the necessarily diachronic
form of the text as an indication that its four books are to be taken, equally simplis-
tically, as being representative of three separate ages followed by a ricorso. As
Verene indicates, Vico's emblem functions as a mnemonic device, a recapitulation
of the major topoi of the memory system and an indication of the basic nature of
their relation to each other.[13]

Metaphysic occupies the central, mediating position in the emblem, with a ray
of light emanating from the divine eye and touching her breast while another, lesser
light moves in turn from her to a statue of Homer. At Homer's feet are what Vico's
"explanation" of the "dipintura" refers to as "hieroglyphs" (*NS* 3) which "denote

Figure 4. Vico's "dipintura." (Frontispiece to Giambattista Vico,
The New Science, 1730/1744)

the world of nations" (*NS* 26). Above are hieroglyphs which "signify the world
of minds and of God" while in the middle, under Metaphysic's feet, is a globe
representing "the world of nature which the physicists later observed" (*NS* 26).
Standing in metonymic relation to the *specula*/tive allegory of which it is a part,
the "dipintura" affords the reader an opportunity for the exercising of categories
as s/he trains to achieve the noetic experience of Vichian "semiophany" toward
which *The New Science* moves. If not a *Lectio divina* because of the fundamental
defectiveness of the human intellect in Vico, the Vichian memory system offers at
least the opportunity for a *Lectio humana* on a grand scale.

Because human knowledge is, for Vico, bounded by divine knowledge, human
inquiry into history and geography through analysis of the language which constitutes both these disciplines (or mythologies, in Vico's terms) as well as all human
knowledge, can lead ultimately to an understanding only of what man himself has
created. In Verene's words, "the human remembers back to the origin of the human
world, but not to the origin or ground of the world itself."[14] In the Joyce system,
however, no such limitation is in evidence. In its place is an almost Augustinian

confidence in the power of the word to generate a world, a confidence which—as we have already seen—shapes Joycean performative discourse according to the contours of liturgical enactment as memory system or, in terms of Ignatian reader response theory, according to the requisites of *Lectio divina*.

Essential to this process in *Finnegans Wake* is Vico's concept of the "Mental Dictionary" with its apparatus of Vichian theory of the origins of speech and writing in primordial time and of memory as a mode of Vico's complex concept of the imagination. Within this new science, what Vico calls "poetic history" and "poetic geography" take their place along with geometry as founding pedagogies, strategies for the recapturing in imagination of humankind's "ideal eternal history" (*NS* 62). If the uttering of this "IDEAREAL HISTORY" (*FW* 262.121) in itself constitutes the condition for entry into the "allaphbed" (*FW* 18.18) of language, the midden of all history, performance—mnemonic enactment—of the system is a means of repealing the law of cause and effect analogous to Vico's long struggle against the ascendancy of Cartesian logic. Taking a strongly anti-Scholastic turn, however, Vico's argument in the *De Sapientia veterum* is very different from the Joycean one, a difference which has radical consequences for the Joyce system. "Thinking," Vico argues,

> is not, indeed, the cause of my being a mind, but a sign of it, and a sign is not a cause. Thus the wise skeptic will not deny the certainty of signs, but he will deny that of causes.[15]

Because of its postlapsarian limitations, human intelligence can apprehend neither God the ultimate cause nor every link in the causal chains of daily life. Thus by virtue of its displacement of the divine final cause to a realm by Vichian definition beyond speculation, Vico's essentially logological system binds itself to ontotheology. Although this precautionary maneuver had the advantage of safeguarding Vico's life during the Neapolitan Inquisition, it does have the disadvantage of pulling the Vichian system against its own semiotic bias and inhibiting the systematic translation of theological to logological codes. By rejecting this suppression of the god-term, the Joyce system makes possible a logological rereading of "providential divining" (*FW* 599.13) through the vehicle of "this new book of Morses" (*FW* 123.35), *Finnegans Wake*. Following a "commodius vicus of recirculation" (*FW* 3.02) from the "strandentwining cable of all flesh" (*U* 3.37) extended in *Ulysses*, *Finnegans Wake* reads Vichian new science back through its originary maneuvers and through its own terms to the "Verb umprincipiant" (*FW* 594.02), first recombinant seme of the Joyce system.

"Through the trancitive spaces": *speculum* and allegory

Referring to that stage in the history of the encyclopedia which we have identified with the medieval *speculum*, Umberto Eco writes that "a maze does not need a Minotaur: it is its own Minotaur: in other words *the Minotaur is the visitor's trial-and-error process*."[16] The same could be said of Vichian autotelic "science." As we enter the maze, an array of memory tasks surrounds us. Before we can proceed, we must complete these tasks; we must exercise memory. Without such interpretive guides at hand, we will not be able to make our way with understanding through the maze although our information will change as, at each turn, the structure repeatedly defines itself and instructs us in the principles of maze navigation. We begin to perceive that we have entered a vast series of overlapping hermeneutic circles. However, there is no "horizon" or anything so fixed as a "perspective" or even an "oscillating perspective." As in the Vichian "dipintura," we are given the keys (*FW* 628.15) though we can't always find the locks. Following the familiar, we may find ourselves seeking out what seems to be the referential and beginning to collate allusions and stabilize what seem to be plot- and character-functions. Thereby we create our own Minotaur to drive out fear and bewilderment as the text—a maze sufficient unto itself—reiterates its instructions for its own processing. As Vico says, whenever humans "can form no idea of distant and unknown things, they judge them by what is familiar and at hand" (*NS* 122).

Both Vichian and Joycean systems are variations on an ancient mode, that of the *specula*/tive allegory which, in taking the form of an enormously complicated memory theater, demands of the reader-exercitant skills which the post-Enlightenment encyclopedia—with its literary heritage in the ascendancy of referential mimesis—rendered almost obsolete. The rhizome-text is, then (to shift Eco's point), "incomprehensible"[17] in terms of the capitalist ontotheology of the encyclopedia, of "science" in its post-Vichian sense, but not in terms of the maze which manifests it—in other words, not in terms of the Porphyrian forest to which it is native. If, as Maureen Quilligan has argued, allegories are always performance-texts, then we might say that rhizomes exist for the processing, a mode of readerly experience which Quilligan refers to, in terms of the tradition, as pilgrimage.[18] Seeking a form of enlightenment which would become problematic, the medieval notion of "pilgrimage" is paradigmatically autotelic and processual for the goal was achieved in the daily enactment of transient exile, self-imposed hardship, and ritual performance of prescribed penances. As in the Zen tradition, meaning emerged (or did not) of itself; semiophany was not conceived of as being a planned event.

Logologically speaking, the experience of textual *nembutsu* (as Barthes classified it) in both *The New Science* and *Finnegans Wake* begins with the gesture of acceptance, of "willing suspension of disbelief,"[19] which allows the *speculum*, which acknowledges textual dissemination of topoi and loci across the Joyce system, and which submits to textual programming. Like the *Wake*'s "Eins within a space" (*FW* 152.18), Vico's "Explanation" of the "dipintura" is the *specula*/tive version of "Once upon a time." And, as we have already seen in the case of *Ulysses*, the spacetime dictates of performative discourse condition the noetic experience of synchrony toward which the Joyce system moves. This experience is what Verene sees in Vico as the moment of total apprehension of the system, a moment made possible by the training of "re-collective *fantasia*" through the Vichian memory system. Thus, in Vico, Gothic pedagogy is

> a process of healing. The notion of wisdom as a whole for Vico is not the notion of unity. It is instead the notion of a language for the preservation of fundamental

opposition. Thus philosophical speech comes from the branch of the [mnemonic] image, the branch of the arts of humanity, but speaks of them only in relation to their opposite, the branch of the sciences, the life of the concept. This speech heals the soul by stirring its memory. It heals us from the madness of the concept, the thick night of rationality, with its language of the single sense of meaning, its inability to speak without a specifiable principle of order.[20]

In the Joyce system, that "thick night of rationality" becomes the battlefield of civil strife in which the seeming antinomies of war and peace (as denoted by Michelet and Quinet) are mediated by ricorso. But strife here extends also to the struggle between memory and anamnesis mediated by aboulia, and to that between language and silence mediated by the Vichian "Mental Dictionary" (*NS* 478) and resolved through the agency of catachresis. In this vast dictionary of all language which encompasses the field of enactment, of language *as* performative, the *speculum* serves as "map of the souls' groupography" (*FW* 476.33), but it is a Porphyrian mapping or arborescent cartography which differs from the Enlightenment ency- clopedia of Diderot and d'Alembert with their attempt, in Eco's words, to "trans- form the [Porphyrian] tree into a map"[21] pure and simple. Closer to Blake's "God us keep / From Single vision & Newton's sleep" and his *specula*/tive allegory of Albion,[22] the Joyce system's radical rethinking of the modern heritage of Cartesian ontotheology brings it into line with the work of such contemporary scientists as René Thom and David Bohm.

If, as d'Alembert maintains, there is a cartographic projection for every system of human knowledge, then the projection of choice for both Joycean and Vichian systems is "Cosmos" or what Phineas Fletcher refers to as *The Purple Island*.[23] Fletcher's allegory of the human body as geographical place is motivated precisely by the surrender of referential mimesis, for "a broad mimetic act must move nearly parallel to God's creation," a movement which Leonard Barkan argues is crucial to allegory as genre.[24] When, in Spenser's *Faerie Queen*, this mime of *Genesis* develops a chiasmic structure of body as "multiple world" and world anatomized into body,[25] allegory itself takes on the broad characteristics of catachresis as op- erative strategy. Thus the fundamentally synecdochic relationship of body and world is textually problematized by the bounded implicature of catachresis. Eco's "Model Reader,"[26] programmed in the application of Vichian "poetic geography" (*NS* 741) or Joycean Phoenix Park, is bound into the "implicate order"[27] of the system.

Consider David Bohm's example of this form of order. In the laboratory a trans- parent container is filled with a viscous fluid and is "equipped with a mechanical rotator that can 'stir' the fluid very slowly but very thoroughly."[28] A droplet of insoluble ink is added, the rotator is set in motion, and "the ink drop is gradually transformed into a thread that extends over the whole fluid." The viscous fluid will take on a grey cast but if the rotator is reactivated so that it turns in the opposite direction, the droplet of ink is reconstituted. Bohm's point here is that what appears to be random nevertheless has its own order, an order different from that of, say, another ink droplet placed in a different position within the same container. Bohm calls this kind of order an "enfolded" or "implicate" order and refers to the order created when the rotator is reversed as "explicate" order.[29] Using Bohm's terms, we can see Vichian "new science" as an explicate order insofar as we can recreate for ourselves "ideal eternal history" (*NS* 349) as a whole through our meditation on loci in the memory system.[30] Thus "he who meditates this science narrates to himself this ideal eternal history so far as he himself makes it for himself" (*NS* 349). For Vico, we can gain access to history through systems of implicate order such as the "Mental Dictionary" (*NS* 473), the product of the "mental language common to all nations, which uniformly grasps the substance of things feasible in human social life and expresses it with as many diverse modifications as these same things may have diverse aspects" (*NS* 161). By reversing the rotating blade of history, we can reconstitute the implicate order of language and, through that study, of the dawn of language acquisition in primordial time.[31]

Characteristic of allegory, this "literalization of etymology"[32] which is the central strategy of the "Mental Dictionary" leads Vico to the study of the ways in which familiar phrases contain impacted within them the traces of "ancient wisdom." For example,

> The French say *bleu* for blue, and since blue is a term of sense perception, they must have meant by *bleu* the sky; and just as the gentile nations used "sky" for Jove, the French must have used *bleu* for God in that impious oath of theirs, *moure bleu*! [or *morbleu*!], "God's death!"; and they still say *parbleu*! "by God!" (*NS* 473)

Or as the *Wake* has it, in II.1—a chapter rich in Vichiana courtesy of the fact that the "producer" of this "Mime of Mick, Nick and the Maggies" is "Mr John Baptister Vickar" (*FW* 255.27) himself—"how accountibus for him, morebleu?" (*FW* 253.36) ш is the one being accounted for here in his guise as hero of "gigantesquesque appearance" (*FW* 253.29) interred in the landscape, an incarnation of poetic geography and incorporation of the Vichian requirement that "allegories must be the etymologies of the [first or] poetic languages" (*NS* 403). Since "the first nations thought in poetic characters, spoke in fables, and wrote in hieroglyphs" (*NS* 429), it is not surprising that ш's crucial first fable, by Vichian definition a "true narration" (*NS* 808), should be the much disputed and highly ambiguous tale of his activities with the Cad in Phoenix Park. An allegorical account of the dangers inherent in all linguistic communication, ш's story enacts the Vichian axiom that "song arose naturally under the impulse of violent passions" (*NS* 108), passions recorded in the Ballad of Persse O'Reilly with its scurrilous insinuations about the father's conduct.

The fact that it is ш, rather than any other member of his family, who is subjected to this invective is also an inevitable consequence of the monosyllable which is his linguistic origin. From the thunderwords or names for Jove in the "ancient languages" are descended the primal interjections such as *pa*, from which come *pape* and *patrare*, meaning "to do, make," an activity which is the "prerogative of God" (*NS* 107). Not only is patriarchal power visited upon ш by language alone but the activity which succeeds his first fable is also patriarchally imprinted, for *interpretatio*, initially the interpretation of divine laws, is "as if for *interpatratio*" (*NS* 107), the Vichian variation on the father's no. In the *Wake* that task of interpretation in the patriarchal mode falls, in the absence of convincing speech by Ш, to the even less convincing foursome, Mamalujo (X), the disciples in old age and anamnesis, their oral heritage reduced to a peep show.

This comedown is a Vichian one as well, analogous to Ш's fate as a stutterer, a sign of his originary status, for just as the language of the gods was almost entirely mute and that of heroes an equal mixture of mute and articulate (*NS* 106), so Ш as a partial mute "must have uttered vowel sounds by singing, as mutes do; and later, like stammerers, . . . [he] must have uttered articulate consonantal sounds, still by singing" (*NS* 112–13). The four, however, represent a different stage in this Vichian allegory though one, like all of these "stages" and "phases," coterminous with the others just as the Vichian stages of the post-Flood evolution of landscape into mountains, then plains and finally to the shores of the sea (*NS* 44) are collapsed in the *Wake* into "Howth Castle and Environs" (*FW* 3.03) and "Dreamoneire" (*FW* 280.01). So the four are assigned double duty as bedposts overseeing the activities of the founding parents and as grave markers whose function as guardians is preserved etymologically since, in the "Mental Dictionary," *phylax*, the Greek word for "grave marker," comes from *phyle*, Gr. "tribe," denoting loyalty according to Vico. Echoing the *Scienza Nuova*'s three fundamental principles, the "eternal and universal customs" (*NS* 333) of religion, marriage and burial, the Mamalujo (X) etymological tree also includes such branches as *cippus*, "the Latin name for . . . post [which] came to mean sepulcher, and *ceppo* [which] in Italian means the trunk of a genealogical tree" (*NS* 529). From figurative trunks and literal posts Vico moves to extensions of the family tree: Lat. *stemmata*, referring to the long rows of statues of their ancestors which the ancient Romans placed along the halls of their houses, a custom perpetuated in the usage of *stemmata* to signify "family arms." Thus in the *Wake*, "Arms appeal with larms, appalling" (*FW* 4.07), "huroldry" (*FW* 5.06) and "scutschum" (*FW* 5.08) are always associated with strife and bloodshed in various forms, and all in turn are associated also with patrilineal claims upon the bodies of earth and people.[33] However, it is the conflict of eye and ear to which the four give most urgent witness, a conflict of linguistic *stemmata*, of speech and writing, of memory and its inescapable other term, anamnesis, death.

Like poetic etymologies, hieroglyphs in the Vichian system are traces of the thought of the first humans in primordial time. The earliest records of the "mental language common to all nations," the "*lingua mentale commune*" (*NS* 161), hieroglyphs make the "Mental Dictionary" possible for the following generations of humankind. Preceding speech, this early mute language operated by associating "signs, whether gestures or physical objects" (*NS* 401), with the "ideas" to be expressed. By using "poetic logic," Vico concludes from this sequence that a transfer of power took place between these abstract "signs" and the words which, like hieroglyphs, represented them. Thus, since "*logos*, or word, meant also deed to the Hebrews and thing to the Greeks'' (*NS* 401), the breaking of the semiotic chain linking concept, gesture or representative object with semantic expression became the occasion of physical violence. Accordingly, ''wars are waged for the most part between nations differing in speech and hence mute in relation to each other'' (*NS* 487).

In the *Wake*, the embattled relationship of Mutt and Jute, Stone Age men who have nevertheless mastered Vico's five stages of language acquisition (interjections, pronouns, particles, nouns and verbs [*NS* 109]), enacts the most rudimentary difficulties of the ''sound seemetery'' (*FW* 17.36). The Vichian giants are not long gone but hieroglyphs in the form of runes have emerged and the thunder which sent the giants in terror to their mountain caves (*NS* 122) has also made it possible for Mutt and Jute to do business with each other. As Jute says,

> Bisons is bisons. Let me fore all your hasitancy cross your qualm with trink gilt. Here have sylvan coyne, a piece of oak. (*FW* 16.29)

As ''mental'' signs mutate into pecuniary ones, private property also becomes possible and with it writing, the ''as time went on as it will variously inflected, differently pronounced, otherwise spelled, changeably meaning vocable scriptsigns'' (*FW* 118.26). With ''scriptsigns'' comes print and ''what papyr is meed of, made of, hides and hints and misses in prints'' (*FW* 20.10). An author is an authority, an owner of fields as are the giants who, struck down with fear by Jove's thunderbolts, had first hidden in their caves, then learned to cease wandering and to settle in one place and begin families. As Vico puts it with fine patriarchal spirit:

> So it came about that each of them would drag one woman into his cave and would keep her there in perpetual company for the duration of their lives. Thus the act of human love was performed under cover, in hiding, that is to say, in shame; and they began to feel that shame which Socrates described as the color of virtue. And this, after religion, is the second bond that keeps nations united, even as shamelessness and impiety destroy them. (*NS* 504)

Shame, inevitable consequence of sexual passion after the first age of ''bestial lust'' (*NS* 504), is thus also a consequence of writing in the Vichian system. An *auctor* or landowner is also a *fundus*, founder and—in Swift's term—''fundament'' (*NS* 491). Like **⊏**'s, his products are excremental, his own body his text, a ''continuous present tense integument'' which slowly unfolds all history (*FW* 186.01). The writer in himself writes process and product and is a ''self-consuming artifact''[34] whose cycle begins in family (resident at the house ''O'Shea or O'Shame'' [*FW* 182.30]), is subsumed by religion and, falling victim to strife within his ''dividual chaos'' (*FW* 186.04) or without in the ''*pura et pia bella*'' (*FW* 178.17) of his age, finally succumbs to death and Vico's last mark of civilization, burial. In the *Wake* this is the passage from ''stripture'' (marriage, human sexual experience) to ''scripture'' (religion, writing) and to ''sepulchre'' (burial), a passage also known as ''cycloannalism'' (*FW* 254.26–28) in honor of the regularity of its occurrence.

The problem of causality is, however, a more difficult one, returning us to Vico's conviction that, limited by a fallen intellect, humankind cannot return by way of poetic logic or imagination to the divine first cause but only to the beginning of human thought. The *Wake* ironizes the same problem: ''Now, the doctrine obtains, we have occasioning cause causing effects and affects occasionally recausing altereffects'' (*FW* 482.36). Which is the root paradigm of another familiar *Wake* predicament: ''how one should come on morrow here but it is never here that one today. Well but remind to think you where yesterday Ys Morganas war and that it is always tomorrow in toth's tother's place'' (*FW* 570.10). Thoth's place, the place of writing, is both *The (Egyptian) Book of the Dead* and the ''book of that which is '' (*FW* 570.08), the ''book of the opening of the mind to light'' (*FW* 258.31) and the ''chapter of the going forth by black'' (*FW* 62.27), a ''wolk in process'' (*FW* 609.31) and a forged ''palimpsest'' (*FW* 182.02) inscribed with ⊏'s ''stolentelling'' (*FW* 424.35). In all this, final answers are unavailable: ''Mere man's mime: God has jest. The old order changeth and lasts like the first'' (*FW* 486.09), the reason being not only that explicate and implicate orders are involved with each other but also that ''The mar of murmury mermers to the mind's ear, uncharted rock, evasive weed. Only the caul knows his thousandfirst name. Hocus Crocus, Esquilocus, Finnfinn the Faineant . . . '' (*FW* 254.18).

As the little death of memory lapse breaks the cycle of memory, so name reveals fraud for, as Vico says, '' 'Name' and 'definition' have also the same meaning'' (*NS* 433) and ⨆ is but a pale imitation of Jove, whose interjections, the first thunderbolts, gave birth by onomatopoeia ''to one produced by the human voice: '*pa*!' '' which was soon doubled: ''*pape*!'' (*NS* 448). Papa ⨆'s ''pregross'' (*FW* 284.22) in this respect is commemorated in the eighth of the *Wake*'s thunderwords— ''Pappappapparrassannuaragheallachnatullaghmonganmacmacmaconacmacwhackfallthedebblenonthedubblandaddydoodled'' (*FW* 332.05)—in which the ballads of ''Finnegan's Wake'' (''Whack fall the doodle-o'') and ''Yankee Doodle'' (''daddydoodled'') combine to celebrate the fall of ''pappa the gun'' (*FW* 331.01). Thunderwords are ''last word[s] of perfect language'' (*FW* 424.23) because of the descent which they signal from the mute state of the gods to the articulate one of humankind. With words comes the strife of ''this babbel men dub gulch of tears'' (*FW* 254.17), and, since ''letters and languages were born twins and proceeded apace through all their three stages'' (*NS* 5), with letters comes the disappearance of ''false religions'' (*NS* 25) and the subsequently embattled state of the remaining ''true religion'' (*NS* 365).

This is the conflict of poet and cleric, church and state, arts and sciences which the *Wake* encodes in terms of Patrick and Balkelly, Kells and Irish *kills* (church), ''prout'' and ''poeta.'' Referring to ''Father Prout,'' the pen name of Irish Jesuit F. S. Mahoney, whose poem ''The Bells of Shandon'' is regularly satirized in the *Wake*, the following passage summarizes grammatological history in Ireland, mentioning along the way the coastal raids of the Vikings against the Irish, and the burial of the Book of Kells:

> The prouts who will invent a writing there ultimately is the poeta, still more learned,
> who discovered the raiding there originally. That's the point of eschatology our book

of kills reaches for now in so and so many counterpoint words. What can't be coded can be decorded if an ear aye sieze what no eye ere grieved for. (*FW* 482.31)

In the working out of its polyglot "Mental Dictionary," the *Wake* reinvents Vichian "ideal eternal history," encountering war (Gr. *polemos*) as it anatomizes the city (*polis*, in Vichian poetic etymology [*NS* 588]) and encountering religion (Lat. *ara*, "altar") as it inscribes another aspect of the collective dungheap of "thanacestross mound" (*FW* 18.03), this time plows (*aratrum*) whose moldboard (*urbs*) resolves the Vichian poetic relationship of *ara*, *aratrum* and *urbs* and thus of the interface of urban and rural worlds (*NS* 778). Vichian "true religion" is shown up as a con job (a Prout) with lethal capabilities which must be met by a fit opponent, the *Wake* itself as a "proteiform graph [which] itself is a polyhedron of scripture" (*FW* 107.08). The *eschaton* toward which the new scripture points thus employs "strangewrote anaglyptics" (*FW* 419.19) as well as maps and "letters" (*FW* 478.02) in accordance with the Vichian schema for the evolution of language (*NS* 98). The problems of coding for eye and ear in the *Wake*, however, exceed even Vichian bounds.

A "general theory of the universal unfolding": Quinet and Michelet

"A man," says *The New Science*, "is properly only mind, body and speech, and speech starts as it were midway between mind and body" (*NS* 347). Speech the mediator, however, performs more than simple linguistic acts for in Vico the oral *is* written, the achievement of linguistic fluency *is* the achievement of writing. "All nations began to speak by writing," we are told, "since all were originally mute" (*NS* 97). As to that Enlightenment obsession, the question of the "origin of languages and letters," Vico asserts that the problem is an invention of scholars,

> all of whom regarded the origin of letters as a separate question from that of the origin of languages, whereas the two were by nature conjoined. And they should have made out as much from the words "grammar" and "characters." From the former, because grammar is defined as the art of speaking, yet *grammata* are letters, so that grammar should have been defined as the art of writing. So, indeed, it was defined by Aristotle, and so in fact it originally was; for all nations began to speak by writing, since all were originally mute. (*NS* 429)

Thus the Vichian evolution from the divine, mute language of hieroglyphs to the heroic, symbolic one of signs and "heroic devices" such as coats of arms and, finally, to the human, epistolary language of letters (*NS* 98, 106, 290) in fact reflects a series of coterminous transformations in understanding of the "semiosic web."[35] This shift in the semiotic weighting of icon/hieroglyph, index/heroic device, and symbol/epistle is most obvious during the ricorso or time of reflux, when warfare erupts as a result of nations or peoples having become "mute in relation to each other" (*NS* 119) and reverting to earlier stages of linguistic competence. Thus the resurgence of military insignia and coats of arms in battle is a return to "hieroglyphic writing" with its symbiotic relationship to "duels, raids, reprisals, slavery, and asylums" (*NS* 353). This collapsing of index into icon represents also a temporary suspension of the symbolic/epistolary mode with its grammatological stress upon the balancing and synthesizing of oral/aural and visual systems—in other words, upon the identity of speech and writing.

For Vico, then, the temporary privileging of one sensory modality over others ruptures the balance of a complex communication network grounded in the co/incidence of opposites. Just as speech mediates between "mind" and "body," so grammatology or, more specifically, "arche-writing"[36] as the central morphogenetic function in *The New Science* is the de facto agent of the Vichian monist ontology. Violence thus represents the incursion of Cartesian dualist hegemony of one sensory modality over another, producing a reflux and dissemination both of earlier unitary linguistic modes and of their tautological extensions in Vico, that is, of dualist concepts of body, mind, consciousness, sensory experience, human hegemony within the ecosystem: the structures of "dividual chaos" (*FW* 186.04) resulting from the shattering of the world community. But chaos in Vico is not absolute; it is "order othered" (*FW* 613.14), "aosch" (*FW* 286.02). It is implicate in world order and thus in morphogenesis. In Bohm's terms, "aosch" can be "explicated" and enfolded again within the macrosystem just as "order" can be "othered," implicated into "aosch."

The Vichian variation on René Thom's "general theory of the universal unfolding"[37] is thus fully grounded in a complex process of *anakephalaiösis*, leading not to the moment of salvation (as Karl Löwith has shown, Vichian history is not *Heilsgeschichte*)[38] but to the endless reenfolding into the ecosystem of insoluble materials being endlessly unfolded from or, more properly, "implicated" out of it. To attempt to break the holistic balancing, the homothetic movement, of living beings is, in Vico, to attempt the destruction of language "itself," to attempt anesthesis of a homologous macrosystem. "Who gave you that numb?" Mark asks Mamalujo (*FW* 546.26) not because name is identity but because the act of naming, the originary languaging act pertinent to any being, marks the full enfolding of that life into community in a profound symbiosis which it denies not only at its own expense but, because it is bound into the semiosic web of the universe, at the expense of all other life forms. Vichian history thus works a dramatistic variation on allegory as "cosmos" and situates allegorical text-processing and text-generation within the matrix of universal morphogenesis. Allegory becomes macrotext; the Gothic pedagogical structures of allegorical performative discourse become the basic structures and processual modes of world-understanding.

"*Mundus*," says *The New Science*, first denoted a "slight slope" and then, when the "theological poets" and geographers came to imagine their situation,

> they came to understand that the earth and the sky were spherical in form, and that
> from every point of the circumference there is a slope toward every other, and that
> the ocean bathes the land on every shore, and that the whole of things is adorned

with countless varied and diverse sensible forms, the poets called this universe *mundus* as being that with which, by a beautifully sublime metaphor, nature adorns herself. (*NS* 725)

Since "among the Greeks and Latins 'name' and 'nature' meant the same thing" (*NS* 494), *mundus* may be seen to incorporate *natura*, and *natura* to enfold *logos/* language just as, according to "poetic geography," "Within Greece itself . . . lay the original East called Asia or India, the West called Europe or Hesperia, the North called Thrace or Scythia, and the South called Libya or Mauretania" (*NS* 742). Thus, "in virtue of the correspondence which the Greeks observed between the two," microcosm was applied to macrocosm, Greece to the world (*NS* 742).

Throughout this sequence, the new science of metonymy is set repeatedly within the larger allegorical exchange process of metaphor. Greece is not less Greece (or Greek) for being the world and the world is no less polysystematic, no less otherly ordered, for being set against Greece in juxtaposition or subsumed within Greece in enfoldment. Like Bohm's container of viscous fluid, *mundus* implicates all matter within its bounds and thereby renders possible the "explication" of any of its parts even if those parts should be orderly structures within a disordered or ricorsive system.[39] An instance of disorder becomes, then, one possible configuration within the "universal [explicate] unfolding." Conversely, any instance of "order" also becomes one possible configuration within universal implicate enfolding, and so on through the permutations and combinations of the Vichian system. We can see one bounded instance of this Vichian paradigm in *Finnegans Wake*'s use of Jules Michelet and Edgar Quinet in relation to the mediating figure of Vico allegorized.

In his *Introduction à la Philosophie de l'Histoire de l'Humanité*, Edgar Quinet presents a benign and optimistic variation on the topos of humankind's place in nature, emphasizing the intrinsic harmony of their interrelationship and the transience of any rupture in the scheme of things. History has its roots "dans les entrailles mêmes de l'univers"[40] and humankind's place is a mediating one between the vast harmonies of the cosmos and the individual rhythms of other animate beings who live alongside us in the world. Thus, although human action has its own distinctive "harmonies and contrasts," it is nevertheless analogous in its order and stability to the physical world as a whole. So close is this morphogenetic bond that "les accidents de la vie des fleurs" may serve "à expliquer des phénomènes correspondants dans l'existence des corps politiques."[41] Humankind, however, has been reluctant to accept its place in the processes of the universe, claiming instead the right of hegemony, of absolute power over other life forms.[42] In Quinet's system, the universe is the companion of humans, its laws are our laws, its destiny is our history.[43] The past lives in us, its order animating our lives. As he writes of his own sense of being bound into the evolving order of time:

je me berce de cet espoir, que la puissance qui a su peser et balancer les siècles et les empires, qui a compté les jours de la vieille Chaldée, de l'Egypte, de la Phénicie, de Thèbes aux cent portes, de l'héroïque Sagonle, de l'implacable Rome, saura bien

aussi coordonner ce peu d'instants qui m'ont été réservés, et ces mouvements éphé-
mères qui en remplissent la durée.[44]

In Quinet death is only a moment within the cycle of time, only "une transformation ascendante, la vie des peuples [n'est] qu'un court moment dans la vie
universelle, une feuille d'un arbre, une page d'un livre, où nous nous efforçons de
déchiffrer l'instant présent à travers les révélations du passé."[45] Cities appear and
disappear as their times come and go.[46] "Si promptement les traces de l'homme
sont effacées par le souffle des âges!"[47] Even the epic battles of the past are erased
by the power of time, of the order of the universe as epitomized by the tenacity of
wildflowers growing amid the ruins of ancient empires.[48] This is the context of the
"beautiful sentence from Edgar Quinet"[49] which recurs across *Finnegans Wake*.

> Le moindre grain de sable battu des vents a en lui plus d'éléments de durée que la
> fortune de Rome ou de Sparte. Dans tel réduit solitaire je connais tel ruisseau, dont
> le doux murmure, le cours sinueux et les vivantes harmonies surpassent en antiquité
> les souvenirs de Nestor et les annales de Babylone. Aujourd'hui, comme aux jours
> de Pline et de Columelle, la jacinthe se plait dans les Gaules, la pervenche en Illyrie,
> la marguerite sur les ruines de Numance; et pendent qu'autour d'elles les villes ont
> changé de maîtres et de nom, que plusieurs sont rentrées dans le néant, que les
> civilisations se sont choquées et brisées, leurs paisibles générations ont tranversé les
> âges, et se sont succédé l'une à l'autre jusqu'à nous, fraîches et riantes commes aux
> jours des batailles.[50]

For Quinet, Vico is the philosopher of "les lois universelles de l'humanité," the
creator of "ideal eternal history." The rise and fall of civilizations is only "l'expression du rapport du monde avec cette indestructible cité" of Vichian universals[51]
and, according to their position in the order of time, nations

> entrent en rapport avec cette cité idéale, et s'établissent dans son enceinte; ils la
> parent de leurs couleurs, et, pendant qu'ils existent par elle et en elle, ils lui com-
> muniquent en retour un mouvement apparent; ils la revêtent de tous les emblèmes
> que des époques diverses leur ont apportés: ils promenent quelque temps leur gloire
> ou leur misère, dans ses immuables labyrinthes; ils font entendre en passant leurs
> voix sous ses voûtes silencieuses; quand ils périssent, elle ne périt point: elle se
> dégage de leurs ruines, et reparaît toute radieuse dans la région des idées.[52]

Although Quinet's new science is closer to being a purely Platonic one than is
either Vico's or Joyce's, his sense of the symbiosis of all life forms in the world
and, in particular, of flowers as emblems of that profound interrelationship is crucial
to *Finnegans Wake*. The children's game of colors in II.1, the heliotrope motiv
with its complex of associations with Dublin/Heliopolis, ш as Pharoah, Λ in his
Joussean role of seducer of ⊥ and the "hedge daughters" (*FW* 430.01), and the
recurrent associations of Δ with flowers, leaves and water: these are some of
Quinet's iconic flowers of morphogenesis though their *Wake* lives are more com-
plexly implicate than Quinet's cosmological botany would in itself allow for. Em-

blems of the "dear prehistoric scenes" (*FW* 385.18), the *Wake*'s "botanical calligrams" bind Ireland to Quinet's Egypt, Chaldea and Phoenicia, and Irish antiquity to the classical past:

> Since the bouts of Hebear and Hairyman the cornflowers have been staying at Ballymun, the duskrose has choosed out Goatstown's hedges, twolips have pressed togatherthem by Sweet Rush, townland of twinedlights, the whitethorn and the redthorn have fairygeyed the mayvalleys of Knockmaroon, and, though for rings round them, during a chiliad of perihelygangs, the Formoreans have brittled the tooath of the Danes and the Oxman has been pestered by the Firebugs and the Joynts have thrown up jerrybuilding to the Kevanses and Little on the Green is childsfather to the City (Year! Year! And laughtears!), these paxsealing buttonholes have quadrilled across the centuries and whiff now whafft to us, fresh and made-of-all-smiles as, on the eve of Killallwho. (*FW* 14.35)

With a nod to Lewis Carroll's Lobster Quadrille, the *Wake*'s wildflowers two-step across Ireland from a couple of Dublin's less fashionable suburbs (Ballymun and Goatstown) to Rush in County Wicklow, Knockmaroon in the Moy Valley and back by "whiff" to the *Wake*'s own "indestructible city," the "sound seemetery" (*FW* 17.35) of Chapelizod, Phoenix Park, Dublin Bay, the Liffey, the Wicklow Hills: a Vichian "poetic geography" compound of "Dyoublong" (*FW* 13.04).

Quinet's flowers are also caught up in the battles of ⊏ and Λ for pride of place. At the end of III.1, ⊏'s chapter on Λ the Post, carrier of ▲'s letter (an inscription in "shemletters" of ▲'s "anaglyptics" [*FW* 419.20]), ⊏ consigns his twin brother to the flowers of death: "may the tussocks grow quickly under your trampthickets and the daisies trip lightly over your battercrops" (*FW* 428.26). However, if being battered by buttercups seems an innocent fate, II.2 has worse in store for both of the twins as Quinet's flowers are assigned "THE PART PLAYED BY BELLE-TRISTICKS IN THE BELLUM-PAX-BELLUM MUTUOMORPHOMUTA-TION" (*FW* 281.R1). Here the Quinet sentence is set in the context of the twins' battles in metonymic relation to all of the world's "Enten eller, either or" squabbles with their equally possible "Nay, rather!" conclusions (*FW* 281.29). Flowers become emblematic of these power struggles ("Margaritomancy! Hyacinthous perivinciveness! Flowers. A cloud" [*FW* 281.14]) as the hieroglyphic stage of language takes ascendancy in conflict situations but, lacking the power of homeopathic magic, the cloud of flowers becomes a background to strife: "Bruto and Cassio are ware only of trifid tongues the whispered wilfulness, ('tis demonal!) and shadows multiplicating . . . , totients quotients, they tackle their quarrel" (*FW* 281.15). Later, in II.3, Quinet's flowers are more directly affected by the battles of the "samuraised twimbs" who "had their mutthering ivies and their murdhering idies and their mouldhering iries in that muskat grove but there'll be bright plinnyflowers in Calomella's cool bowers when the magpyre's babble towers scorching and screeching from the ravenindove" (*FW* 354.24). Signaling the end of an explicate time of Babel, the magpie-Phoenix is the pyre from which emerge both the raven of black foreboding and the dove of peace, both murderous ivy and "bright plinnyflowers."

Before babble, scorching and screeching are enfolded into "sound, light and heat, memory, will and understanding" (*FW* 266.18) which must e/merge "in gyrogyrorondo" (*FW* 239.27).

Brutus and Cassius, Browne and Nolan, Bruno of Nola and Nicholas of Cusa, Edgar Quinet and Jules Michelet: opposites bound, since "felixed is who culpas does" (*FW* 246.31), in order constantly othered, *per omnia saecula saeculorum* ("Poor omniboose, singalow singlearum" [*FW* 488.11]). And without "ricocoursing" (*FW* 609.14), "Solitude" (*FW* 246.35) and beginning again in caves of rock or spirit, mind and body are set apart before the coming of reflection (*NS* 236). Hence the Vichian "universal principle of etymology in all languages: words are carried over from bodies and from the properties of bodies to signify the institutions of the mind and spirit" (*NS* 237). Before that fluent deconstruction of body and mind which denotes the coming of grammatology, human institutions remain undeveloped, mute. For Michelet, however, that Vichian state of muteness is the founding condition of all life in the universe:

> Avec le monde a commencé une guerre qui doit finir avec le monde, et pas avant: celle de l'homme contre la nature, de l'esprit contre la matière, de la liberté contre la fatalité. L'histoire n'est pas autre chose que le récit de cette interminable lutte.[53]

Michelet's *Introduction à l'Histoire Universelle*, written, as he said, "on the burning pavements of Paris" during the uprising of July 1830, takes as its purpose the understanding of history "comme l'éternelle protestation, comme le triomphe progressif de la liberté"[54] which he conceived to be a Vichian undertaking. Michelet's Vico is a hero fighting on the side of the masses against the tyranny of the few, a French revolutionary figure whose great proclamation is the claim that the force which directs the "course the nations run" is "mind, for men did it [history] with intelligence; it was not fate, for they did it by choice; not chance, for the results of their always so acting are perpetually the same" (*NS* 1108). Thus Michelet's "strong reading"[55] of the Vichian text effectively destroys the holistic, morphogenetic power of the system, putting in its place a patriarchal and paternalistic claim to ownership of the world and its life forms. Adapting the metonymy of France in relation to the world, Michelet repeats the Vichian transformation of metonymic into metaphoric relation but this time the result is the proclamation of a French colonialist hegemony, a redemptive mission undertaken by France, "le pilote du vaisseau de l'humanité." But, says Michelet,

> ce vaisseau vole aujourd'hui dans l'ouragan; il va si vite, si vite, que le vertige prend aux plus fermes, et que toute poitrine en est oppressée. Que puis-je dans ce beau et terrible mouvement? Une seule chose: le comprendre; je l'essayerai du moins.[56]

—a ⊏ like goal, the inscription of a "letter selfpenned to one's other" (*FW* 489.33), grounded in sometime claims about "the ouragan of spaces" (*FW* 504.14), alas in this century no longer hyperbolic ones.

Michelet's privileging of culture over nature, of France over the world, of the material over the nonmaterial, of ''Liberté'' over ''fatalité,'' represents a rupturing not only of Quinet's vision of benign order but also of the Vichian morphogenetic universe itself. Quinet's Joussean understanding of world-order in terms of an exchange of gestures, a ''rhythmo-catechizing'' interface of human and other life forms in a responsive universe, is thus balanced against a system which pushes that understanding to the limit and which Vichian new science cannot sustain in tension. The forces of violence everywhere threaten the balance of memory (for Quinet's wildflowers are botanical memory systems) and the balance of ''body'' and ''mind'' grammatologically mediated. That balance, so easily broken, requires that the warring twins—whether Quinet and Michelet or ⊏ and ∧ —be subsumed within a larger system, that their explicate disorder be resolved, at least temporarily, into text. That text must then invoke all the rivers of the world and all the words for peace which it can muster, for those ''MUTUOMORPHOMUTATION[S]'' (*FW* 281.R1)—like the ''*lingua commune mentale*'' which the *Wake* seeks—are components of a memory system which, in its drive toward all-inclusiveness, takes as goal the Vichian recognition of words as deeds, of reading acts which draw on ''memory, will and understanding'' (*FW* 266.19).

''The Vico road goes round and round to meet where terms begin'' says ∧ rolling down the Liffey in his barrel (*FW* 452.21). The snag in that watery progress is, however, not only the postman's ''sunsickness'' (*FW* 452.35) but also his threatened experience of aboulia (loss or impairment of willpower) and consequent failure at his task, the delivery of ▲'s letter. ''Well, to the figends of Annanmeses with the wholeabuelish business!'' (*FW* 452.34) he exclaims, threatening anamnesis into the bargain. Again in the play produced by ''Mr John Baptister Vickar'' in II.1, ''a deep abuliousness'' (*FW* 255.27) not only is threatened but does ''descend upon the Father of Truants,'' Ш, and on ▲ in their pantomime guise.

Like the association of anamnesis with ▲, the marking of aboulia with Vico's stamp draws upon theory of memory in *The New Science*, Vico's *Autobiography*, and his *On the ancient wisdom of the Italians*. Indeed, memory is one of Vico's great themes and, as Donald Phillip Verene has shown, the central morphogenetic principle of the Vichian system. ''Memory is the same as imagination'' (*NS* 699)[57] and both powers are therefore located ''in the head.'' The ''mother of the Muses; that is, of the arts of humanity'' (*NS* 699), memory is divided by Vico into three branches or aspects: *memoria* ''when it remembers things,'' *fantasia* or imagination ''when it alters or imitates them,'' and *ingegno* or invention ''when it gives them a new turn or puts them into proper arrangement and relationship'' (*NS* 819).[58] In the *De sapientia* Vico speculates further on the conjunction of imagination and memory, ''which stores within itself the perception of the senses'':

Was this [conjunction] because we can neither imagine something unless we have remembered it, nor remember anything unless we perceive it through the senses? Certainly, painters have never depicted any kind of plant nor any living thing which nature has not produced, for their hippogriffs and centaurs are truths of nature mingled with what is false. [. . .] Through their fables, therefore, the Greeks handed down their belief that the Muses, which are virtues depicted by the imagination, were the daughters of Memory.[59]

The product of Greek oral tradition, "Homer left none of his poems in writing" (*NS* 850) but was a "stitcher-together of songs," one of many rhapsodes who sang the songs which came to be referred to as Homeric (*NS* 851). Thus,

> the blindness and the poverty of Homer were characteristics of the rhapsodes, who, being blind, when each of them was called *homéros*, had exceptionally retentive memories, and, being poor, sustained life by singing the poems of Homer throughout the cities of Greece; and they were the authors of these poems inasmuch as they were a part of these peoples who had composed their histories in the poems.[60]

In this sense, then, "Homer was an idea or a heroic character of Grecian men insofar as they told their histories in song" (*NS* 873).

If Homer, writing during the "childhood of the world" (*NS* 1032), represents the apogee of mnemonic power, early childhood itself represents memory's first period of strength and "vividness of imagination" but a strength which can turn to "corpulence of the imaginative faculty."[61] Care must be taken to ensure that young people study "physics, which leads to the contemplation of the corporeal universe and [which] has need of mathematics for the science of the cosmic system."[62] Plane geometry should also be included in the regimen since it "is in a certain sense a graphic art which at once invigorates memory by the great number of its elements, refines imagination with its delicate figures . . . , and quickens perception. . . . "[63] It should be taught "not by numbers or genera but by forms," that is, by using the "synthetic" method which teaches that "we should make truths rather than discover them."[64] Rhetoric or "Topics," "the art of finding in anything all that is in it," will help young people to make discoveries since Topics furnishes their minds with "matter" which will later help them to form sound judgments. In all these studies, "they should first apprehend, then judge, and finally reason . . . ," a sequence which the *Wake* faithfully follows in II.2 as ⊏ and ▲ practice Euclid's Proposition Two and apply it to the universe. In the course of this lesson, the twins also exhibit the Vichian notion that "the first faculty to manifest itself is that of seeing likenesses," though perhaps not the Vichian corollary, that the nature of children "is purer and less corrupted by persuasion or prejudice" than that of their elders.

Like the Vichian "dipintura," ▲'s "geomater" (*FW* 297.01) diagram is the graphic presentation of an allegory of cosmos,[65] the visual image of a complex memory theater from which the discourse system of the whole may be generated in performance, whether ∧'s lifting of the "maidsapron" to reveal Anna Livia's "quincecunct" (*FW* 206.35)—in Euclidean terms, simply an articulation of what was always there—or the reader's programmed enactment of the *Wake*'s performative discourse. Bringing the aboulia of ricorso, the Vico of both *The New Science* and *Finnegans Wake* must also be the vehicle of memory in its triple role of rememoration, mimesis and invention. So the knowable universe of plane geometry becomes also a field of discovery and invention, a topos from which the exercising of the **▲** principles of generativity and anamnesis, memory and forgetting, can be undertaken. Thus the "dipintura's" patterns of transmission of understanding— from God to Metaphysic, from Metaphysic to Homer and to the world—inscribe an implied triangulation of interests such as we see in the "geomater" diagram in terms of a "poetic geography" whose founding principle is *mundus*, the allegorical catachresis of body and place. At the macrostructural level, "Oh Kosmos! Ah Ireland!" (*FW* 456.07) replicating the Vichian understanding of Homeric Greece; at the microstructural, "A is for Anna like L is for liv" (*FW* 293.18).

That poetic geography in the *Wake* is epitomized in the geomater diagram's "Vieus Von DVbLIn" (*FW* 293.12), where the "doubling bicirculars" meet (*FW* 295.31) and where the memory wheel is turned (*FW* 69.05). Like Vico's "dipintura" a sign of community and agent of communal exchange, the geomater diagram is also the locus of identity-shifting and -questioning within "Dyoublong" (*FW* 13.04). Summed up in one of the *Wake*'s great descriptions of its own morphogenetic operations, that processual drive becomes an ovine production line, pouring chicken-and-egg questions along its course:

> Our wholemole millwheeling vicociclometer, a tetradomational gazebocroticon (the "Mamma Lujah" known to every schoolboy scandaller, be he Matty, Marky, Lukey or John-a-Donk), autokinatonetically preprovided with a clappercoupling smelting-works exprogressive process, (for the farmer, his son and their homely codes, known as eggburst, eggblend, eggburial and hatch-as-hatch can) receives through a portal vein the dialytically separated elements of precedent decomposition for the very-petpurpose of subsequent recombination so that the heroticisms, catastrophes and eccentricities transmitted by the ancient legacy of the past, type by tope, letter from litter, word at ward, with sendence of sundance, since the days of Plooney and Columcellas when Giacinta, Pervenche and Margaret swayed over the all-too-ghoul-ish and illyrical and innumantic in our mutter nation, all, anastomosically assimilated and preteridentified paraidiotically, in fact, the sameold gamebold adomic structure of our Finnius the old One, . . . as sure as herself pits hen to paper and there's scribings scrawled on eggs.
> Of cause, so! And in effect, as? (*FW* 614.27)

The Vichian three ages of gods, heroes, and humans and the ricorso; the four old men as guardian bedposts-cum-grave markers, watching over creation and death; the major characteristics of each of the Vichian cycles, ever (re-)generative in ovine analogy, less viscous than Bohm's fluid medium but equally prone to ex- and implication; the Vichian stages of language from mute signs to hieroglyphs to letters; Quinet's flowers of ecosystemic and temporal balance presiding over the endless cycles of anastomosis and recombinant semes: all leading to Finn, avatar of **Ш** alias Finnegan, in other words to the inscription of writing on the fluid medium of eggs soon rendered viscous and eventually solid when subjected to heat alias energy. But then, following Vico, we must return through all of these "associational clusters"[66] (and many more), questioning all assumptions of causal connection, scrutinizing every apparent "effect," reconsidering our acculturated assumptions which lead us so relentlessly to "first causes." "Of cause, so!—And in effect, as?" (*FW* 615.11)

What we have in both *The New Science* and the *Wake* is not causal sequence but the endless cycle of "precedent decomposition" and "subsequent recombination," of forgetting and remembering, of performative discourse within a knowable world. If the new science is akin to geometry insofar as the latter, "when it constructs the world of quality out of its elements, or contemplates that world, is creating it for itself" (*NS* 349), then Vichian geometry is a mode of processual mimesis, a performative discourse like *The New Science* itself (*NS* 349). The same could be said of *Wake* geometry in its role as icon of the reading act inscribed in and prescribed by the text—"eggtentical" (*FW* 16.36) in other words. Thus anamnesis is bound into the cycle of memory, "IDEAREAL HISTORY" into Joussean gesture,[67] text production into text consumption ("His producers are they not his consumers?" [*FW* 497.01]), ▲ into Dublin Bay and the "roturn" of the tide (*FW* 18.05).

> What has gone? How it ends?
> Begin to forget it. It will remember itself from every sides, with all gestures, in each our word. Today's truth, tomorrow's trend.
> Forget, remember! (*FW* 614.19)

"Traumscrapt": *Somnium* and *Visio*

"In the night of thick darkness enveloping the earliest antiquity," Vico writes, "there shines the eternal and never failing light of a truth beyond all question: that the world of civil society has certainly been made by men, and that its principles are therefore to be found within the modification of our own mind" (*NS* 331). To the exploration and articulation of those principles *The New Science* is dedicated, its task the formulation of an "ideal eternal history" which, as we have seen, is classified by Vico as a performance-system which becomes itself in enactment as the performer "makes it for himself" (*NS* 349). In this, Vichian science is like geometry. As the former

> constructs the world of quantity out of its elements, or contemplates that world, [it] is creating it for itself, just so does our Science . . . [create for itself the world of nations], but with a reality greater by just so much as the institutions having to do with human affairs are more real than points, lines, surfaces, & figures are. (*NS* 349)

Incorporating Vichian geometry into the dark night of civil strife, *Finnegans Wake* inscribes ricorsive language across the field of dream, assigning to the hieroglyphs ("The Doodles family" [*FW* 299.F4]) focal roles in this "mar of murmury" (*FW* 254.18). Geometric insignia, these glyphic indicators serve as directional markers, pointing the way through this new-scientific *speculum*, a Phoenix Park which opens to us the "childhood of the world" (*NS* 1032) and its regenerative cycles operated by "mind, for men did it with intelligence; it was not fate, for they did it by choice; not chance, for the results of their always so acting are perpetually the same" (*NS* 1108).

Vico's hieroglyphs mediating *scienza* and geometry are William Warburton's mediating writing and dream. In ancient Egypt, as Warburton wrote in his *The Divine Legation of Moses Demonstrated*, priests "believed that their Gods had given them *hieroglyphic writing*" and dreams, and that "the same mode of expression [was employed] in both revelations."[68] Both hieroglyphs and dreams were subject to "onirocritic," a mode of "interpretation" grounded in an understanding of dreams as allegorized texts. Like writing, dream encodes a knowable world, and in this system writing is to world as dream is to writing. Within the convention of the *specula*/tive allegory, then, *scienza* (whether Vico's science or Warburton's hermeneutics of revelatory writing) gives access to the human world composed, as it is in these systems, of language: the semiotics of congruent word and world. If, then, both dream and *scienza* serve as vehicles for the regeneration of past impacted within present, of forgetting within memory, the art of onirocritic is in itself a ricorsive tactic, enabling the interpreter to articulate dream as history, history as dream. Dream becomes the sound of memory turning in the dark, and memory a glyphic condensation of gesture known and susceptible to enactment within the liturgy or performative code of the dream narrative. So in its manifold inventions of *scienza*, the Joyce system reinvents the ancient onirocritic of Gothic pedagogy.

Interlacing of patterns across the text or development of discrete sequences, dissemination of one glyph or of a glyphic cluster across one or several texts, fragmentation of established textual paradigms:[69] these are all common strategies in *specula*/tive allegory, whether of the onirocritical kind or not. Equally, they are strategies of that form of medieval "glyphic" narrative known as the dream vision in which the single most important mimetic gesture is the adoption of the dream convention itself. As Constance Hieatt has argued, the dream vision "is a device to lend credence to the marvellous."[70] In other words, dream functions as legitimizing strategy, as semantic sanction of invention in nonreferential modes. Thus J. B. Stearns writes of this genre in classical times that

> In general, the dream fills the role of a messenger between the divinities or the spirits of the dead and living mortals. Consequently, the poet, who often regards himself as a priest of the gods, sometimes receives inspiration by means of dreams, or, at least, assigns a dream as his reason for composing.[71]

Accordingly, the dreamer in many dream poems "both is and is not the same as the writer who names him as 'I' in the poem."[72] Or, the writer both is and is not a dreamer, a singer of fabulous tales, a Homer in Vico's sense, a disseminator of information across codes, a codemaker by invention, a network of loci and topoi in a memory theater, a text awaiting an exercitant, an autotelic pedagogy teaching only itself. Or the dreamer/narrator is the text bound in self-consuming processual diegesis—a dream which is "a scene of writing,"[73] manifesting its own telos, a glyph of its own substance endlessly performative of its own process/ing, endlessly instructive and instructing, a rhizome-epiphany, a performative gnomon motiv/ated across the manifold catachresis of a plurivocal text. Not a "monolook interyerear" (*FW* 182.20) but a "drama parapolylogic" (*FW* 474.05), a techne for the production of process, for morphogenesis, for retrieving the "Mental Dictionary" which is *Mundus*, the world (*NS* 725).

But the dream narrative as genre may also be more restrictively categorized in terms of, for example, the five subdivisions presented by the fourth-century writer Macrobius in his *speculum*, the *Commentary on the Dream of Scipio*, one of the most influential of medieval onirocritical texts. Macrobius supplies five categories of dream narrative: the *somnium* (Gr., *oneiros*) or "enigmatic dream"; the *visio* (Gr., *horama*) or "prophetic vision"; the *oraculum* (Gr., *chrematismos*) or "oracular dream"; the *insomnium* (Gr., *erypnion*) or "nightmare"; and, finally, the *visum* (Gr., *phantasma*) or "apparition."[74] A single dream may be classified under several of these headings, perhaps synthesizing *visio* and *visum* if a dream is both prophetic and concerned with the apparition of a figure of wisdom such as a deceased parent who had lived an exemplary life. A *visio* does not require interpretation since "future events are depicted in the dream exactly as they will occur"[75] while, in contrast, a *somnium* is an "allegorical dream"[76] which requires exegesis and possesses "the global character of dream revelation at its highest. . . ."[77] *Insomnium* refers to interrupted dreams "produced by mental or physical distress"[78] and, like the *visum*, is of little interest to Macrobius, whose focus is on the analysis of the *somnium* presented in Cicero's text *Somnium Scipione*. In the course of that analysis, Macrobius ranges from geometry to cosmology and from Pythagorean number theory to neoplatonic metaphysics, working inventions on the recombinant semes of his *speculum* and modeling a *specula*/tive paradigm to which authority would be attributed for a millennium.

In his dissertation on the *somnium*, F. X. Newman has catalogued a number of other major features of this genre as it developed in the wake of Macrobius as well as of the equally influential Boethius, and the ongoing modeling of the form through particular exemplars. Among the standard features of the dream narrative catalogued by Newman is the employment of circular structure, bringing the dreamer back to where he (seldom she) started but in better harmony with the world around him after suffering a period of confusion or dislocation. Typically, the dreamer returns to a world of springtime with May being the favored month, and benefits from his dream revelation in proportion to his moral and spiritual qualities. "Evil men," in fact, "see only vain and delusive fantasies"[79] in their dreams, while the dreamer who wakes at the outset of his dream and then falls asleep again is thought to be experiencing "the opening of the spiritual eye of the heart."[80] Through the agency of his imagination, "the mediating instrument between truth and the dreamer's ignorance,"[81] he transcends corporeal vision and acquires spiritual insight, a process often imaged in terms of the crossing of a river or lying down to sleep beside it or of encountering a many-branched river which occasions a choice on the part of the dreamer.[82] These choices form part of the pedagogical structure of the dream narrative and are frequently presented in terms of debates between dreamer and guide or of the whole narrative structured as a debate.[83] Thus *specula*/tive knowledge on a grand scale might be inculcated or presented in such a way that the ingenuity of the onirocritic was challenged and the narrative might take on the characteristics of a puzzle to which the keys were given and the intermediate steps left to the exegete's skill.

Such is the case with the *Wake*'s dream narrative, principally employing the *somnium* and the *visio* along with traditional details of landscape both human and ecological. Thus we have the river not only as emblem of generation and dissolution but as generator of text, and not only the muddled voices of half-awake dreamers marking the passing of the night—

> Hark!
> Tolv two elf kater ten (it can't be) sax.
> Hork!
> Pedwar pemp foify tray (it must be) twelve.
> And low stole o'er the stillness the heartbeats of sleep. (*FW* 403.01)

—but also the confusion of dreamers emerging from sleep near dawn and rehearsing the terms of revelations experienced at that traditionally crucial dream moment. Hearing the stirrings of their children, the parents begin the narrative of their own death as a movement into anamnesis:

> A cry off.
> Where are we at all? and whereabouts in the name of space?
> I don't understand. I fail to say. I dearsay you too. (*FW* 558.32)

Meanwhile **Λ** rests on the hillside in his pilgrim's attire ("brief wallet to his side, and arm loose, by his staff of citron briar, tradition stick-pass-on" [*FW* 474.03]), tired after his experiments in rhythmo-catechizing with **⊥** and the "hedge daughters" and after his denunciation of **Ϲ** with its ultimate consignment of him to the region toward which their parents are also moving: "Walk while ye have the light for morn, lightbreakfastbringer, morroweth whereon every past shall fall fost sleep. Amain" (*FW* 473.23). Attempting to fill the role of prophetic figure in **Ϲ**'s dream, **Λ** utters the traditional injunction to repent and be saved before the coming of the end, the mutation of mo(u)rning. Classified as "drama" rather than "dream monologue" (*FW* 474.04) given the performative nature of his narrative, **Λ**'s own early morning dream enacts the pilgrim's vivid experience of guilt occasioned by recognition of sin:

> —Dream. Ona noonday I sleep. I dreamt of a somday. Of a wonday I shall wake. Ah! May he have now of here fearfilled me! Sinflowed, O sinflowed! Fia! Fia! Befurcht Christ! (*FW* 481.07)

Λ's fear, expressive of the revelation he experiences as part of his *visum*, contrasts sharply with the peaceful world of the Ass, modeled on Langland's Piers Plowman, as he drifts with a clear conscience into sleep ("Methought as I was dropping asleep somepart in nonland" [*FW* 403.18]) and, "as I was jogging along in a dream as dozing as I was dawdling, arrah, methought broadtone was heard" (*FW* 404.03).[84] This is the prologue to **∧** 's appearance as false prophet in the *visio* dreamt by the Ass: "When lo (whish, O whish) mesaw mestreamed, as the green to the gred was flew, was flown, through deafths of durkness greengrown deeper I heard a voice, the voce of Shaun . . . " (*FW* 407.11). Thus the violent world of Michelet again intersects with the gentle, ecological view of Quinet with its heritage of medieval pastoral.

Michelet's dark world is further invoked in the *Wake*'s "dreambookpage[s]" (*FW* 428.16) through the *somnium* in which **Ш** drifts, "somnolulutent" (*FW* 76.30), and which **∧** calls down upon **⊏** as he points the "deathbone" at him: "*Insomnia, somnia somniorum. Awmawm*" (*FW* 193.29). Wandering in this vast "semitary of somnionia" (*FW* 594.08), which persists after the invocation to dawn commencing Book IV, we are bound still in the "somnione sciupiones" (*FW* 293.07) which serves as a label for the geomater diagram with its neo-Macrobian "aletheometry" (*FW* 370.13). An episode of insomnia resulting from the erotic unrest of the **Ш** children, II.2 resolves itself into their bitter "Nightletter" wishing "best youlldied greedings to Pep and Memmy" (*FW* 308.21), a moment of respite in the long series of catechetical paradigms in the form of debates which stretches across the *Wake* from the first encounter of Mutt and Jute (*FW* 16–18) to its metonymic sequel, the debate of Patrick and Balkelly in Book IV.

In that "triptych vision" (*FW* 486.32) or *visio*, the *Wake* finally rejects the "opposition of dream to wakefulness . . . [which] is a representation of metaphysics"[85] and thematizes the processual course set out in *Portrait* and *Ulysses*. In the opposition of memory and forgetting, the triptych generates its own third term and resolves in its own processing the binarism which structures the debate. It is a techne which Albrecht Dürer identified as "dreamwork" (*Traumwerk*), writing that "Whoever wants to do dreamwork, must mix all things together."[86] Dürer's immediate reference is to his use of the ancient practice of surrounding a "central" image of a saint or deity with a border or frame of interlaced figures, a semiosic web of nonreferential data. Like the Tunc page of the Book of Kells which is woven into the geomater diagram of the *Wake* as well as into the voyeurism of Mamalujo and the motiv of "invagination"[87] across the narrative, Dürer's dreamwork pages have Gothic pedagogical ends in view. The erosion of boundaries and categories, the ambiguation of binary structures, the induction of allegory and medieval dream narrative into the performative discourse of the text: these are among the lessons of "dreaming" in the *Wake* and of *Traumwerk* in Dürer.

Motiv/ated by Vichian morphogenesis, the *Wake*'s "traumscrapt" (*FW* 623.36) maps a Porphyrian forest of tree stories as it fulfills the ancient injunction to "hand on the matter worthily,"[88] preface to the reader's bond, the "earning"[89] of the work through induction into the text's programmatic strategies of invention. As we enter the system by way of its geometric mnemonics, we come to discover that— like *The New Science*—*Finnegans Wake* offers us the possibility of a radical restructuring of our still-Cartesian world. Privileging the geomater diagram over its ancient type, the *melothesia* or emblem of "Vitruvian man,"[90] the *Wake* opts for "order othered" (*FW* 613.14), for Dürer's concept of dreamwork rather than for Freud's ontotheological one, and for a central morphogenetic principle which is closer to that of medieval dream narrative than to either the psychological novel or "Realist" fiction. This is the apogee of the Joyce system's antihumanist rejection of ideological structures complicit in hegemony. And it marks the final stage of the initial induction into Gothic pedagogy with its quadrivial components troped through the agency of Vichian morphogenesis. Deconstructive geometry, mathematics and cosmologically oriented astronomy have occupied us thus far. What remains is music.

V

MOUSIKÉ/MEMORY: SOUND/SIGN:
FROM JOYCE TO ZUKOFSKY

> "Sounds pass quickly away but numbers remain."
>
> —*Ignoto*

> "Dog can sometimes be read backwards, and reading the letters forwards and backwards is the world."
>
> —Zukofsky, *Bottom: On Shakespeare*

Modern: a twelfth-century term designating an extreme form of Scholastic thought.[1] *Modern*: a mode of invention, a processual calculus governing Gothic pedagogy. In Louis Zukofsky's terms, the poem as an "object in process"[2] inscribing performative utterance, requiring enactment of the particulars[3] upon which the text invents its variations, Gothic in its drive toward sequence and simultaneity. Refuting infinity—defining it out—through the binding of music to speech ("music perceived as history,"[4] the product of all possible speech acts) and of sound to story and *mathémata* in Zukofsky's poetic integral in his great long poem "*A*." Refuting stasis not through the imposition of a false finitude (the encyclopedia) but through the inscription of "everything / . . . moving / and mixing / with everything else" ("*A*" 634–35) which is the *speculum*, an "alphabet of subjects"[5] each becoming its own fugue, arborescent in processual mimesis, numbers performed and become *mathémata*, the codes of the world.

For Foucault, an epistemic shift: the "modern" closes the gap opened by the Enlightenment's privileging of concepts of subjectivity, causality, referentiality, which culminate in those ontotheologies which we may label, metonymically, Freud, "Realism" and commodity capitalism with its humanist declarations of individual freedoms in the midst of denial and exploitation of those who choose, in terms of two of the Joyce system's categories, Quinet over Michelet, botanical calligram over encyclopedia. Reaching back across the rift opened by two centuries of "Reason," modernity reinvents the Gothic pedagogy of Scholasticism, once again choosing catechism and catachresis as operative strategies, challenging language to reveal the structures of the world through the application of Vichian new science grounded in a semiotics of the perceived environment, of that world of "civil society which has certainly been made by men, and . . . its principles are therefore to be found within the modifications of our own human mind" (*NS* 331), its riddles synaptically encoded, susceptible to the "poetic logic" of the *speculum*, the resolution always already "there" in a potentially knowable and known world.

Setting aside the picture of the self which held us captive[6]—the picture of a Cartesian world paradoxically haunted by mystery, its texts kerygmatic proclamations of darkness requiring a new light for their interpretation; setting aside with that great Scholastic thinker of modernity, Ludwig Wittgenstein, the possibility of enacting finitude upon process, modernity reaches across "beginnings" and "endings," across the Book of Kells and Bach and the *Odyssey* and Dogon masks, until perhaps like Tinguely's machines dismantling themselves by the pool at the MOMA, what is left is what was *there* to "begin" with—a preposition dangling into a knowable world to which we return with astonishing effort, seeing in Dachau, My Lai, Sharpeville, Chernobyl, Shatila the apocalyptic effects of the post-Cartesian heritage of the Enlightenment.

"To deconstruct . . . is to do memory work,"[7] as Derrida has said. The urgency of that memory work in both the Joyce and the Zukofsky systems is the urgency of modernity's return to connection with a pre-Enlightenment semiotics of word as act, of language in and of the world. Not a theological but a logological enterprise, this memory work concerns itself not with a nostalgia for origins but, rather, with a need to learn again a mnemonic repertoire which is grounded in what we have called the ecosystemic motiv in the Joyce system. Thus in Zukofsky the "utterance of construction" which is "the sounding of . . . [the sentences'] grammatical and typographical morphology by the voice," or "speech growing into song,"[8] inscribes catachresis across its field of enactment and configures its gestural codes according to the laws of "Musemathematics" (*U* 11.834).

Our project in this chapter is the invention of a *specula*/tive music which, incorporating some of the principles of such different textual machines as those of Louis Zukofsky and John McCarthy, will approach the Gothic pedagogical goal of the production of a *manifestatio* of *specula*/tive modernity. We begin with the two major categories offered by the quadrivium—the curricular structure of Gothic pedagogy—under the heading of "music": *musica practica*, or the craft of music making, and *musica speculativa*, or *specula*/tive music. Encompassing music not only as a branch of philosophy but also as a rhetoric having logical relations to other rhetorical arts, *musica speculativa* conceives music as a language, a grammatology which may be applied and which is amenable to what we have been referring to as the tradition of Augustinian speech act theory.

Consider the medieval distinction between the workman whose skill is applied in the actual construction of a building, and the architect whose knowledge of mathematics, philosophy, theology and so on enables him to design a structure as God designs the world. While the workman operates within the frame of *musica practica*, the architect, theorizing the structure of the building, operates within *musica speculativa*. The analogy is an ancient one. As in Vichian poetics, it is the morphogenetic operation which is stressed in medieval music and architecture: the *language* of the treatise or formula, the summa or *specula*/tion on number theory, which is performative, its embedded gestural codes determinative of that form of enactment which is the sounding of music, the physical specificity of the building. As the *Wake* puts it, "Mere man's mime: God has jest" (*FW* 486.09). In playing a musical instrument or using a carpenter's tool, we mime the lavish and sometimes whimsical gestures of the divine workman whose morphogenetic principles and operations are best understood by the divine theorist. Thus the playing of music or the building of cathedrals is, according to medieval epistemology, a secondary activity, a *practice*, while the conceptual activities involved in the generation of such structures (in both cases, mathematical activities governed by logological theory) are thought to be at a higher level, approaching divine cognition more closely.

Musica speculativa is, then, concerned precisely with the problematic of processual mimesis and with the operation of techne, while *musica practica* with its quotidian concerns is grounded in the particularity of specific techniques applied in specific situations. Where, during and after the Renaissance, *musica practica* assumed dominance with its armory of instructional handbooks and exercises leading not to logothesis but to better fingering or improved rhythm, by the end of the Middle Ages *musica speculativa* had mutated into cosmological, mathematical and linguistic studies, only to experience its own rebirth in the twentieth century courtesy of Webern, Schoenberg, Berio, Cage and Xenakis among many others in music as well, of course, as in the work of those post-Einsteinian physicists who pursue that great neo-medieval project, a "theory of everything" (TOE) or a "general theory of the universe" (GUT). In their more restricted and technologically different forms, TOEs and GUTs become that extraordinary synthesis of neurolinguistics, brain chemistry, computer engineering and physics which we know as Artificial Intelligence.

To construct an expert system is, in part, to construct a catechism, a fixed, dialogic repertoire whose roots are in hard-wired transformations of neural circuitry and in general theories of universal evolution at the cognitive level. But before we can conclude that the Joyce system is, among other things, a kind of expert system, we need to consider medieval theories of *musica speculativa* in more detail and to filter that information through the terministic screen of one of modernity's greatest exercises in what Vico might have called "poetic music," Louis Zukofsky's *speculum* entitled "*A*." Like the Joyce system, Zukofsky's poem is involved in the inscription of *musica practica* within the morphogenetic paradigm of *musica speculativa*. And like the Joyce system, "*A*" foregrounds its musical intertexts, leaving us with the problematic of "poetic music" rather than with the identification of intertexts, a process which, in any case, would not meet the questions posed by *musica speculativa*. Attempting to attach the system analyzed to those extradiegetic plot- and character-functions which it produces as telos, *musica practica* as analytic strategy almost inevitably seeks to turn Gothic pedagogy against itself. Rejecting that strategy, we return again by way of Augustine, following a "commodius vicus"

(*FW* 3.02) back to the *Wake* with its eye/ear code and to "*A*" with its poetic integral, compound of speech and song.

"Beyond memory": *Musica speculativa*

Letters (*grammata*), says Augustine, are "signs of sounds made by the articulate voice with which we speak."[9] Other signs "pertain to the sense of sight [. . .] and very few to the other senses." Thus, banners, military standards, and manual gestures "are like so many visible words"[10] though words have a richer signifying capacity than do such purely visual tokens. However,

> because vibrations in the air soon pass away and remain no longer than they sound, signs of words have been constructed by means of letters. Thus words are shown to the eyes, not in themselves but through certain signs which stand for them.[11]

Written or "visible words" contrast with invisible words, the product of "voice [which] is air struck (*verberatus*) by the breath, from which circumstance words (*verba*) also receive their name," as Isidore of Seville puts it in his great *speculum*, the *Etymologiarum*.[12] For Plato in the *Philebus*, mastery of the classification and performance of sound—the skills of re*verb*eration—constitutes the summit of *paideia*, the educational process:

> when you have learned what sounds are high and what low, and the number and nature of the intervals and their limits or proportions, and the systems compounded out of them . . . under the name of harmonies; and the affections corresponding to them in the movements of the human body, which when measured by numbers ought, as they say, to be called rhythms and measures . . . ; when, I say, you have learned all this, then, my dear friend, you are perfect. . . . [13]

As Eric A. Havelock argues in his *Preface to Plato*, the emphasis in this passage on the acquisition of mnemonic paradigms which include such kinesthetic components as dance and gesture is typical of what the Greeks meant by *mousiké*. Thus "Greek 'music' exists only to make the words more recollectable, or rather to make the undulations and ripples of the meter automatically recollectable, in order to free psychic energy for the recall of the words themselves."[14] Rediscovering the choreography of gesture devised by Marcel Jousse, Havelock catalogues the various gestural components of the mnemonic repertoire which is *mousiké*, including the physical movements of the vocal organs as well as of hands and feet, ears and torso. "The entire nervous system," he concludes, "is geared to the task of memorisation."[15]

For the Greeks that task was facilitated by the structuring of language through the vehicle of the *stoicheion* or vowel sound,[16] a developmental stage preceding that of the *grammata* or letters to which Augustine refers several centuries later. Serving to organize the production of speech and melody around tone and pitch, this sounding process renders all linguistic and musical experience dependent upon "sense-perception and memory" for, as Aristoxenus writes in the *Harmonic Elements*, "we must perceive the sound that is present and remember that which is past."[17] Amplifying this doctrine, Augustine states in the *De musica* that "rhythms which are in the effect sustained by the ears, *passio aurium*, are brought to them by sound, and removed by silence,"[18] and he notes that this passion of the ears is shared by humans and animals just as memory itself is.[19]

To study *mousiké*, then, is to acquire language and achieve competence in its use through performance of a mnemonic repertoire. But, as the *Etymologiarum* has it, since "the world itself is said to be composed by a certain harmony of sounds and heaven revolves in harmonic modulation . . . music extends to all things."[20] Reaching back through Boethius's *De Musica* to the *Timaeus*, Isadore recalls the Platonic axiom that "the soul of the universe is united by musical concord"[21] and that "music is number made audible."[22] Here Pythagorean number theory fuses with neoplatonic cosmology, a synthesis at the root of medieval music theory from the time of Boethius and persisting, as we shall see, into the seventeenth century. Macrobius, for example, argues that

> Every soul in this world is allured by musical sounds so that not only those who are more refined in their habits, but all the barbarous peoples as well, have adopted songs by which they are inflamed with courage or wooed to pleasure; for the soul carries with it into the body a memory of the music which it knew in the sky. . . . Consequently it is natural for everything that breathes to be captivated by music since the heavenly soul that animates the universe sprang from music.[23]

—a passage which both anticipates Vico's theory of the stages of language acquisition and recalls Augustine's of "number and dimensions" which the memory "contains" in spite of the fact that these principles cannot be the product of sensory perception.[24] Distinguishing between sound per se and what sounded words call up in the memory, Augustine writes that "the words [signifying number and dimension] may sometimes be spoken in Latin and at other times in Greek, but the principles are neither Greek nor Latin. They are not language at all."[25]

Beyond language, beyond memory, is "the principle of number . . . [which] is not an image of the things we count, but something which is there in its own right."[26] Beyond number is God for Augustine and Boethius, the World-Soul for the neoplatonic tradition following the *Timaeus*. In the Pythagorean tradition, however, number and the operations of its principles in mathematics serve as "the representation of fundamental truth"[27] for, according to Stobaeus, "Truth is the proper innate character of number." And as Plotinus puts Augustine's eminently traditional, neoplatonic point, "The variety of sense-objects merely recalls to the soul the notion of number."[28] Number signifies that form of finitude which we have already classified in terms of the *speculum* just as its comprehensiveness, its specification of every aspect of its vast system, is evident in Pythagorean assertions of the Monad as the principle of both limit and unity, while the Duad—associated with such negative elements as the female principle, even numbers ("weaker" than odd numbers), excess and defect, diversity and multiplicity which dare to break away from the unity of the Monad[29]—is associated with infinity.

"The infinite," writes Proclus in the *Elements*, "is not cognate with the One but alien from it. . . . The manifold of gods is therefore not infinite but marked by a limit." And for Plotinus in the *Enneads*, the beauty of the universe is sustained "only so far as the [principle of] unity holds it from dissipating into infinity."[30] In other words, infinity is the vacuum which nature abhors (and which attracts makers of encyclopedias and repels makers of *specula*). Learning to enact the *speculum* of his culture, the Greek student of *mousiké* acquired knowledge not only of its limits but also of his own relationship with it, performing his own harmonic relation to the concords and discords of the universe as he danced, sang, played the cithara or the lyre, and caused the words of his ancestors' harmonies to re*verb*-erate the harmony of his own being.

Playing the music of the spheres on his monochord, Pythagoras became the emblem for the Middle Ages of the reconciliation of concord and discord in what Boethius classified as *musica mundana* or earthly music, through which an approach might be made to *musica divina*, the heavenly music of God. *Musica mundana* comprehends the music of the spheres, the fundamental harmony of the physical world including the operation of the four elements and seasons, and the movements of the heavens. *Musica divina* comprehends the beauty and proportion of God, known to the human world through *musica divina*'s reflection not only in the har-monies of the earth but also in *musica humana*, signifying those relationships of balance and proportion earlier referred to the Greek *mousiké*. Thus *musica humana* was interpreted both physically and spiritually in Boethius's binary system:

> In the first sense, reference is made [by Boethius] to the external symmetry of the human body, the balance of its members and their placement; in addition, there is the beauty of the internal organs and their arrangement, as well as the harmony between their functioning and man's well-being. On the other hand, there is also a harmonious relation between the body and the soul, a harmony seen in the health of the body and the functions of the soul—intelligence, love, etc. These relationships are a form of music, for they are, like music, founded on the same numerical laws.[31]

Boethius's subset of *musica humana* is the lowest member of the system and is classified as *musica instrumentalis*, referring to the actual playing of instruments, a category which later was incorporated into *musica practica*, the workmanlike realm of those who, like the flute-girls of Plato's time, were without status, being unable to perform the intellectual calisthenics which Alanus de Insulis displays in the following passage from the *De planctu naturae*, in which he integrates the topos of the *concordia discors* into the fourfold subsets of *musica humana* and *mundana*:

> just as the concordant discord, singular plurality, consonant dissonance, discordant accordance of the four elements unite into one whole the structure of the worldly

kingdom, so also do the similar dissimilarity, unequal equality, deformed conformity, divided identity of the four humours join together the edifice of the human body.[32]

Thus although the full apprehension of the divine signified lies beyond human memory and performance, through music which *is*—thanks to Plato and the Pythagoreans—mathematics, and through the experience of the beauty of the world which *is* the experience of number (since "all things that are beautiful are subject to the power of number and can be explained by it," in Boethius's system),[33] at least partial access to the "soul of the universe"[34] is possible.

Since *mousiké* was primarily verbal in its emphasis—a paradigm retained throughout the Middle Ages as *musica* acquired its subclassifications—Pythagorean understanding of the inscription of limitation within the Monad was transformed into a semiotics of predictable double-coding in which verbal and musical elements existed in a symbiotic, sometimes parasitic, relationship. St. John Chrysostom exemplifies the latter in his advice that "even though the meaning of the words be unknown to you, teach your mouth to utter them meanwhile. For the tongue is made holy by the words when they are uttered with a ready and eager mind."[35] Symbiosis is apparently more likely to occur after death, however, for after "entering into God's sacred choir . . . you may yourself become a cithara, . . . making a full harmony of mind and body."[36] Thus is the experience of the infinite sanctioned and rendered conceivable within the code of the finite.

However, double-coding need not be externalized to be operant within this system. "One may also sing without voice," John writes, "the mind resounding inwardly."[37] But an outward resounding is equally possible, noted by Guido of Arezzo six centuries later in the *Micrologus* as he contemplated the "concordant and mutually congruous lines" often seen in verse and wondered "at a certain harmony of language. And if music were added to this, with a similar internal congruity, you would be doubly charmed by a twofold melody."[38] This "melody" is, in a sense, already present in words which are, as Augustine observed, *sounds*, and which—if encountered in letters—must be reverberated in air or played, performed, just as the neumes of medieval musical notation were crystallized breaths, moments of *pneuma* sounding on the page.[39] "Consider, then," argues Guido, "that just as everything which is spoken can be written, so everything that is written can be made into song. Thus everything that is spoken can be sung. . . ."[40]

The divorce between sound and musical notation expressed by Isadore of Seville with his sense of sounds perishing because they cannot be written down is less urgently felt by Guido not because neumes were any closer to sound for him but because, as the inventor of solfège, he had solved the problem of translating between aural and chirographic modes through the introduction of a fixed mnemonic system which was widely available and, written beneath the neumes, would serve to enable one familiar with the system "to sing a verse without learning it beforehand"[41] from another singer's performance. Thus sound was harnessed to writing and made to sing through vowels, a chirographic adaptation of the *stoicheion* system of *mousiké*. Guido also devised a variation on this early Gothic pedagogy, generating music out of the vowels of the literary text by "placing the five vowels . . . in repeated succession under the letter of the monochord (i.e., the great scale, or gamut, ranging from *G* up to *á*) and then allowing . . . [the] text to write the melody'' for him.[42]

A similar strategy was used some three centuries later in the development of the isorhythmic motet during the French Ars Nova period. However, here the concern is not so much with Guido's simple series of transcoding operations but rather with a much more complex series of superimpositions involving the application of the *talea*, or ''cutting,'' to the *color*, a melody which ''was taken as a series of pitches, without rhythm and without necessity for retention of a specific melodic shape.''[43] In its privileging of disjunction between the *color* and the *talea*, the isorhythmic motet differs from the standard motet form of the *Ars antiqua*. ''Thus if the melody included twenty notes, for example, and the rhythmic pattern decided upon used only fifteen of these, the *color* would begin its repetition after the *talea* had recommenced; there would be an overlapping of the first part of the *talea* with the last of the *color*.''[44] Five repetitions of the *talea* and four of the *color* would therefore be necessary in order to bring the structure to a point of final coincidence. Since neither the length of *color* and *talea* nor the number of repetitions or of variations in rhythmic pattern was fixed, numerous combinations were possible and the form has been said to anticipate the development of tone rows in twentieth-century serial music with its principle of ''combinatoriality.''[45]

The fact that the melodies employed in the construction of such motets were frequently taken from other musical sources and integrated into new forms through variation in context or rhythm also associates the form with that of the *contrafactum* or song to which ''a new set of words has been fitted,'' often with ''precise syllabic equivalence.''[46] With the development of polyphony in the thirteenth century, more complex effects based upon these forms became possible and three centuries later, Johannes Kepler was able in his *Harmonices Mundi* (1619) to associate the discovery with the playing of ''the everlastingness of all created time in some short part of an hour by means of an artistic concord of many voices'' by which the composer ''might to some extent taste the satisfaction of God the Workman with his own works, in that very sweet source of delight elicited from this music which imitates God.''[47]

Kepler—like Augustine, Boethius, Alanus de Insulis, and innumerable others before and, to a lesser extent, after him—wrote in the tradition of *musica speculativa* which developed out of both Platonic speculation on *mousiké* and Pythagorean number theory with its exfoliations into every level of medieval thought. In his *Plain and Easy Introduction to Practical Music* (1597), Thomas Morley defined *musica speculativa* as ''that kind of music which, by mathematical helps, seeketh the causes, properties and natures of sounds, by themselves and compared with others proceeding no further, but content with the only contemplation of the art.''[48] It is this ''high semiotics''[49] of *specula*/tive music which forms one basis for the development of Gothic architecture as earthly *manifestatio* of sound and number, word and music, in polyphonic figures of the world.

''I have seen lines drawn by architects,'' Augustine observed in the *Confessions*, ''and they are sometimes as fine as the thread spun by spiders.''[50] Like music for

Augustine, architecture was *"scientia,"*[51] a mode of knowledge, and its practi-
tioners—until the rise of the great Gothic cathedrals in the thirteenth century brought
about a social transformation in their role—were theorists (*"theoreticus"*) emu-
lating the compositional tactics of the divine architect[52] or, as Alanus de Insulis
called him, *"elegans architectus."*[53] Through Vitruvius's association of Pythagorean concepts of harmony in music with the harmony and proportion of the human
body and of harmony in architecture, the master builders of the Gothic cathedrals
conceived of themselves as building theology,[54] imitating in stone "the single,
delightful concordance of one superior, well-tempered harmony," in the words of
Abbot Suger, traditionally assumed to be the first of the great builder-architects. [55]
Augustine's arachnid lines became a sounding in stone of the world-harmonies
evident in all creation, from simplest to most complex forms, and a proclamation
of the triumph of processual mimesis within the Gothic pedagogy of architecture
and music, the "aural geometry" which is the *manifestatio*, the elucidation in time
and space, of those principles of enactment which are explicit in the paradigm of
mousiké/musica humana and which become the evolving paradigm of liturgical
enactment throughout the Middle Ages from the time of Augustine to the Thomist
resolution of form as act.

In *Gothic Architecture and Scholasticism*, Erwin Panofsky has identified totality,
homology, and "multiplicity" or combinatoriality as the three major characteristics
of the High Gothic style.[56] The totalizing force of this style is seen as an attempt
"to embody the whole of Christian knowledge, theological, moral, natural, and
historical, with everything in its place and that which no longer found its place,
suppressed."[57] The resulting synthesis of architectural motivs and elimination of
such elements as the crypt, galleries and towers other than the two in the front of
the structure, produced through "extreme linearization" what Jean Bony has referred to as "an intensely rationalistic approach to the play on forms."[58] Characteristic of this approach is the "uniform division and subdivision of the whole
structure" in such a way that homology serves as its operant principle. "The whole
is thus composed of smallest units—one might almost speak of *articuli*—which
are homologous in that they are all triangular in [the] groundplan and in that each
of these triangles shares its sides with its neighbors."[59]

This principle of multiplicability or "progressive divisibility"[60] resulted in a
configuring of the whole system in terms of regular series of replicating units. Thus
at the height of what is classified as the Rayonnant style of Gothic, "supports were
divided and subdivided into main piers, major shafts, minor shafts, and still [more]
minor shafts; the tracery of windows, triforia, and blind arcades into primary,
secondary, and tertiary mullions and profiles; ribs and arches into a series of mold-
ings."[61] Everywhere the emphasis was on the flattening of surfaces and the can-
celing out of depth, preserving only enough relief "to make the linear systems
perceptible."[62] Thus, as Jean Bony maintains, by masking a broken roofline with
"an austere screen of wall," the architects of Mantes cathedral created "something
as pure and abstract as a Le Corbusier of the 1920s. . . . "[63]

The counterpart to this statement of "scholasticism in stone" (*JJII*, 515) is "the
classic *Summa* with its three requirements of (1) totality (sufficient enumeration),

(2) arrangement according to a system of homologous parts and parts of parts (sufficient articulation), and (3) directness and deductive cogency (sufficient inter-relation) . . . enhanced by . . . suggestive terminology, *parallelismus membrorum*, and rhyme."[64] Distinctness, deductive cogency and mutual inferability are the marks of this form according to Panofsky, who hypothesizes that someone trained in Scholastic methodology—or Gothic pedagogy at its medieval apogee—"would not have been satisfied had not the membrification of the edifice permitted him to re-experience the very processes of architectural composition just as the membrification of the *Summa* permitted him to re-experience the very processes of cogitation." As Panofsky concludes, processual mimesis demands "a maximum of explicitness."[65] For the inscription of words as "signs of sounds" is no less than the scoring of *musica speculativa*, the embedding of memory and forgetfulness in the codes of the world.

"An alphabet of subjects": Toward Zukofsky

Inheritor of Gothic pedagogy, Zukofsky recapitulates through Bach and Boethius the *musica speculativa* of the Joyce system, resolving words and music into the poetic integral of "*A*" as emblem of the world. Here Bach becomes a taxonomy of *specula*/tive paradigms, corollary of the Joyce system's use of liturgical enactment in the service of Gothic pedagogy. Here the Augustinian injunction in both systems that words not *follow* music but *be* music demands processual mimesis in the production of a Vichian "Mental Dictionary" of *mousiké* in all its replicating paradigms. "Verbivocovisuality," then, demands not only *musica speculativa* but, *da capo*, both synesthetic co/incidences and ricorsive movements along Moebius loops of words which, as notes, are numbers and defy infinity in their explicitness. In "*A*":

> words you
> count what
> words you
>
> leave out
> that count
> go backwards ("*A*" 315)

—and in *Ulysses*:

> They list. Three. They.
> I you he they.
> Come, mess. (*U* 447)

"The mind is capable of performing an endless process of addition" ("*A*" 46), a process which is the performative enactment of the text, its "nature" as "creator" and "created" ("*A*" 734)—*naturans* and *naturata*—bound into the "inertial systems" ("*A*" 735), of flower and leaf, the "figurate notation"[66] of Aquinas's handwriting.

In Zukofsky's great *speculum* entitled *Bottom: On Shakespeare*, invention takes at least four forms: "an invention of sound that follows a thinking on singing, or an invention that follows a thinking on seeing, or that invention which is finally a thinking on thinking . . . "[67] Invention is also "music as 'number, a felt relation of counting,' [. . .] Bach's feet dancing his fugue at the organ."[68] In *Finnegans Wake* this is the Quinet motiv; in *Ulysses* at/one/ment, the moment when words (*suck, foetus*) are epiphanized in *Portrait*. It is gesture, a metonym for *mousiké* alias *musica humana*, operant in all of its multiplicative sets in the eye/ear code of the *Wake*, summed up in the Gothic pedagogical motto, "What can't be coded can be decorded if an ear aye seize what no eye ere grieved for" (*FW* 482.34). Composition is invention and "action" is "place," for "these eyeing intimacies of print are all actions." Thus Joycean composition of place intersects with Zukofskian composition of and as process. Enacting place, poems or "acts upon particulars" are process.[69] Inventing "place," we enact the process delineated by textual program, a process which is "music": *specula*/tive, Pythagorean in its abhorrence of infinity, architectural in its deployment of number and homology. One of the most fully developed examples in the Joyce system of invention which functions in this way and synthesizes the codes of eye and ear, setting them into homologous relations with each other, is the "verbivocovisual" code, one of the foundations of *musica speculativa* in *Finnegans Wake*.

In its privileging of an Augustinian sounding of words and of recursive modes of mnemonic processing, the Joyce system's eye/ear paradigm serves as a kind of solfège enabling us to perform one repertoire with competence early in our learning of the text. A contrafacted set, its components function in much the same way as a series of transputers or individual processors, each programmed to perform a particular operation or to process a specific portion of a problem. The initial division is simply between *eye* and *ear*, or *I* and *ere*. Subsequent homonymic transformations are from *I* to German *Ei* and Middle English *ey* with a variant in *ay/aye*. Another subset is introduced with *eye* variants in such languages as Dutch (*Oog*), German (*Auge*), Icelandic (*Auga*), and Dano-Norwegian (*Øye*), the connector here being simple translation as transcoding device. A more complex instance of the eye code occurs with the transformation to *egg* (German *Ei*) and with the introduction of the pronominal category as an agent of transformation (from *eye/I* to *you*), and then a return to homonym as agent with the transformation of *you* to *yew* and *Ewe*.

In the ear code, a similar series of transformations occurs, again with the initial homonym *ere*, followed by translations into Dutch (*Oor* and *Aar*), German (*Ohr*), and Dano-Norwegian (*Øre*). The homonymic subset *Eire/air* follows the pattern of vowel transformation (from *o* to *a*) while retaining an inaudible element of the eye code (*Ei/re*). Between these two arrays of subsets is the mediating term or shifter, French *oreille/oeil*, like *Ei/eye/egg* an example of catachresis. Code-switching here produces such examples of Vichian morphogenesis as "Ere ore or ire in Aarland"

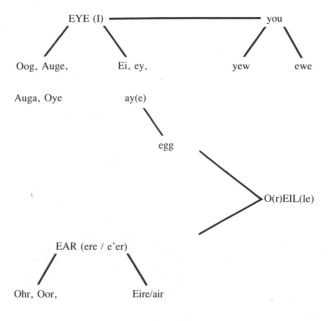

Figure 5. The eye/ear paradigm in *Finnegans Wake*

(*FW* 69.08), "if an ear eye seize what no eye ere grieved for" (*FW* 482.34), "he could talk earish with his eyes shut" (*FW* 130.19), "Ear! Ear! Not ay! Eye! Eye! For I'm at the heart of it" (*FW* 409.03), "Erin's ear" (*FW* 467.32; cf. Ireland's Eye), and "in my mine's I" (*FW* 425.25). This is geometric music, perhaps "audible geometry," one of the Joyce system's variants on Zukofskian *natura naturata*, an integral of eye and ear inscribed within the resolute homology of parallax. This sequence of operations may be diagrammed as shown in figure 5. Thus the Ballad of Persse O'Reilly is resolved into an invention on the themes of the verbi/voco and the visual, *specula*/tively balanced against each other in dialogic enactment. Like the similar resolution of number in its various forms, including geometry, into music (and vice versa) in the Pythagorean tradition as in the Joyce system, the transcoding of eye and ear in the *Wake* subsumes sequence and simultaneity, cause and effect, diachronic and synchronic within each other in recursive enumeration of the recombinant semes of the system.

"What has gone? How it ends?" (*FW* 614.19) Artificial Intelligence provides a model fulfilling Augustine's dream of cognitive mapping beyond memory and analogous to those emblematic Temples of Speculative Music which are a medieval invention on the theme of contemporary research on brain function. Given that strict analogies are made by some cognitive scientists between brain function and computer function and that computer architecture (that is, the configuration of the computer's processing operations) is increasingly modeled upon what is known, for

Figure 6. "The Temple of Speculative Music." (From Robert Fludd,
Utriusque Cosmi . . . Historia, Tomus primus, 1617)

example, about information-relay operations in the brain, it is not surprising that
modernity's drive toward holistic models of the semiosic web should result in Gothic
pedagogical systems. Since some branches of Artificial Intelligence are concerned
with the problem of the semiotics of processual mimesis in text "environments"
of various kinds, the field also has the advantage of providing both a lexicon and
an array of inquiry procedures which are useful in this context. In fact, the operations
of John McCarthy's system, "LISP," provide another way of configuring that fugal
arborescence of textual paradigms which is characteristic of *Portrait* and which, as
we have seen, remains a principal structuring mode in *Ulysses* and *Finnegans Wake*
as well.

    Terry Winograd has argued that "all language use can be thought of as a way
of activating a procedure within the hearer. We can think of any utterance as a
program—one that indirectly causes a set of operations to be carried out within the

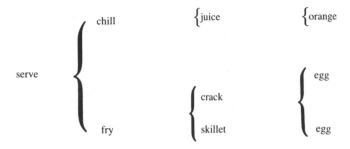

Figure 7. A LISP tree. (From John Haugeland, *Artifical Intelligence: The Very Idea*)

hearer's cognitive system."[70] Distinctive in terms of both its memory organization and its control structure, McCarthy's LISP employs hierarchical (rather than linear) structure which produces the ordering of data by results and prerequisites built into the system and not by time of entry into it.[71] Using a "tree-like" memory organization, LISP defines "new functions in terms of other functions that are already defined,"[72] building on "primitive" or basic functions, configured according to the Y-braiding or nodal structure of a LISP tree. Since LISP nodes are not symmetrical, the branches (or sockets in this sequence of Y-connectors) are explicitly designated left or right. Thus, having identified the required tree and determined the path one's mnemonic sequence will follow, any continuous sequence of left and right turns may be selected in order to reach the designated node from the chosen root function.[73] LISP memory thus operates in terms of a sequencing of lists built as trees whose structures develop as programmed and according to required configuration, storing not only the final term or result of the sequence but also all of the connections among the nodes in the tree or list. The mnemonic hierarchy works by moving back from results to prerequisites or requirements and thus fixes a hierarchy of goals much as the "verbivocovisual" or eye/ear code does in *Finnegans Wake*.

John Haugeland provides a simple example of a LISP tree, based upon a scenario which begins with a breakfast order (chilled orange juice, two fried eggs) being given in a restaurant. The kitchen or McCarthy machine must then work back to prerequisites, or "arguments" in mathematical parlance, having established the goal or "values" (juice, eggs) required. Haugeland's version of this LISP tree is shown in figure 7.[74] The task has been subdivided into a series of "subroutines" which must be performed (chill, crack, fry) before the goal (breakfast) can be achieved by way of presentation of the appropriately prepared materials (orange, eggs). In other words, a list of lists must be prepared and each must be configured according to the mnemonic repertoire. of the system. Since "whenever a LISP function gets an argument [or prerequisite/s], it assumes that the argument is actually specified via another function," each function must first be "evaluated" or scrutinized in order to determine its position within the system. Further, since the LISP machine accepts "only LISP trees as arguments and returns only LISP trees as values . . . it is possible to define a single complex function that will return any . . . [designated] transform as its value, for any input. LISP is therefore universal"[75]—or, in terms of Gothic pedagogy, finitely recursive since the maximum number of branching maneuvers is already bounded within the system. It will be obvious, then, that McCarthy's machine is a thoroughly *specula*/tive one, concerned with a version of processual mimesis and bound by the multiplicative drive of its sets and subsets to reenact the operations of the system.

In LISP, form *is* act in all senses, and act a recombinant sequence of recursive definitions. Thus "in defining a function, that function itself may be used, as long as there's an escape clause that eventually stops the regress."[76] However, lest it seem that this "escape clause" is LISP's version of an encyclopedic infinity, it is important to note that one "escapes" from or "exits" the system, having reached its boundary, and that such transcoding maneuvers can also be built into the system through the insertion of a "NIL" element, a blank or empty set, as a term of a list. Since "LISP programs and LISP memory units ('data structures') have exactly the same underlying form,"[77] it is possible to inscribe such "NIL" nodes in both program and mnemonic repertoire and thus, in Gothic pedagogical fashion, inscribe *in absentia* terms within the system. Thus, like black holes and memory holes, "NIL" tokens serve in the Joyce system as contained universes which have "escaped" and are occasions of regeneration through forgetting. As "*A*" puts it,

> To begin a song:
> If you cannot recall,
> Forget ("*A*" 140)

As we have seen, in *Finnegans Wake* dream functions as narrative sanction of processual mimesis and of "forgetting" or anamnesis within the system. Thus in its last great rejection of the codes of Enlightenment propriety in fictive form, the system displaces us to the margin,[78] to the operations of *Wake* language, to learning again how to exercise the system's exercises. On such occasions we may find ourselves in the midst of what computer architects refer to as the "return-from-subroutine problem," which involves how to return "home" via the "return address" when one is out on a limb of one's memory tree. In Joycean terms, this is the problem of how to keep both ends of parallax going at the same time, or how to operate catechetical paradigms outside *Ulysses* III.2, or how to ensure that catachresis predictably operates according to its morphogenetic program. The simple answer is repetition, but how does repetition function to achieve its text-designated goal? There are at least two responses in terms of computer architecture, the first involving one solution to the "return-from-subroutine" problem as explained by Haugeland:

> Whenever a portion of your program calls a subroutine it first puts its return address on the top of the stack [a "last-in-first-out" memory system] and then branches. Whenever any subroutine finishes its job, it removes whatever address is on top of the stack and branches back there. The result is that any subroutine always returns automatically to the most recent call that has not yet been answered. . . . Thus

subroutine calls can be nested (sub-subroutines calling sub-subroutines and so on) arbitrarily and without distinction.[79]

This is how motiv systems operate in the Joyce system, replication producing branching which leads into the whole paradigm composed of a subsystem of nested motivs. So each motiv system is a subroutine addressed to its components, as we have seen in the case of the ear/eye paradigm in *Finnegans Wake*.

But the dialogical structure of both catechetical paradigms and catachresis demands a more complex procedure. In computer lexicon, this is an "expert system" which requires a well-defined "micro-world"[80] such as a textual system is. There are several other requisites, all having to do with the criterion of practicality since expert systems are typically devised in such cases as medical diagnostic situations where large amounts of data particular to, for example, chemotherapy options relevant to a specific form of cancer, are to be systematized in such a way that a diagnostician may consult the system about a particular array of variables in a specific situation (for example, a negative response to a particular combination of drugs at a specific stage of treatment). Expert systems operate on the basis of semiotic analyses of ranges of semic clusters and serve as filters for arrays of information too complex for the diagnostician to deal with efficiently in any other way. Such systems clearly also facilitate the comparison of a specific situation with a vast repertoire of other data relevant to a specific factor or group of factors.

Employing interactive programs, expert systems are fundamentally catechetically based pedagogical machines in which a LISP-like hierarchy may be used. Proceeding, as *Ulysses* III.2 instructs, from the known to the unknown, the user of the Joycean expert system encounters not only the nested subroutines of the motiv system and the relatively fixed catechetical paradigms but also the much more complex situations of catachresis where the inscription of ictus, or an *in absentia* element, within the structure produces at least a momentary cognitive gap. Here the textual program functioning as expert system provides an array of solutions or responses designated as appropriate or "felicitous" by the system on the basis of its homologous patterning. However, textual "felicity conditions" are met more easily in the "micro-world" of the Joyce system than in Austin's speech act environment for here response paradigms are fixed and comprehension is a corollary of finite, performative competence—finite not only because of the evident limits of the text and the fixed orders of its paradigms and elements but also in a musical sense for, as we have seen, *musica speculativa* abhors a vacuum and *mousiké/ musica humana* demands full gestural enactment.

All of which is to argue, at least in part, that High Gothic cathedrals are architectural expert systems and that the modernity of Gothic[81] is rooted in mathematical paradigms which are also typical of *musica speculativa*. Modified in a variety of ways by both the Joyce and Zukofsky systems, those paradigms not only recur in the twentieth century but again constitute the core of modernity. Gothic pedagogy is, then, the crucial techne of the modern wherever it occurs, peculiar neither to the specific mode from which it takes its name nor to the Joyce system's enactment of it. A dramatistic strategy which, in its Joycean variation, derives its terministic screens from logologically grounded performative operations including liturgical enactment, catachresis, and *musica speculativa*, Gothic pedagogy takes as motto Beckett's apprehension that "Joyce came to see that the fall of a leaf is as grievous as the fall of man"[82]—both alive, both fallen, falling: homologous portions of a world living, breathing, dying, ceaselessly. The ecosystemic motiv again.

"An Hieroglyphical and Shadowed Lesson of the Whole World": Zukofsky and the Lessons of the Joyce System

Returning to the golden section as architectural module, Le Corbusier redis-covered Vitruvian Pythagoras, proclaiming that "a house is a machine to live in"[83] (built on a human scale, its geometry a set of nested figures). A text is also a machine: in the case of the Joyce system, a McCarthy machine though with a repertoire of variations exceeding LISP's wildest dreams. Learning the rules, de-ducing Joycean game theory, we acquire performance-competence. Exercising the exercises, we are trained in *mousiké* and experience that "semiophany" which Augustine locates "beyond memory," a realm to which *musica speculativa* gives access. Remembering where we are, we discover forgetting, anamnesis—finite boundary, memory hole, closure out of which the system reinvents itself "in soandso many counterpoint words" (*FW* 482.34) according to textual program, until the end.

"To begin a song: / If you cannot recall, / Forget" counsels "*A*"-12. A prosody handbook[84] like Augustine's *De Musica*, Zukofsky's long poem "*A*" is also a *speculum* and a Gothic pedagogy of contrafacted sequences, incorporating the Py-thagorean quadrivium as strategy of world-building or of architecture as *scientia*. *Bottom* serves as foil to and commentary not only on "*A*" and Zukofsky's complete production but also on the life and works of Shakespeare. It is one of the great metacritical texts in the English language. In both "*A*" and *Bottom* (or "*B*"), Pythagoras's four mathematical disciplines are resolved into that "ideational music"[85] which is evident in the geometric triumph of the Gothic cathedral, in the fugues of Bach and the works of Shakespeare, and in the structure of the universe, whether of text or "nature." In Zukofsky's recurrent citation of Bach, "The order which rules music is the same order that controls the placing of the stars and the feathers in a bird's wing."[86] Replicating the movements of nature, "He who creates / Is a mode of these inertial systems— / The flower—leaf and leaf wrapped around the center leaf . . . ," as one voice in "*A*"-24 puts it ("*A*" 735).

Poems, like flowers, are in constant process of enactment: "Poems are only acts upon particulars. Only through such activity do they become particulars them-selves—i.e., poems." Like leaves wrapped around each other, letters—those "eye-ing intimacies of print [—] are all actions" as well and are bound, like flowers, into a larger system. Quoting Christopher Smart in *Bottom*, Zukofsky writes:

> For there is a language of flowers.
> For there is a sound reasoning upon all flowers. . . .

> For flowers are medicinal.
> For flowers are musical in ocular harmony.[87]

Botanical "reasoning" involves not only soundness of logic but also reasoning through sound, the logic of both music and flowers being that of "nature" whose "ocular harmony" is interfaced with musical harmony. In Zukofsky, "botanical calligrams" have become audible; so is the work of Shakespeare though in a *specula/ tive* as well as practical sense. Thus in *Bottom*, Shakespeare "is not a metaphor for music—a matter of what the eyes see flowing away in the mind,"[88] not a metaphor restricted to a mode of optic intellection but, rather, the nonfigurative reality of "presence joined by the fixed curve" or Blakean "bounding line" of *musica mundana*, the limits of human music intersecting the boundary of *musica divina*. So "music avoids impossibility"[89]—avoids the "infinite" in the Pythagorean (negative) sense, and, like memory, is bound into the cycle of forgetfulness.

For Zukofsky as for Vico (*NS* 461–63), "man sung before he spoke"[90] and words remain sounds. Sounding the letters, we articulate an Augustinian music as

> The syllables of *Pericles* are brought together like notes. And if that intellective portion of mind that is music can make poetry and prose interchangeable, because there is a note always to come back to a second time—sung to the scale the "subjects" of speech are so few and words only ring changes one on another, the differences perceived by their fictions are so slight music makes them few. Up, down, outwards— for even inversions and exact repetitions move on—are the melodic statement and hence the words' sense: or after syllables have been heard before in contiguity, they may also be augmented or diminished, or brought to crowd answer on subject in a great fugue, as in [*Pericles*] V, i.[91]

Music mimes nature's modes of processual operation and enactment, moving as nature moves according to John Scotus Erigena as cited in *Bottom*: "Nature is eternal . . . but . . . dynamic, moving by the dialectical process of division and return."[92] Fugue form provides a restricted model of this process: "everything must grow out of the subject and there must be nothing new [. . .], there being a unity in spite of infinite multitude, and an infinite multitude in spite of unity."[93] Thus music, nature, and memory function as correlatives within this stable system in which creator and created exist in a relation of exchange which is not only dialectical but also, and more importantly, dialogical:

> Natura naturans— / Nature as creator / Natura
> Naturata— / Nature as created ("*A*" 734)

Verbal music and semantic data exist in a similar tension since "the sound and pitch emphasis of a word are never apart from its meaning."[94] In turn, this exchange relation is replicated in poems whose "forms are achieved as a dynamics of speech and sound, that is, as a resolution of their interacting rhythms—with no loss of value to any word at the expense of the movement."[95]

Miming nature's operations, art becomes for Zukofsky a part of nature. As he states in *Bottom*,

> That art is "good" which does not presume or run out on the world but becomes part of visible, audible, or thinkable nature: an art reached with scaled matter, when it is, as in Shakespeare with words, in Bach with sounds, in Euclid with concepts, or in Ravenna mosaic with small colored stones.[96]

In Zukofsky as in the tradition of *musica speculativa* upon which he draws, all matter is "scaled," constructed according to scale, occupying its place though that "place" be in movement. As Scotus Erigena explains in a passage from *The Division of Nature* quoted in *Bottom*:

> Dialectic begins with essence . . . to which it returns. Geometry . . . with the point from which all figures are developed and into which it is resolved. Astronomy . . . with the moment from which all motion is developed and into which it is resolved. Metaphysics begins and ends with God. In nature . . . division is creation, by successive states from the divine unity. All things flow constantly from God as water flows from a spring . . . as water tends ever to return to its level.[97]

Like "*A*," nature contains its own "omissions" which are part of the poem, delineates the boundaries of its black holes, reconfigures an ultimately fixed system, permits broken symmetries within a world enacting "mind's music" ("*A*" 606), *musica humana* which is "chances of / ordered changes changes of ordered chances . . . " ("*A*" 406). Thus in "*A*"-24,

> I feel
> that everything
> is moving
> and mixing
> with everything else ("*A*" 633–34)

as the other four voices of this Masque move and mix with each other according to a set performance ritual:

> The metronome markings for the music determine the duration of each page for all the voices on each page. The speed at which each voice speaks is correlated to the time-space factor of the music. The words are NEVER SUNG to the music. ("*A*" 564)

But Handel's "Harpsichord Pieces" serve primarily as an *aide-mémoire* in "*A*"-24, sending us *da capo*, back through "recurrence," "forgetfulness," and "L. Z."

("*A*" 806), the code of authorial inscription from A to Z, and into that "nature" which is in process of being and becoming in "*A*," which *is* the poem at any moment when the wheel of memoration stops and we peer into Platonic anamnesis, searching for a way to start again. However, "Thanks to the dictionary,"[98] there is always a way in Zukofsky's system; no sensory modality is lost. Dante, following the same path, provides an exemplum for when he " 'thinks' a metric foot in *De Vulgari Eloquentia* a human foot stalks him like Cressid's. So the visible reference persists 'tangibly' as print, as the air of the voice in handwriting as notes."[99] Dante's metrics are Augustinian *musica speculativa*, his "notes" the *visibile parlare* of the *Purgatorio*. Synthesizing Augustine and Scotus Erigena on the subject of "musical" form in his essay "An Objective," Zukofsky stresses that a poem is "a context associated with 'musical' shape, musical with quotation marks since it is not of notes as music, but of words more variable than variables, and used outside as well as within the context with communicative reference."[100]

That all script is musical notation in a *specula*/tive sense is crucial to both the Joyce system and to Zukofsky's theory of the integral, which, as "*A*"-12 states, is his "poetics" whose "lower limit" is speech and "upper limit music" ("*A*" 138). However, those fixed limits to the scale which are denoted by this poetic integral undergo a seriès of permutations from "*A*"-12 to "*A*"-14. The first occurs later in "*A*"-12 where the original version—

$$\int \frac{\text{music}}{\text{speech ("}A\text{" 138)}}$$

becomes

$$\int_{-1}^{1} \int \frac{\text{sound}}{\text{story—eyes: thing thought ("}A\text{" 173)}}$$

Sound is to music as story is to speech or as story is to eyes, but here we may construe the dash preceding "eyes" in alignment with the negative quantity (-1) of the lower limit of the corresponding integral. Thus, story minus eyes is to sound (working from lower to upper limit) as speech is to music. The music of an oral narrative is, as the repeated stress upon the dialectic of aural/oral and visual presented above would seem to indicate, incomplete without the stimulus of the visual. A story without the involvement or voice of the eyes is equivalent to a "thing thought."

The second permutation of this system, in "*A*"-14, will help us here:

lower limit music
upper limit *mathémata*
swank for things ("*A*" 349)

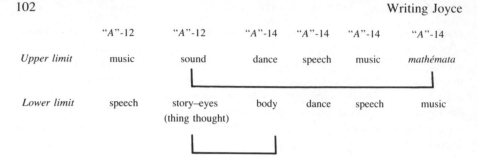

Figure 8. Zukofsky's integral

Things become music when they are thought; Pythagorean *mathémata* become mathematics through the energy of *mousiké*. Acting upon the particulars of things, music is the upper limit of speech in its most fully articulated (harmonized, mnemonically encoded) form, that of poem or "story." As the rest of the second permutation from "*A*"-14 has it:

> lower limit body
> upper limit dance
> lower limit dance
> upper limit speech
> lower limit speech
> upper limit music ("*A*" 349)

If we align the terms of the initial version of the integral with their equivalents in its two permutations, another paradigm emerges as shown in figure 8. Nonreplicating terms are thus *sound* and *mathémata* from the upper limit of the integral, and *story–eyes* with its correlative *thing thought* followed by *body*. A chiasmic interrelationship is evident: *mathémata* ("swank for things") is aligned with *thing thought* and thus with *story–eyes* while *sound* is aligned with *body*. But we know from a passage earlier in "*A*"-12 that

> Music does not always
> Call on the human voice
> Only free (often wordless)
> Men are grateful to one another ("*A*" 130)

Like the debt of gratitude to Celia Zukofsky (Celia the music maker after her hagiographic namesake, patron of musicians) which is acknowledged and celebrated at the end of "*A*," gratitude here is an aspect of freedom and of that love—of family, of Bach, of words and music—which is invoked again and again across the poem and which, as reflection of *musica divina*, is the sustaining force when words are "blown" by the wind's harmonics beyond the range of the human ear. Bodies may not always be capable of receiving sound nor may thoughts always impinge upon things (or vice versa) or things upon things. Things may exceed the reach of eyes or of stories (as those objects known as stories or poems may summon eyes but not thoughts). But within the dialogical poetics which Zukofsky's integral encodes, we move nonetheless through a consistent series of parallel scales bounded in each case by parallel lower limits (*speech, story–eyes/thing thought, body, dance, music*) and by parallel upper limits (*music, sound, dance, speech, mathémata*). Speech *is* music, story *is* sound, body *is* dance, music is *mathémata* is speech—a recapitulation of *musica speculativa* which, with several extra terms, is a version of the "*nine/men's/morris*" dance which occurs in "*A*"-21 ("*A*" 445), echoing Joyce's SD in *Ulysses* I:2:

> this
> is
> my
> form
>
> a
> voice
> blown ("*A*" 445)

writes Zukofsky; and Joyce:

> Across the page the symbols moved in grave morrice, in the mummery of their letters
> [. . .]: so: imps of fancy of the Moors. Gone too from the world, Averroes and
> Moses Maimonides, dark men in mien and movement, flashing in their mocking
> mirrors the obscure soul of the world, a darkness shining in brightness which bright-
> ness could not comprehend. (*U* 2.155)

It is a version of Bach's triad of music, stars, and feathers: the music of all spheres—some stellar, some avian—bound into a world fugue which is Zukofsky's book, Joyce's Moorish algebra transposed into *Ulysses* and *Finnegans Wake*. But

> . . . What book?
> what book?
> entire enough
> to take
> the place
> of all
> the books
> and of
> the world itself ("*A*" 423)

—a riddle to which one answer is the world as book, the ancient topos grounded in an understanding on the part of medieval grammarians of author, *auctor*, as one who "performed the act of writing. He brought something into being, caused it to 'grow,' " or, in Augustinian terms, caused words to be sounded. As A. J. Minnis writes in his study of *Medieval Theory of Authorship*, the term *auctor* was thought to have been derived from the Latin verb *agere*, "to act or perform," *augere*, "to grow," and *auieo*, "to tie," as well as from the Greek noun *autentim*, "authority."[101] Thus authors were imaged also by such poets as Virgil and Lucan as tying together their verses with feet and meters or, in Augustine's terms, with sounding words. So in performing "*A*"-24, we grow the work from A to Z, *da capo*, learning as we perform according to the visual and aural/oral directives provided by Zukofsky's vast "performance-system,"[102] learning to tie our notes together and keep time. Foregrounding its Gothic pedagogical goals, Zukofsky's system articulates Joycean operations, voicing explicitly the lessons of the Joyce system.

Not a metaphoric sequence but a homologous one:

> *musica speculativa* (*mousiké*)/architecture (geometry)/
> text (word, sound)/world (memory system)

A taxonomy of recombinant technai, a "Mental Dictionary." Or a calculus in which the logic of topoi ("topo-logie") is a subset of *musica speculativa*; in which troping the performative discourse of the text is a musical strategy involving "an interpolation, textual or musical, into an already existing composition;"[103] in which *contrafactum* engages the system in endless recirculation by the river of dream narrative; in which "dream" is an element in an isorhythmic motet which starts with Vico's Homer practicing *mousiké* and proceeds by way of Ignatian exercises to composition of place, speech become music become *mathémata*, sounding its *specula*/tive world.

Memory is a stomach, says Augustine.[104] In the *Confessions*,

> "*ego sum, qui memini, ego animus.*"

Animus nourishes and digests *ego* in the continuous present-tense process of being I, *ego sum*, which drives the stomach of memory in peristalsis, alimentary desire. Subsuming *ego* within itself, *qui memini*—centered, relative clause balancing *sum* against *animus*—*verb*alizes its own action in ongoing rememoration. So composition is act (*sum, memini*) and place or locus of enactment (*ego, animus*), the product of the repertoire of encoded mnemonic paradigms. Recapitulation—*anakephalaiōsis*, multiplicability, combinatoriality—drives the system.

> See this. Remember.
> [. . .]
> Listen. (*U* 9.294)

"Astronomically fabulafigured" (*FW* 596.29), the Joyce system flaunts its quadrivial music while dispatching Model Readers on allusive expeditions. Perhaps when their backs are turned, the system "is epiphanised," a recapitulative moment like that which Lethaby imagines of a Gothic cathedral which *rings* when a mason taps a pillar to make its stress audible.[105] The note is the world.

NOTES

1. Configuring the System

1. Paul Ricoeur defines *techne* as "something more refined than a routine or an empirical practice . . . in spite of its focus on production, it contains a speculative element, namely a theoretical inquiry into the means appplied to production. It is a method; and this feature brings it closer to theoretical knowledge than to routine" (*The Rule of Metaphor*, trans. Robert Czerny with Kathleen McLoughlin and John Costello, S.J. [Toronto: Univ. of Toronto Press, 1977], p. 28).

2. Umberto Eco, *The Role of the Reader* (Bloomington: Indiana Univ. Press, 1979), p. 11.

3. On *kerygma* see Frank Kermode, "Novel and Narrative," in *The Theory of the Novel: New Essays*, ed. John Halperin (New York: Oxford Univ. Press, 1974), p. 156, and *The Genesis of Secrecy* (Cambridge, Mass.: Harvard Univ. Press, 1979). Cf. Pierre Macherey's concept of the "*postulate of depth* which has been the principal inspiration of all traditional criticism" (*A Theory of Literary Production*, trans. Geoffrey Wall [London: Routledge and Kegan Paul, 1978], p. 81; Macherey's emphasis). For a good example in Joyce criticism, consider Patrick McCarthy's comment that "we substitute the self-consciousness of the *book* for that of the *characters*" in *Finnegans Wake* (" 'A Warping Process': Reading *Finnegans Wake*," in *Work in Progress: Joyce Centenary Essays*, ed. Richard F. Peterson, Alan M. Cohn and Edmund L. Epstein [Carbondale: Southern Illinois Univ. Press, 1983], p. 50; McCarthy's emphasis). On the distinction between dictionary and *speculum* with its *specula/* tive characteristics, see Vincent Descombes, "Variations on the Subject of the Encyclopedic Book," *Oxford Literary Review* 3:2 (1978), pp. 54–60, and Michel Beaujour, *Miroirs d'Encre* (Paris: Seuil, 1980), pp. 30–35. For a traditional approach to Modernist encyclopedism, see Edward Mendelson, "Encyclopedic Narrative: From Dante to Pynchon," *MLN* 91:6 (Dec. 1976), pp. 1267–75.

4. See Jacques Derrida on "specular dispossession," in *Of Grammatology*, trans. Gayatri Chakravorty Spivak (Baltimore: Johns Hopkins Univ. Press, 1976), p. 141. *Specula/* tive forms are precisely those which do not denote the speculary ontology of the encyclopedia with its narcissistic attempt to be definitive.

5. See Ricoeur's discussion in chapter 1 of *The Rule of Metaphor* of Aristotelian *mimēsis physēos* as what I refer to here in terms of processual mimesis. Ricoeur notes that "it is only through a grave misinterpretation that the Aristotelian *mimēsis* can be confused with imitation in the sense of copy" (p. 39). "To present men '*as* acting' and all things '*as in act*'—such could well be the ontological function of metaphorical discourse," Ricoeur concludes (p. 43). Cf. Joyce's annotation of Aristotle's "*e tekhne mimeitai ten physin*—This phrase is falsely rendered as 'Art is an imitation of Nature.' Aristotle does not here define art; he says only, 'Art imitates Nature' and means that the artistic process is like the natural process" (*The Paris Notebook*, 27 March 1903; in *The Workshop of Daedalus*, ed. Robert Scholes and Richard M. Kain [Evanston: Northwestern Univ. Press, 1965], p. 54). Thus the selection of the term *technic* in both the Gilbert and the Linati schemas for *Ulysses*.

6. Jacques Derrida's shorthand definition of the performative, given in a lecture in his "Political Theology of Language" seminar at the International Summer Institute for Semiotic and Structural Studies, Toronto, June 1987.

7. Maria Corti's phrase in *An Introduction to Literary Semiotics*, trans. Margherita Bogat and Allen Mandel (Bloomington: Indiana Univ. Press, 1978), p. 123. Consider performance as *ars inveniendi*. In the context of theatrical performance, Patrice Pavis refers to the "performance-text: the *mise en scène* of a reading and any possible account made of this reading by the spectator" ("Reflections on the Notation of Theatrical Performance," trans. Susan Melrose, in Pavis, *Languages of the Stage: Essays in the Semiology of the Theatre* [New York: Performing Arts Journal Publications, 1981], p. 127).

8. Gregory L. Ulmer's phrase in *Applied Grammatology: Post(e)-Pedagogy from Jacques Derrida to Joseph Beuys* (Baltimore: Johns Hopkins Univ. Press, 1985). Ulmer notes that "applied grammatology will be characterized by a picto-ideo-phonographic Writing that puts speech back in its place while taking into account the entire scene of writing" (p. 157).

9. Umberto Eco, *Semiotics and the Philosophy of Language* (Bloomington: Indiana Univ. Press, 1984), p. 148.

10. Susan Oyama, *The Ontogeny of Information* (Cambridge: Cambridge Univ. Press, 1985), p. 168.

11. This is one aspect of John Searle's definition of fiction in "The Logical Status of Fictional Discourse," in *Expression and Meaning* (Cambridge: Cambridge Univ. Press, 1979), pp. 58–75. Note, however, that Searle's concept of "serious" utterance and his argument with respect to the Austinian requirements of seriousness and intentionality for performative (specifically, illocutionary) acts to be said to have taken place introduces precisely the limitations of Austinian speech act theory which are rejected here in favor of the revisionist views of Benveniste and Johnson as well as of a logologized Augustinian semiotic. Searle's inscription of "truth," in other words, renders possible the logological inscription of "meaning" across the system.

12. For Burke on act and enactment, see chapter III of *A Grammar of Motives* (Berkeley: Univ. of California Press, 1962), pp. 227–74.

13. My thanks to Wladimir Krysinski for pointing this out and to my students at ISISSS 87 in Toronto for vigorously reinforcing it. Readers who prefer to remain in that state which I classify here as nostalgia may, of course, choose to incorporate such elements as Joyce's biography, Irish sociopolitical and cultural history and so on into a reading of the system following a social semiotic model of the sort developed by, e.g., Michael Halliday. While I reject the subjectivist bias which seems to me to be fundamental to such a model, I do concede the logical possibility of reading/writing the system in this way, as exemplified by Cheryl Herr's fine book *Joyce's Anatomy of Culture* (Urbana: Univ. of Illinois Press, 1986). Finally, it should be noted that readers in search of Joycean sanction for the importation of sigla into the analysis of *Ulysses* need only look at the Buffalo Notebooks for numerous examples of Joyce's use of "S. D.," e.g., Notebook VI.c. 3–63 and VI.c. 4–101, 103 (vol. 27, *The James Joyce Archive*, ed. Michael Groden [New York: Garland Publishing, 1978]) and VI.c. 12–81, 82, 211 (*Archive*, vol. 19); and of "L.B.," e.g., Notebook VI A (*Archive*, vol. 56, pp. 209, 213, 217, 228, 231). Naming operations are polyvalent throughout *Ulysses* and are repeatedly drawn into the nonreferential ontology of the system. See chapter III.

14. See Roland McHugh, *The Sigla of "Finnegans Wake"* (Austin: Univ. of Texas Press, 1976). Although I agree with McHugh's textually based arguments supporting the use of the sigla, I completely reject what seems to me to be a logical non sequitur in his argument, that is, McHugh's attempt to reinscribe Realist concepts of character and plot upon the sigla. This attempt is consonant with his referential-mimetic reading of *Finnegans Wake*, of course, but I regard that strategy as a rejection of the text.

15. On "oscillating perspectives" see John Paul Riquelme, *Teller and Tale in Joyce's Fiction* (Baltimore: Johns Hopkins Univ. Press, 1983). Consider, for example, Riquelme's assertion that in both *Portrait* and *Ulysses* "the reader translates the third person into 'I' during the reading process" (p. 54), his discovery that *Portrait* has "navels" which afford "evidence of a presence that hides and reveals itself in the vertiginous forms of the narration" (p. 84), and his equation of referential mimesis with narrative as well as with that mode of action which, for him, characterizes narrative. Thus for Riquelme, " 'Circe' is not organized like a conventional realistic narrative with seemingly real characters in a recognizable setting

acting and thinking in believable ways. I would not deny the referential component completely. Without it, the episode would give no impression of action; it would not be part of a narrative'' (p. 137). For Wolfgang Iser's theory of horizons and wandering viewpoints, see "Patterns of Communication in Joyce's *Ulysses*," in *The Implied Reader* (Baltimore: Johns Hopkins Univ. Press, 1978), pp. 196–233, and *The Act of Reading* (Baltimore: Johns Hopkins Univ. Press, 1978), chapter III. Note that as the reader "operates the 'fusion of the horizons,' . . . he produces an experience of reality which is real precisely because it happens, without being subjected to any representational function" (*Implied Reader*, p. 227) yet *Ulysses* is said to "evoke constantly changing 'pictures' of everyday life" which make "demands on the reader's creativity" because of their number and complexity (ibid., p. 232). Thus "Even though he will never find the object of his search, on his way he [the reader] will meet with a vast array of possible conceptions, through which the reality of everyday life will come alive in a corresponding number of ways" (ibid., pp. 232–33).

16. Eco, *Semiotics*, p. 163.

17. Kenneth Burke, *The Rhetoric of Religion* (Berkeley: Univ. of California Press, 1961), p. 1.

18. Ibid.; p. 3.

19. For an example of Burke's use of this procedure, see Kenneth Burke, "Fact, Inference, and Proof in the Analysis of Literary Symbolism," in *Terms for Order*, ed. Stanley Edgar Hyman and Barbara Karmiller (Bloomington: Indiana Univ. Press, 1964), pp. 145–72.

20. Jurij M. Lotman, "The Dynamic Model of a Semiotic System," trans. Ann Shukman, *Semiotica* 21:3/4 (1977), pp. 193–210. Lotman states that "self-description creates the history of the object from the point of view of its own model of itself" (p. 200), a procedure followed in *Writing Joyce* insofar as the Joyce system functions in such a way as to render systemic what Lotman classifies, in Ann Shukman's translation, as "extrasystematic" (i.e., extrasystemic). See also Lotman, *The Structure of the Artistic Text*, trans. Ronald Vroon (Ann Arbor: Michigan Slavic Contributions no. 7, 1977). Lotman's model has an antecedent in the work of Jan Mukarovsky. See Peter Steiner on Mukarovsky's concept of "semantic gesture," in "The Conceptual Basis of Prague Structuralism," in Ladislaw Matejka, ed., *Sound, Sign and Meaning: Quinquagenary of the Prague Linguistic Circle* (Ann Arbor: Michigan Slavic Contributions no. 6, 1976), pp. 372–77. Other variations on the theme of dynamic or processual models in semiotics include the polysystem theory of Itamar Even-Zohar, the semiotics of drama developed by Patrice Pavis, and the semiotics of gesture of Adam Kendon. Processual semiotic models have been slow to come to literary semiotics in English, in part because of the impact of Greimassian neo-Structuralism and of its subjectivist counterpart which is now particularly evident in American and British semiotics of cinema. See, for example, Kaja Silverman, *The Subject of Semiotics* (New York: Oxford Univ. Press, 1983).

21. It remains for anyone interested in this project to do an archeology of the system by exploring the relations of *Dubliners* and *Exiles*, in particular, to the Joyce system as conceived in *Writing Joyce*. One way of working with *Exiles* is briefly indicated in chapter II, and I suspect on evidence of this sort that a narratological model might be useful in the first instance.

22. Joseph Frank, "Spatial Form in Modern Literature," in *The Widening Gyre* (Bloomington: Indiana Univ. Press, 1968), pp. 3–62.

23. Kenneth Burke, "Terministic Screens," in *Language as Symbolic Action* (Berkeley: Univ. of California Press, 1966), pp. 44–62.

24. John Deely's phrase, *Introducing Semiotic* (Bloomington: Indiana Univ. Press, 1982), p. 10.

25. Umberto Eco, "Dreaming of the Middle Ages," in *Travels in Hyperreality*, trans. William Weaver (San Diego: Harcourt Brace Jovanovich, 1986), p. 70.

26. Ibid.

27. Ibid.

28. Georges Poulet, "Phenomenology of Reading," *NLH* I:1 (Fall 1969), p. 54.

29. Ernst Curtius, *European Literature and the Latin Middle Ages*, trans Willard R. Trask (Princeton: Princeton/Bollingen, 1973), p. 254.

30. Ibid., p. 484.

31. Ibid., p. 490.

32. See Eugène Vinaver, *The Rise of Romance* (Oxford: Clarendon Press, 1971), p. 98; Paul Zumthor, *Speaking of the Middle Ages*, trans. Sarah White (Lincoln: Univ. of Nebraska Press, 1986); Eugene Vance, "Mervelous Signals: Poetics, Sign Theory, and Politics in Chaucer's *Troilus*," *NLH* X:2 (Winter 1979), pp. 293–337. See also Hans Robert Jauss, "The Alterity and Modernity of Medieval Literature," *NLH* X:2 (Winter 1979), pp. 181–227, a classic essay which takes a hermeneutic approach to the subject. Mary T. Reynolds notes in *Joyce and Dante: The Shaping Imagination* (Princeton: Princeton Univ. Press, 1981) that "both Dante and Joyce, placing the artist at the center of their work, made poetic invention itself the subject and tested the limits of their art" (p. 148). Like Beckett, Reynolds here foregrounds the system as *ars inveniendi* although she does not develop this crucial observation. Cf. Patrick A. McCarthy's sense in *The Riddles of "Finnegans Wake"* (London: Associated Univ. Press, 1980) that precisely this aspect of *FW* is "one of its many riddlelike qualities" (p. 154) and that "the purpose of a riddle is to mislead and confuse the listener, at least temporarily, and to illustrate the ingenuity of the riddler" (p. 18), especially because "riddles throughout Joyce's works are never meant to be answered correctly" (p. 20). McCarthy has quite precisely missed Beckett's point. Cf. Jean-Michel Rabaté, "Lapsus ex machina," on *Finnegans Wake* as "performative utopia" (in *Poststructuralist Joyce*, ed. Derek Attridge and Daniel Ferrer [Cambridge: Cambridge Univ. Press, 1984], pp. 79–101).

33. M. M. Bakhtin, *The Dialogic Imagination*, ed. Michael Holquist, trans. Caryl Emerson and Michael Holquist (Austin: Univ. of Texas Press, 1982), p. 51.

34. I am indebted to my colleague Patricia Merivale, who uses this phrase in a very different sense in her article "Learning the Hard Way: Gothic Pedagogy in the Modern Romantic Quest," *Comparative Literature* 36:2 (Spring 1984), pp. 146–61.

35. See Julia Kristeva, *Semeiotikè: Recherches pour une sémananalyse* (Paris: Seuil, 1969), pp. 255ff.

36. Eco, *Travels*, p. 84.

37. On *contrafactum*, see chapter V.

38. On *manifestatio*, see chapter V.

39. Michel Foucault, *The Order of Things*, trans. anon. (London: Tavistock, 1974), p. 387.

40. Eco, *Travels*, p. 84.

41. Andreas Huyssen, *After the Great Divide: Modernism, Mass Culture, Postmodernism* (Bloomington: Indiana Univ. Press, 1986), p. 202. See in particular chapters 9 and 10.

42. Gregory Ulmer's phrase, *Applied Grammatology*, p. 42 where the moiré effect is defined as "One of the effects of interlacing . . . the flicker produced when two grids are superimposed or made to overlap in a dissymmetrical or off-centered way."

43. On the history of semiotics, see John Deely, *Introducing Semiotic*. On Derrida and the Rabbinical tradition, see Jacques Derrida, "Edmond Jabès and the Question of the Book," in *Writing and Difference*, trans. Alan Bass (Chicago: Univ. of Chicago Press, 1978), pp. 64–78. See also Susan A. Handelman, *The Slayers of Moses: The Emergence of Rabbinic Interpretation in Modern Literary Theory* (Albany: State Univ. of New York Press, 1982), chapter 7, and Handelman, "Jacques Derrida and the Heretic Hermeneutic," *Diacritics* IV (1983), pp. 98–129. For Derrida on Joyce, see, e.g., "Two Words for Joyce," trans. Geoff Bennington, in *Poststructuralist Joyce*, pp. 145–58.

44. For an introduction to some of the principles of cognitive science invoked in this book, see Jean-Pierre Changeux, *Neuronal Man: The Biology of Mind*, trans. Laurence Garey (New York: Oxford Univ. Press, 1985), and Patricia Smith Churchland, *Neurophilosophy: Toward a Unified Science of the Mind-Brain* (Cambridge, Mass.: Bradford Books, 1986). For related concepts in Artificial Intelligence, see Marvin Minsky, *The Society of Mind* (New York: Simon and Schuster, 1985).

45. My thanks are due to Peter Wilkins and Hilary Clark whose theses on the encyclopedia focused my attention on the problem sufficiently to provoke a countertheory. See Peter Wilkins, "Transformations of the Circle: An Exploration of the Post-Encyclopedic Text"

(M.A. thesis, Univ. of British Columbia, 1985), and Hilary Clark, "The Idea of a Fictional Encyclopedia: *Finnegans Wake, Paradis*, the *Cantos*" (Ph.D. diss., Univ. of British Columbia, 1985).

2. Barthes' *Loyola*/Joyce's *Portrait*

1. Jorge Luis Borges, "Kafka and His Precursors," in *Labyrinths: Selected Stories and Other Writings* (Harmondsworth: Penguin Books, 1970), p. 236.

2. Michel Foucault, *The Archeology of Knowledge*, trans. M. M. Sheridan Smith (New York: Harper and Row, 1976), p. 23. See David Hayman, "Nodality and the Infra-Structure of *Finnegans Wake*," *James Joyce Quarterly* 16:1–2 (Fall 1978/Winter 1979), pp. 135–49, for a different approach to Joycean nodality. See also Hayman, "The Joycean Inset," *James Joyce Quarterly* 23:2 (Winter 1986), pp. 137–55.

3. Cf. Hans Walter Gabler's statement in his essay "The Seven Lost Years of *A Portrait of the Artist as a Young Man*" that "chapters II and IV [of *Portrait*] take on a centripetal and centrifugal direction, and the religious retreat becomes, literally and structurally, the dead center of the novel" (in Thomas F. Staley and Bernard Benstock, eds., *Approaches to Joyce's "Portrait"* [Pittsburgh: Univ. of Pittsburgh Press, 1976], p. 51).

4. Derrida, *Grammatology*, p. 162 (Derrida's italics).

5. I capitalize this term henceforward in order to signal its exclusive use here in the sense defined by Barthes, to be radically distinguished from the Pound/Imagiste usage. I have in most cases in this chapter preferred "Stephen Dedalus" to "Stephen," introducing a frequently awkward usage in order to preserve a distance, to stress both literal/semantic and allegorical/anagogic texts.

6. Barthes refers here to topography and "a rhetorical tradition" exemplified in Cicero's recommendation that, "when speaking of a place, [one should consider whether it is] . . . flat, mountainous, harmonious, rough, etc. (exactly what Ignatius says); and Aristotle, stating that in order to remember things one must recognize where they are, includes place (topos), common or particular, in his rhetoric of the probable . . . " (*B* 55). The "rhetorical tradition" is that of *ars memoria*, here represented by its Classical phase as reconstructed by Frances Yates, *The Art of Memory* (Harmondsworth: Peregrine Books, 1969), pp. 17–62.

7. See Florence L. Walzl, "The Liturgy of the Epiphany Season and the Epiphanies of Joyce," *PMLA* LXXX:4 (Sept. 1965), pp. 436–50. Perhaps the best study of motifs of sight in *Portrait* is Lee T. Lemon's "*A Portrait of the Artist as a Young Man*: Motif as Motivation and Structure," *Modern Fiction Studies* XII (Winter 1966–67), pp. 439–50. On Joyce's experience of Jesuit educational methods, see Kevin Sullivan, *Joyce among the Jesuits* (New York: Columbia Univ. Press, 1958), and Bruce Bradley, S.J., *James Joyce's Schooldays* (Dublin: Gill and Macmillan, 1982).

8. Cf. Ramón Saldívar's reading of this phrase as "in itself neutral and . . . [exerting] no modification of the surrounding elements of the sentence within which it occurs" in *Portrait* (*Figural Language in the Novel: The Flowers of Speech from Cervantes to Joyce* [Princeton: Princeton Univ. Press, 1984], pp. 197–99). See also John B. Smith's assertion that "the dynamic patterns of associations among images on the page reflect the developing structure of Stephen's mind" (*Imagery and the Mind of Stephen Dedalus* [Lewisburg: Bucknell Univ. Press, 1980], p. 17).

9. As identified by Richard Ellmann, *Ulysses on the Liffey* (New York: Oxford Univ. Press, 1972), p. 25.

10. Cf. David Hayman, "Stephen on the Rocks," *JJQ* 15:1 (Fall 1977), pp. 5–17.

11. Meditation on the name of the Buddha, analogous to *Lectio divina* (*B* 59).

12. As we are elliptically informed by the retreat director's statement that "Hell [epicenter of the retreat and the novel] is the centre of evils and, as you know, things are more intense

at their centres than at their remotest points" (*P* 134). "Still point" is T. S. Eliot's phrasing of *nembutsu* in "Burnt Norton." See *The Complete Poems and Plays of T. S. Eliot* (London: Faber, 1969), p. 173.

13. The source of this sermon is Giovanni Pietro Pinamonte. See Elizabeth F. Boyd, "Joyce's Hell-Fire Sermons," *Modern Language Notes* LXXV:7 (Nov. 1960), pp. 561–71; James Doherty, "Joyce and *Hell Opened to Christians*: The Edition He Used for His Sermons," *Modern Philology* 61 (1963), pp. 110–19; and James R. Thrane, "Joyce's Sermon on Hell: Its Sources and Backgrounds," *Modern Philology* 57 (1960), pp. 177–98. On the *speculum*, see chapter III.

14. "The great and golden rule of art, as well as of life, is this: That the more distinct, sharp, and wirey [*sic*] the bounding line, the more perfect the work of art . . . "; in *The Complete Writings of William Blake*, ed. Geoffrey Keynes (Oxford: Oxford Univ. Press, 1966), p. 585 ("A Descriptive Catalogue," no. XV).

15. *Logodaedalus*. Obs. "One who is cunning in words" (*Oxford English Dictionary*).

16. Fig. 12 in Yates is a reconstruction of this memory system in Bruno's *De umbris idearum* (1582). In *De la Causa*, Bruno wrote that "you must know that it is by one and the same ladder that nature descends to the production of things and the intellect ascends to the knowledge of them; and that the one and the other proceeds from unity and returns to unity, passing through the multitude in the middle." Yates comments that the aim of the Brunian memory system is "to establish within, in the psyche, the return of the intellect to unity through the organization of significant images" (p. 224) rigorously classified upon the mobile wheels of the system. See Yates, pp. 209–227. This is a crucial, and much ignored, aspect of Bruno's importance for the Joyce system.

17. Foucault argues that literature post-Mallarmé "breaks with the whole definition of genres as forms adapted to an order of representations, and becomes merely a manifestation of a language which has no other law than that of affirming—in opposition to all other forms of discourse—its own precipitous existence; and so there is nothing for it but to curve back in a perpetual return upon itself, as if its discourse could have no other content than the expression of its own form; it addresses itself to itself as a writing subjectivity, or seeks to re-apprehend the essence of all literature in the movement that brought it into being . . . " (*The Order of Things*, p. 300).

3. From Catechism to Catachresis

1. Joseph Frank, "Spatial Form," in *The Widening Gyre*, p. 19.

2. Gérard Genette, "La Littérature et l'espace," in *Figures II* (Paris: Seuil, 1969), p. 47.

3. Frank, *Widening Gyre*, p. 7.

4. Ibid., p. 8.

5. Ibid., p. 13.

6. Ibid., p. 16.

7. Ibid., p. 19. Cf. A. Walton Litz, "The Genre of 'Ulysses,' " in *The Theory of the Novel: New Essays*, ed. John Halperin (New York: Oxford Univ. Press, 1974), p. 116.

8. Genette, *Figures II*, p. 19. Frank notes that Genette was unaware of his essay at the time of composition of "La Littérature et l'espace" ("Spatial Form: Thirty Years After," in *Spatial Form in Narrative*, ed. Jeffrey R. Smitten and Ann Daghistany [Ithaca: Cornell Univ. Press, 1981], p. 243).

9. Genette, *Figures II*, p. 48.

10. Gérard Genette, *Narrative Discourse: An Essay in Method*, trans. Jane E. Lewin (New York: Cornell Univ. Press, 1980), p. 34.

11. A. J. Greimas's terms in *Structural Semantics*, trans. D. McDowell, R. Schleifer, and A. Velie (Lincoln: Univ. of Nebraska Press, 1983), pp. 143ff.

12. Genette, *Narrative Discourse*, pp. 164, 234.

13. Umberto Eco, *A Theory of Semiotics* (Bloomington: Indiana Univ. Press, 1979), p. 62.

14. Genette, *Narrative Discourse*, p. 164.

15. See Edmund Husserl, *Ideas: General Introduction to Pure Phenomenology*, trans. W. R. Boyce Gibson (London: Collier Books, 1962), chapter 9 on "Noesis and Noema."

16. Frank, *Widening Gyre*, p. 8.

17. Paul Ricoeur, *Hermeneutics and the Human Sciences*, trans. and ed. John B. Thompson (Cambridge: Cambridge Univ. Press, 1981), p. 205.

18. Kenneth Burke, "Biology, Psychology, Words," in Burke, *Dramatism and Development* (Barre, Mass.: Clark Univ. Press, 1972), p. 18.

19. John Freccero, "The Significance of Terza Rima," in *Dante: The Poetics of Conversion* (Cambridge, Mass.: Harvard Univ. Press, 1986), pp. 266–67. See also Freccero on Burke, in the same volume, p. 260.

20. On ekphrasis see Murray Krieger, "The Ekphrastic Principle and the Still Movement of Poetry; or *Laokoön* Revisited," in Krieger, *The Play and Place of Criticism* (Baltimore: Johns Hopkins Univ. Press, 1967), pp. 105–128. See also Svetlana Alpers, *The Art of Describing: Dutch Art in the Seventeenth Century* (Chicago: Univ. of Chicago Press, 1983), p. 136, and Wendy Steiner, *The Colors of Rhetoric: Problems in the Relation between Modern Literature and Painting* (Chicago: Univ. of Chicago Press, 1982), p. 41.

21. Eliot, *Complete Poems and Plays*, p. 175.

22. Hans Urs von Balthasar, *Man in History* (New York: Sheed and Ward, 1968), p. 116, quoted in Freccero, *Dante*, p. 266. See also ibid., p. 269.

23. John Freccero, "Logology: Burke on St. Augustine," in *Representing Kenneth Burke*, ed. Hayden White and Margaret Brose (Baltimore: Johns Hopkins Univ. Press, 1982), p. 60.

24. Freccero, "Logology," p. 62.

25. Steiner, *Colors of Rhetoric*, p. 191.

26. Freccero, "Logology," p. 66. Freccero's emphasis.

27. H. P. Grice, "Logic and Conversation," in *Syntax and Semantics*, vol. 3: *Speech Acts*, ed. Peter Cole and Jerry L. Morgan (New York: Academic Press, 1975), pp. 44–47.

28. Jurij Lotman, *The Structure of the Artistic Text*, p. 292.

29. Joseph Frank, "Spatial Form: An Answer to the Critics," *Critical Inquiry* 4:2 (Winter 1977), p. 237. See also Erich Auerbach, "Figura," trans. Ralph Manheim, in *Scenes from the Drama of European Literature* (Minneapolis: Univ. of Minnesota Press, 1984), pp. 11–76.

30. Gérard Genette, *Introduction a l'architexte* (Paris: Seuil, 1979).

31. See Genette, "Proust palimpseste," in *Figures* (Paris: Seuil, 1966), pp. 39–67. Cf. Joseph Kestner, "Virtual Text/Virtual Reader: The Structural Signature Within, Behind, Beyond, Above," *James Joyce Quarterly* 16:1/2 (Fall 1978/Winter 1979), pp. 27–42. Derived by Wyndham Lewis from Wilhelm Worringer quoting Gottfried Semper, the phrase "Scholasticism in stone" is cited approvingly by both Worringer and Joyce. "As a matter of fact," Joyce responded to Lewis, "I do something of that sort in words" (*JJII*: 515; Worringer, *Form in Gothic*, rev. ed. and trans. Herbert Read [New York: Schocken, 1957] p. 162).

32. Ricoeur, *Rule of Metaphor*, pp. 35–43.

33. See Foucault, *Order of Things* and Derrida, *Grammatology*, part I.

34. Ricoeur, *Rule of Metaphor*, p. 43. Ricoeur's emphasis.

35. John Freccero's phrase in a lecture on "Augustine and Oedipus," "Augustine of Hyppo" Conference, University of British Columbia, 9 Nov. 1984.

36. See Kenneth Burke, *A Grammar of Motives* (Berkeley: Univ. of California Press, 1969), p. 227, citing St. Thomas: "*forma per se ipsum facit rem esse in actu.*" For a theological discussion of this principle, see Etienne Gilson, *The Christian Philosophy of St. Thomas*, trans. L. K. Shook, C.S.B. (New York: Random House, 1956), pp. 177–86.

37. Ricoeur, *Rule of Metaphor*, p. 28.

38. Ibid., p. 39.

39. John Freccero's phrase, "Augustine and Oedipus" lecture.

40. Ricoeur, *Rule of Metaphor*, p. 209.

41. Marshall McLuhan, *Understanding Media* (Toronto: Signet, 1964), p. 23.

42. Ricoeur, *Rule of Metaphor*, p. 55.

43. Ricoeur, *Hermeneutics and the Social Sciences*, p. 205. Ricoeur's phrase is "action-event" which I abbreviate here for reasons which will be evident as the discussion of *act* develops in this chapter. Cf. Joseph M. Powers's assertion that "the entire context of the reality of the bread [in the Eucharist] is that of a sign-act" (*Eucharistic Theology* [New York: Herder and Herder, 1967], p. 175). It would then be reasonable to assert, using Karl Bühler's terminology, that the liturgy is a sustained "act history" (*Akt-Geschichte*). See Robert E. Innis, *Karl Bühler: Semiotic Foundations of Language Theory* (New York: Plenum Press, 1982), p. 121.

44. Joseph P. Jungmann, S.J., *The Mass of the Roman Rite: Its Origins and Development*, trans. Francis A. Brunner, C.S.S.R., rev. Charles K. Riepe, rev. and abridged ed. (London: Burns and Oates, 1959), p. 134.

45. Emile Benveniste, *Problems in General Linguistics*, trans. Mary Elizabeth Meek (Coral Gables: Univ. of Miami Press, 1971), p. 237. Note Austin's statement that "performative is both an *action* and an *utterance*" and, with respect to distinctions between performative and constative, "There would perhaps be no great harm in not distinguishing them, if by degrees we were brought to see, in every phase of ordinary language, an implicit performative utterance" ("Performative-Constative," in *Philosophy and Ordinary Language*, ed. Charles E. Caton [Urbana: Univ. of Illinois Press, 1963], pp. 24 and 34).

46. O. B. Hardison, Jr., *Christian Rite and Christian Drama in the Middle Ages* (Baltimore: Johns Hopkins Univ. Press, 1965), p. 67.

47. Harold Scheub, "Body and Image in Oral Performance," *NLH* 8 (1977), p. 354.

48. Ibid., p. 355. Cf. the systems of hand gestures used by *devadasi* temple dancers and codified in the *Nathashastra*, thought to have been written in the second or third century. Such systems are characteristic also of the South Indian *kathakali* as well as the *kathak* dance of North India. For more information about *mudras*, see Ernest T. Kirby, *Ur-Drama: The Origins of Theatre* (New York: New York Univ. Press, 1975), pp. 40ff. It is interesting to note that the term *patterning* is also applied to the fixed gestural routines used by therapists who train autistic children and stroke victims who have suffered paralysis. For a detailed semiotic analysis of a counting system using hand/arm gestural codes, see Drid Williams, "The Arms and Hands, with Special Reference to an Anglo-Saxon Sign System," *Semiotica* 21:1/2 (1977), pp. 23–73.

49. Powers, *Eucharistic Theology*, p. 175. See also E. Schillebeeckx, O.P., *The Eucharist*, trans. N. D. Smith (New York: Sheed and Ward, 1968), pp. 78–80.

50. Powers, *Eucharistic Theology*, p. 175.

51. Harold Scheub, "Oral Narrative Process and the Use of Models," *NLH* 6 (1974), p. 371.

52. Walter J. Ong, *Rhetoric, Romance, and Technology* (Ithaca: Cornell Univ. Press), p. 291. See also Jeff Opland on "Oral Poetics and Oral Noetics," in Opland, *Xhosa Oral Poetry: Aspects of a Black South African Tradition* (Cambridge: Cambridge Univ. Press, 1983).

53. Walter J. Ong, *Interfaces of the Word: Studies in the Evolution of Consciousness and Culture* (Ithaca: Cornell Univ. Press, 1977), p. 196.

54. Walter J. Ong, *Orality and Literacy: The Technologizing of the Word* (London: Methuen, 1982), p. 36.

55. Ibid.

56. Ibid., pp. 37–41.

57. Ibid., p. 46.

58. Ibid., p. 49.

59. Ibid., p. 53. See A. R. Luria, *Cognitive Development: Its Cultural and Social Foundations*, trans. Martin Lopez-Morillas and Lynn Solotaroff (Cambridge, Mass.: Harvard Univ. Press, 1976), p. 86.

60. Frank Kermode, "Novel and Narrative," in *Theory of the Novel*, ed. John Halperin, p. 156. See also Kermode, *The Genesis of Secrecy*. *Kerygma* is Rudolf Bultmann's term. See Bultmann et al., *Kerygma and Myth: A Theological Debate*, ed. Hans Werner Bartsch, trans. Reginald A. Fuller, 2d ed. (London: S. P. C. K., 1964).

61. Genette, *Narrative Discourse*, p. 164.

62. Emile Benveniste, *Problèmes de linguistique générale* (Paris: Gallimard, 1966). My translation. Cf. Benveniste, *Problems in General Linguistics*, p. 237. In his essay "Semiotics of Theatrical Performance," Eco assimilates this mode of performance into the category of ostension (*Drama Review* 21:1 [March 1977] p. 110).

63. Gérard Genette, *Mimologiques: Voyage en Cratylie* (Paris: Seuil, 1976), p. 9.

64. Burke, *Grammar of Motives*, p. 227.

65. Marcel Jousse, *L'Anthropologie du geste* (Paris: Resma, 1969), p. 18.

66. Marcel Jousse, *La Manducation de la Parole* (Paris: Gallimard, 1975), p. 127. Ong defines *secondary orality* as "both remarkably like and remarkably unlike primary orality. Like primary orality, secondary orality has generated a strong group sense, for listening to spoken words forms hearers into a group, a true audience. . . . But secondary orality generates a sense for groups immeasurably larger than those of primary oral culture—McLuhan's 'global village.' Moreoever, before writing, oral folk were group-minded because no feasible alternative had presented itself. In our age of secondary orality, we are group-minded self-consciously and programmatically. . . . In a like vein, where primary orality promotes spontaneity because the analytic reflectiveness implemented by writing is unavailable, secondary orality promotes spontaneity because through analytic reflection we have decided that spontaneity is a good thing" (Ong, *Orality and Literacy*, pp. 136–37).

67. Jousse, *La Manducation*, pp. 27 and 127.

68. A phrase from lecture notes by Marcel Jousse, quoted in G. Baron, *Marcel Jousse: Introduction à sa vie et à son oeuvre* (Paris: Casterman, 1965), p. 237.

69. Jousse, *La Manducation*, p. 66.

70. Ibid., passim.

71. Ibid., p. 272. Cf. Louis Marin's study of Transsubstantiation as enunciation within the Eucharistic theology of the Port-Royal Logic ("Un chapître dans l'histoire de la théorie sémiotique: La théologie eucharistique dans 'La Logique de Port-Royal' [1683]," in *History of Semiotics*, ed. Achim Eschbach and Jürgen Trabant [Amsterdam: John Benjamins, 1983], pp. 127–44).

72. Jousse, *La Manducation*, p. 233. For a more detailed discussion of Jousse, see my article "The Choreography of Gesture: Marcel Jousse and *Finnegans Wake*," *James Joyce Quarterly* 14:3 (Spring 1977), pp. 313–25.

73. Patrice Pavis, *Language of the Stage*, p. 127.

74. Ong, *Orality and Literacy*, p. 34.

75. A. Walton Litz, "The Genre of *Ulysses*," in *Theory of the Novel*, ed. John Halperin, p. 116.

76. Hugh Kenner, *Ulysses* (London: George Allen and Unwin, 1980), p. 157.

77. Fredric Jameson, "*Ulysses* in History," in *James Joyce and Modern Literature*, ed. W. J. McCormack and Alistair Stead (London: Routledge and Kegan Paul, 1982), p. 138.

78. Macherey, *Theory of Literary Production*, p. 81.

79. Beaujour, *Miroirs d'encre*, p. 34.

80. Ibid., p. 31.

81. Descombes, "Variations on the Subject of the Encyclopaedic Book," p. 56.

82. See Foucault, *Order of Things*.

83. Descombes, p. 56.

84. Ibid. Descombes' emphasis.

85. Beaujour, p. 32. See also Michel Lemoine, "L'oeuvre encyclopédique de Vincent

de Beauvais,'' in Maurice de Gandillac et al., *La pensée encyclopédique au moyen âge* (Neuchatel: Editions de la Baconnière, 1966), pp. 78–85.

86. Beaujour, p. 34.

87. Ibid., pp. 34–35. On Gothic architecture and modernity, see chapter V.

88. See Florence L. Walzl, ''The Liturgy of the Epiphany Season and the Epiphanies of Joyce,'' *PMLA* 80:4 (Sept. 1965), pp. 436–50. Throughout this discussion of *Ulysses* I have preferred book and chapter numbers to the Homeric chapter titles of the Gilbert/Linati schemas. Bringing into alignment the classification of chapters in both *Ulysses* and *Finnegans Wake*, this procedure seeks also to avoid the Realist domestication of the text which Gilbert/Linati as well as Campbell/Robinson and Glasheen titles now customarily evoke. Though his lexicon is not mine, I agree with Daniel Ferrer's assertion that ''upon . . . [the] symbolic framework [of each techne], a huge imaginary construction rises,'' and it is the conceptual architecture of that structure which we must explore. See Ferrer, ''Echo or Narcissus?'' in *James Joyce: The Centennial Symposium*, ed. Morris Beja, Phillip Herring, Maurice Harmon, and David Norris (Urbana: Univ. of Illinois Press, 1986), p. 73.

89. Lancelot Andrewes, *Sermons on the Nativity* (Grand Rapids: Baker Book House, 1955), Sermon XV, p. 254.

90. Nicholas of Cusa, *Of Learned Ignorance*, trans. Germain Heron (London: O. F. M., 1954), p. xiv.

91. See, e.g., *A Catechism of Catholic Doctrine* (Dublin: M. H. Gill, 1951), p. 77: ''A sacrament is a sensible or outward sign instituted by Christ to signify grace and confer it on our souls.'' Cf. Richard E. Madtes' position that the ''interrogative [catechetical] method'' evolves ''ultimately from the fundamental curiosity of inquisitive man in an incomprehensible universe'' (*The ''Ithaca'' Chapter of Joyce's ''Ulysses''* [Ann Arbor: UMI Research Press, 1983], p. 67). Madtes here quite precisely misses the point of the whole chapter.

92. Barbara Johnson, *The Critical Difference: Essays in the Contemporary Rhetoric of Reading* (Baltimore: Johns Hopkins Univ. Press, 1980), pp. 143–44.

93. Lotman, *The Structure of the Artistic Text*, p. 9.

94. *Hypogram* is Michael Riffaterre's term. See his *Semiotics of Poetry* (Bloomington: Indiana Univ. Press, 1978), p. 168, fn. 16.

95. Johnson, *Critical Difference*, p. 144.

96. Cusa, *Of Learned Ignorance*, p. 157.

97. See, e.g., S. L. Goldberg, *The Classical Temper* (London: Chatto and Windus, 1961).

98. Marin quoted in Beaujour, p. 308, fn. 3.

99. Cf. Joyce's letter to Olga Howe, 23 May 1930: ''Now does not every word we use represent a Trinity: it has a sense, a sound, a power to evoke pictures. One does not feel it as [*sic*] rule unless 'something goes wrong,' i.e. either the sense is stupid, or the picture obsolete, or the sound false. Would it not be possible to write a book where all these three elements of literature are segregated and dissociated? A device can be used, a most commonplace banal device to prove it: a pun. [. . .] I wonder if there is anything wrong in attempting to make this process of reconstruction of the LOGOS conscious?'' In Robert H. Deming, ed., *James Joyce: The Critical Heritage*, vol. 2 (London: Routledge and Kegan Paul, 1970), p. 532.

100. Derrida's phrase. See *Margins of Philosophy*, trans. Alan Bass (Chicago: Univ. of Chicago Press, 1982), p. 256.

4. Performing the Dreamwork

1. Eco, *Semiotics and the Philosophy of Language*, p. 59.

2. Ibid., p. 64.

3. Ibid., p. 68.

4. Ibid., p. 83, referring to Deleuze and Guattari's concept of the rhizome.

5. Foucault, *Order of Things*, p. 135.

6. René Thom, *Structural Stability and Morphogenesis*, trans. D. H. Fowler (Reading, Mass.: W. A. Benjamin, 1975), p. 5.

7. See Douglas R. Hofstadter, *Gödel, Escher, Bach: An Eternal Golden Braid* (New York: Vintage Books, 1980), on "recombinant ideas" (p. 657) and concepts of recursivity.

8. Donald Phillip Verene, *Vico's Science of Imagination* (Ithaca: Cornell Univ. Press, 1981), p. 192. See also Giorgio Tagliacozzo. "Epilogue," in *Giambattista Vico: An International Symposium*, ed. Giorgio Tagliacozzo and Hayden White (Baltimore: Johns Hopkins Univ. Press, 1969), pp. 599–600, fn. 3. A. Walton Litz was the first to point out the pun on "viricordo." See "Vico and Joyce," in ibid., p. 253.

9. Giambattista Vico, "On the ancient wisdom of the Italians," in *Vico: Selected Writings*, ed. and trans. Leon Pompa (Cambridge: Cambridge Univ. Press, 1982), p. 55.

10. Ibid.

11. For the approach to the *dipintura* taken here I am indebted to Margherita Frankel, "The 'Dipintura' and the Structure of Vico's *New Science* as a Mirror of the World," in *Vico: Past and Present*, ed. Georgio Tagliacozzo (Atlantic Highlands, N.J.: Humanities Press, 1981), pp. 43–51. The dipintura was designed under Vico's direction by Domenico Antonio Vaccaro and engraved for the frontispiece of the 1730 edition. It was reproduced in subsequent Italian editions but omitted from the abridged version of the Bergin/Fisch English translation. See Gianfranco Cantelli, "Myth and Language in Vico," trans. Margaret Brose, in Giorgio Tagliacozzo and Donald Phillip Verene, ed., *Giambattista Vico's Science of Humanity* (Baltimore: Johns Hopkins Univ. Press, 1976), p. 62.

12. See Frankel, pp. 44–49.

13. Verene, *Vico's Science*, pp. 178–92. See also Donald Phillip Verene, "Vico's Philosophical Originality," in *Vico: Past and Present*, ed. G. Tagliacozzo (Atlantic Highlands, N.J.: Humanities Press, 1981), pp. 142–43.

14. Verene, "Vico's Philosophical Originality," p. 137.

15. Vico, *Selected Writings*, p. 59.

16. Eco, *Semiotics*, p. 81. Eco's emphases.

17. Ibid., p. 83.

18. Maureen Quilligan, *The Language of Allegory: Defining the Genre* (Ithaca: Cornell Univ. Press, 1979), p. 29.

19. Samuel Taylor Coleridge, *Biographia Literaria* (London: J. M. Dent, 1906), p. 147.

20. Verene, *Vico's Science*, pp. 220–21.

21. Eco, *Semiotics*, p. 82. Isaiah Berlin was the first to point out the performative nature of language in Vico. See *Vico and Herder* (London: Hogarth Press, 1976), pp. 50–51. See also Verene, "Vico's Philosophy of Imagination," on Vico's mode of "presentational thought" (*Vico and Contemporary Thought*, ed. Giorgio Tagliacozzo, Michael Mooney, and Donald Phillip Verene [London: Macmillan, 1980], p. 31, fn. 27).

22. William Blake, *Complete Writings*, p. 818.

23. Angus Fletcher, *Allegory: The Theory of a Symbolic Mode* (Ithaca: Cornell Univ. Press, 1964), pp. 108–120.

24. Leonard Barkan, *Nature's Work of Art* (New Haven: Yale Univ. Press, 1975), p. 205.

25. Ibid., p. 276.

26. Eco, *The Role of the Reader*, pp. 3–11.

27. David Bohm, *Wholeness and the Implicate Order* (London: Routledge and Kegan Paul, 1980), p. 149.

28. Ibid.

29. Ibid. p. 150.

30. Verene, "The New Art of Narration: Vico and the Muses," *New Vico Studies* (1983), pp. 28–29, 36.

31. Verene, *Vico's Science*, pp. 152–153. On the simultaneity of the Vichian stages see

Giorgio Tagliacozzo and Margherita Frankel, "Progress in Art? A Vichian Answer," in *Vico: Past and Present*, p. 241; and Eco, *Semiotics*, p. 108. Although most Joyceans still assume the Vichian stages of history to be sequential, few Vico scholars any longer adhere to this position. Verene's work, in particular, marks a breakthrough in the understanding of Vico in terms applicable to the Joyce system.

32. Quilligan, *Language of Allegory*, p. 135.

33. Cf. Michael J. O'Shea, *James Joyce and Heraldry* (Albany: State Univ. of New York Press, 1986), p. 3 and passim.

34. Stanley Fish, *Self-Consuming Artifacts: The Experience of Seventeenth-Century Literature* (Berkeley: Univ. of California Press, 1972).

35. Eco, *Semiotics*, p. 148.

36. Derrida's phrase in *Grammatology*, p. 92.

37. Thom, *Structural Stability*, p. 33.

38. Karl Löwith, *Meaning in History* (Chicago: Univ. of Chicago Press, 1949), p. 225, fn. 1.

39. See R. W. Sperry, "Orderly Function with Disordered Structure," in *Principles of Self-Organization*, ed. Heinz von Foerster and George W. Zopf, Jr. (New York: Pergamon, 1962), pp. 279–89, for an elaboration of this concept.

40. Edgar Quinet, *Oeuvres Complètes* (Paris: Pagnerre, 1857), vol. II, p. 368.

41. Ibid.

42. Ibid., pp. 369–70.

43. Ibid., p. 370.

44. Ibid.

45. Ibid., p. 351.

46. Ibid., p. 389.

47. Ibid., p. 352.

48. Ibid., p. 367.

49. See Joyce's letter of 22 Nov. 1930 to Harriet Shaw Weaver. In *Letters of James Joyce*, ed. Stuart Gilbert (London: Faber and Faber, 1957), p. 295. On Quinet in *FW* see Clive Hart, *Structure and Motif in "FW"* (London: Faber, 1962), pp. 182–200. Joyce's version of the Quinet sentence differs slightly from the original, as noted by Atherton, *The Books at the Wake* (London: Faber, 1959), p. 276.

50. Quinet, pp. 367–68.

51. Ibid., p. 355.

52. Ibid.

53. Jules Michelet, "Introduction à l'histoire universelle," in *Introduction à l'histoire universelle: Tableau de la France—Préface à l'histoire de France* (Paris: Bibliothèque de Cluny, Libraire Armand Colin, 1962), p. 39.

54. Ibid., p. 1.

55. See Harold Bloom, *The Anxiety of Influence* (New York: Oxford Univ. Press, 1973), on "clinamen" (pp. 19–45). It is important to note that the Michelet of the *Introduction à l'histoire universelle* became, a decade later, a naturalist whose ecological views were similar to Quinet's. The *Wake* preserves the Quinet/Michelet struggle by ignoring this later transformation. On this aspect of Michelet, see Linda Orr's excellent study *Jules Michelet: Nature, History, and Language* (Ithaca: Cornell Univ. Press, 1976).

56. Michelet, *Préface à l'histoire de France*, p. 3.

57. Cf. Frank Budgen's report that he "once broached the question of imagination with Joyce. He brushed it aside with the assertion that imagination was memory" (Budgen, *Myselves When Young* [London: Oxford Univ. Press, 1970], p. 187). Condillac's version constitutes yet another variant: "Imagination is memory itself, brought to the full vivacity of which it is capable" (*Traité des Sensations*, quoted in Hans Aarsleff, *From Locke to Saussure* [Minneapolis: Univ. of Minnesota Press, 1982], p. 212.

58. See Verene, *Vico's Science*, p. 105, on the translation of *ingegno*.

59. Vico, *Selected Writings*, p. 69.

60. Cf. Berkley Peabody: "An oral tradition does not retrieve actions from the past; it performs actions that were also performed in the past" (*The Winged Word* [Albany: State Univ. of New York Press, 1975], p. 430, fn. 16).

61. Giambattista Vico, *The Autobiography of Giambattista Vico*, trans. Max Harold Fisch and Thomas Goddard Bergin (Ithaca: Cornell Univ. Press, 1944), p. 145.

62. Ibid., p. 124.

63. Ibid., p. 74.

64. Ibid. In the 1730 edition of *NS*, Vico advises "younger readers" that "it is necessary that you should have acquired the habit of reasoning geometrically and that you should neither open these [geometry] books in any arbitrary place, in order to read them, nor dip into them here and there, but follow their teaching from start to finish" (quoted by Leon Pompa, "Imagination in Vico," in *Vico: Past and Present*, p. 167).

65. For a detailed discussion of this map see Lorraine Weir, "Phoenix Park in *FW*," *Irish University Review* 5:2 (Autumn 1975), pp. 230–49.

66. Kenneth Burke's phrase in *The Philosophy of Literary Form*, 3d ed. (Berkeley: Univ. of California Press, 1973), p. 20.

67. J.-M. Rabaté has commented on the relation between Joussean *geste* and *gesta*, the transformation of history into memory, in the *Wake* ("Vico: Croce. Joyce: Jousse" Session, Vico and Joyce Conference, Venice, 19 June 1985).

68. William Warburton, *The Divine Legation of Moses Demonstrated (1765)* (New York: Garland Publishing, 1978), vol. III, p. 192. See also Jacques Derrida, "Scribble (writing-power)," *Yale French Studies* 58 (1979), pp. 117–47. Stephen K. Land notes the "affinity" between Vico and Warburton in *From Signs to Propositions: The Concept of Form in Eighteenth-Century Semantic Theory* (London: Longman, 1974), p. 62.

69. Eugene Vance, "Pas de Trois: Narrative, Hermeneutics, and Structure in Medieval Poetics," in *Interpretation of Narrative*, ed. Mario J. Valdés and Owen J. Miller (Toronto: Univ. of Toronto Press, 1978), pp. 118–34.

70. Constance Hieatt, *The Realism of Dream Visions* (The Hague: Mouton de Gruyter, 1967), p. 18.

71. J. B. Stearns, *Studies of the Dream as a Technical Device in Latin Epic and Drama* (1927), pp. ix–x, quoted in Hieatt, p. 20. Mary T. Reynolds notes that "Joyce's decision to cast the entire book [*FW*] in the shape of a dream may owe something to his reading of Dante's *Paradiso*." See *Joyce and Dante*, p. 199.

72. A. C. Spearing, *Medieval Dream-Poetry* (Cambridge: Cambridge Univ. Press, 1976), p. 19.

73. Derrida's phrase in *Grammatology*, p. 316.

74. Macrobius, *Commentary on the Dream of Scipio*, trans. William Harris Stahl (New York: Columbia Univ. Press, 1952), p. 88.

75. Francis Xavier Newman, "Somnium: Medieval Theories of Dreaming and the Form of Vision Poetry" (Ph.D. diss., Princeton University, 1963), p. 108.

76. Ibid., p. 109.

77. Ibid., p. 79.

78. Ibid., p. 71.

79. Ibid., pp. 258–59.

80. Ibid., p. 183.

81. Ibid., p. 299.

82. Ibid., p. 290.

83. Ibid., pp. 318–19.

84. See William Langland, *Piers Plowman: The B Version*, ed. George Kane and E. Talbot Davidson (London: Athlone Press, 1975), pp. 227–28.

85. Derrida, *Grammatology*, p. 316.

86. Quoted in E. H. Gombrich, *The Sense of Order* (Oxford: Phaidon Press, 1979), p. 251, from Albrecht Dürer, *Dürers Schriftlicher Nachlass*, ed. K. Lange and F. Fuhse (Halle a.S., 1893), p. 357. Cf. Margot Norris's discussion of "the animation of a pun" as a "dream

technique'' in *FW* (*The Decentered Universe of "Finnegans Wake"* [Baltimore: Johns Hopkins Univ. Press, 1974], p. 17). It is interesting to see that in spite of her use of psychoanalysis in analyzing *FW*, Norris maintains that ''there is ample evidence to suggest that . . . [*FW*] is designed precisely to refute the realist epistemology that has dominated prose fiction since the eighteenth century'' (p. 11). In a book which was not available to me until *Writing Joyce* was completed, John Bishop links Freudian ''Traumwerk'' with Vichian and argues that ''Vico gave . . . [Joyce] the dream-work by which he spun out *Finnegans Wake*'' (*Joyce's Book of the Dark* [Madison: Univ. of Wisconsin Press, 1986], p. 185). Paradoxically, however, while maintaining that the *Wake* ''devastates as completely as the condition of sleep the whole notion of discrete individuality'' (p. 214), Bishop employs a subjectivist epistemology throughout his book, thus deflecting his reading of dreamwork away from Vichian materialist semiotics and toward kerygma.

87. See Jacques Derrida, ''The Double Session,'' in *Dissemination*, trans. Barbara Johnson (Chicago: Univ. of Chicago Press, 1981), pp. 173–285. For Derrida on catachresis, see ''White Mythology,'' pp. 230–57, in *Margins of Philosophy*, trans. Alan Bass (Chicago: Univ. of Chicago Press, 1982), and *Glas*, trans. John P. Leavey and Richard Rand (Lincoln: Univ. of Nebraska Press, 1986), p. 2.

88. Vinaver, *The Rise of Romance*, p. 54.

89. Kenneth Burke, *Attitudes toward History*, 3d ed. (Berkeley: Univ. of California Press, 1984), p. 246.

90. See Barkan, *Nature's Work*, p. 37. See also Kenneth Clark, *The Nude* (London: John Murray, 1956), p. 13.

5. Mousiké/Memory : Sound/Sign

1. Eugene Vance, ''The modernity of the Middle Ages in the future,'' *Romanic Review* 64 (1973), p. 140.

2. Zukofsky, ''On Objective,'' *Prepositions*, 2d ed. (Berkeley: Univ. of California Press, 1981), p. 15. *Calculus* is Zukofsky's term. See his analysis of the calculus which structures ''*A*''-8, reprinted in Marcella Booth, *A Catalogue of the Louis Zukofsky Manuscript Collection* (Austin: Humanities Research Center, Univ. of Texas, 1975), p. 53.

3. Zukofsky, *Prepositions*, p. 18.

4. Louis Zukofsky, *Bottom: On Shakespeare* (Berkeley: Univ. of California Press, 1987), vol. 1, p. 92. Subsequent references to *Bottom* are to vol. 1 in all cases.

5. Ibid., p. 94.

6. Ludwig Wittgenstein, *Philosophical Investigations*, trans. G. E. M. Anscombe (Oxford: Basil Blackwell, 1968), p. 48 (115).

7. Jacques Derrida, *Memoires: For Paul De Man*, trans. Cecile Lindsay, Jonathan Culler, and Eduardo Cadava (New York: Columbia Univ. Press, 1986), p. 73.

8. First two passages from Louis Zukofsky and René Taupin, ''The Writing of Guillaume Apollinaire,'' in *Westminster Magazine* XXIII:1 (Spring 1934), pp. 9–10; third passage (''speech growing into song'') quoted in Booth, *Catalogue*, p. 235, from a note by Zukofsky offering ''*A*''-12 to *Botteghe Oscure* for consideration.

9. Saint Augustine, *On Christian Doctrine*, trans. D. W. Robertson, Jr. (New York: Liberal Arts Press, 1958), p. 103.

10. Ibid., p. 35.

11. Ibid., p. 36.

12. Isidore of Seville, ''Etymologiarum,'' in *Source Readings in Music History*, ed. Oliver Strunk (New York: Norton, 1950), p. 95.

13. Edward A. Lippman, *Musical Thought in Ancient Greece* (New York: Columbia Univ. Press, 1964), p. 100.

14. Eric A. Havelock, *Preface to Plato* (Cambridge, Mass.: Belknap Press of Harvard Univ. Press, 1963), p. 150.

15. Ibid., p. 151.

16. Lippman, *Musical Thought*, p. 101.

17. Aristoxenus, "Harmonic Elements," in Strunk, *Source Readings*, p. 30.

18. Saint Augustine, *De Musica*, ed. W. F. Jackson Knight (Cambridge: R. I. Severs, 1942), p. 87.

19. Ibid., p. 13; *Confessions*, trans. R. S. Pine-Coffin (Baltimore: Penguin Books, 1961), p. 224.

20. Quoted in Jesse Gellrich, *The Idea of the Book in the Middle Ages* (Ithaca: Cornell Univ. Press, 1985), p. 85.

21. Boethius, "De institutione musica," in Strunk, *Source Readings*, p. 80.

22. Albert Seay, *Music in the Medieval World*, 2d ed. (Englewood Cliffs, N. J.: Prentice-Hall, 1975), p. 19.

23. Macrobius, *Commentary on the Dream of Scipio*, pp. 195–96.

24. Augustine, *Confessions*, p. 219.

25. Ibid.

26. Ibid.

27. Vincent Foster Hopper, *Medieval Number Symbolism* (New York: Columbia Univ. Press, 1938), p. 45.

28. Stobaeus; and Plotinus, *Enneads*, quoted in Hopper, *Medieval Number Symbolism*, p. 46.

29. Hopper, *Medieval Number Symbolism*, p. 40.

30. Ibid., p. 41.

31. Seay, *Music in the Medieval World*, p. 20.

32. Gellrich, *Idea of the Book*, p. 82.

33. Seay, *Music in the Medieval World*, p. 19.

34. Boethius, from the "De institutione musica," in Strunk, *Source Readings*, p. 80.

35. St. John Chrysostom, "Exposition of Psalm XLI," in ibid., p. 69.

36. Ibid., p. 70.

37. Ibid.

38. Quoted in John Stevens, *Words and Music in the Middle Ages: Song, Narrative, Dance and Drama, 1050–1350* (Cambridge: Cambridge Univ. Press, 1986), p. 385.

39. Derrida, *Grammatology*, p. 249.

40. Quoted in Stevens, *Words and Music*, p. 384.

41. Guido of Arezzo, "Epistola de ignoto cantu," in Strunk, *Source Readings*, p. 122.

42. Stevens, *Words and Music*, pp. 383–84. Cf. the system devised to enable singers and players to sing Seiklos's Skolion or round-song, which, because of the antimetric rhythm of its verses set against a regular music pattern (i.e., a *tala* in Indian music), required a shorthand notation to facilitate performance. Thus a horizontal dash above the note indicated two units; an angle ⌐, three; ⊔, four; and ⊔⊔, five units. A small upright angle ∧ signified a rest, stood for lambda, and was sometimes replaced by an arc ∩. See Curt Sachs, *The Rise of Music in the Ancient World East and West* (New York: Norton, 1943), pp. 264–65. Joycean numerologists may wish to speculate on the extent to which this system is applicable to *Finnegans Wake* with its virtually identical sigla.

43. Seay, *Music in the Medieval World*, p. 133. For an introduction to medieval forms of numerical composition, see Curtius, *European Literature and the Latin Middle Ages*, pp. 501–509.

44. Seay, *Music in the Medieval World*, p. 133.

45. Charles Rosen, *Schoenberg* (London: Marion Boyars, 1976), p. 101. Rosen notes Webern's version of Frank's ekphrastic principle in 1912. "Writing down the twelve notes of the chromatic scale in his notebook and then crossing off the individual notes as they appeared in one of his miniature pieces," Webern wrote that he " 'had the feeling that when the twelve notes had been played, the piece was over' " (Rosen, pp. 70–71).

46. Stevens, *Words and Music*, p. 506. On *contrafactum* see also Paul Zumthor, *Langue et techniques poétiques à l'époque romane, XIe–XIIIe siècles* (Paris: Klincksieck, 1963), pp. 172–73.

47. Quoted in John Hollander, *The Untuning of the Sky: Ideas of Music in English Poetry, 1500–1700* (New York: Norton, 1970), p. 40.

48. Quoted in ibid., p. 20.

49. Deely, *Introducing Semiotic*, p. 18.

50. Augustine, *Confessions*, p. 219.

51. Augustine, *De Musica*, p. 13.

52. Otto von Simson, *The Gothic Cathedral* (New York: Pantheon, 1956), p. 31.

53. Quoted ibid. See also ibid., p. 36, fn. 38.

54. Ibid., p. 133.

55. Quoted in Gellrich, *Idea of the Book*, p. 79.

56. Erwin Panofsky, *Gothic Architecture and Scholasticism* (New York: Meridian, 1976), pp. 48ff.

57. Ibid., pp. 44–45.

58. Jean Bony, *French Gothic Architecture of the Twelfth and Thirteenth Centuries* (Berkeley: Univ. of California Press, 1983), p. 377.

59. Panofsky, *Gothic Architecture*, p. 46.

60. Ibid., p. 48.

61. Ibid.

62. Bony, *French Gothic Architecture*, p. 377.

63. Ibid., p. 154.

64. Panofsky, *Gothic Architecture*, p. 31.

65. Ibid., p. 59.

66. Zukofsky, *Bottom*, p. 184.

67. Ibid., p. 37.

68. Ibid., p. 426. Richard Ellmann comments that for Joyce "all music aspires to the condition of language" (*Ulysses on the Liffey* [New York: Oxford Univ. Press, 1972], p. 104). For Luciano Berio, "musical thought" is "the discovery of a coherent discourse that unfolds and develops simultaneously on different levels" (*Luciano Berio: Two Interviews*, trans and ed. David Osmond-Smith [New York: Marion Boyars, 1985], p. 84). So "music" is, among other things, a rhetorical mode, an *ars inveniendi*—a stance increasingly taken by semioticians of music. See, e.g., Ivanka Stoianova, *Geste-Texte-Musique* (Paris: Inédit, 1978). Cf. Jean-Michel Rabaté's statement that "classical rhetorics can describe all these musical figures [of II.8] as well [as], if not better than, the vocabulary of musicology" ("The Silence of the Sirens," in *James Joyce: The Centennial Symposium*, pp. 82–83).

69. Zukofsky, *Bottom*, p. 442; *Prepositions*, p. 18. For a detailed discussion of the Joyce system's eye/ear codes, see Lorraine Weir, "Permutations of Ireland's Eye in *Finnegans Wake*," *Canadian Journal of Irish Studies* 5:2 (1978), pp. 23–30.

70. Quoted in Hofstadter, *Gödel, Escher, Bach*, p. 629.

71. John Haugeland, *Artificial Intelligence: The Very Idea* (Cambridge, Mass.: MIT Press, Bradford Books, 1985), p. 147.

72. Ibid., pp. 154–55.

73. Ibid., p. 148.

74. Ibid., p. 152.

75. Ibid., pp. 153–54.

76. Ibid., p. 156.

77. Ibid., p. 155.

78. See Shari Benstock, "At the Margin of Discourse: Footnotes in the Fictional Text," *PMLA* 98 (1983), pp. 204–225.

79. Haugeland, *Artificial Intelligence*, pp. 144–45.

80. Ibid., p. 193.

81. On Gothic modernity, see J. Bony, *French Gothic Architecture*, p. 1.

82. Guy Davenport, "Au Tombeau de Charles Fourier," in *Da Vinci's Bicycle* (Baltimore: Johns Hopkins Univ. Press, 1979), p. 98.

83. Le Corbusier (1921), quoted in Stanislaus von Moos, *Le Corbusier: Elements of a Synthesis* (Cambridge, Mass.: MIT Press, 1979), p. 81.

84. Peter Quartermain, " 'I am different, let not a gloss embroil you,' " rev. of "*A*," *Paideuma* 9:1 (Spring 1980), p. 205.

85. Zukofsky, *Bottom*, p. 276.

86. Louis Zukofsky, "The Effacement of Philosophy," in *Prepositions*, p. 55.

87. Zukofsky, *Bottom*, p. 197.

88. Ibid., p. 184.

89. Louis Zukofsky, *Anew*, 2, in *All* (New York: Norton, 1965), p. 85.

90. Zukofsky, "About the Gas Age," in *Prepositions*, p. 172.

91. Zukofsky, *Bottom*, p. 432.

92. Ibid., p. 118.

93. Ibid., p. 210.

94. Zukofsky, "An Objective," in *Prepositions*, p. 17.

95. Ibid., p. 22.

96. Zukofsky, *Bottom*, p. 182.

97. Ibid., p. 118.

98. Louis Zukofsky, *It Was* (Kyoto: Origin Press, 1961), p. 99.

99. Zukofsky, "About the Gas Age," in *Prepositions*, p. 172. See Dante, *Purgatorio* 135. John Freccero commented on Augustinian philosophy of language in terms of speech act theory in his unpublished lecture, "Augustine of Hyppo" Conference, Univ. of British Columbia, 9 Nov. 1984.

100. Zukofsky, "An Objective," in *Prepositions*, p. 16.

101. A. J. Minnis, *Medieval Theory of Authorship: Scholastic Literary Attributes in the Later Middle Ages* (London: Scolar Press, 1984), p. 10.

102. Corti, *Introduction*, p. 123.

103. Stevens, *Words and Music*, p. 511.

104. Augustine, *Confessions*, pp. 220, 223.

105. William R. Lethaby, *Architecture: An Introduction to the History and Theory of the Art of Building* (3d ed., 1955), quoted by Zukofsky in *Bottom*, pp. 183–84. (Source identified by Peter Quartermain in " 'Not at all surprised by science': Louis Zukofsky's First Half of 'A'-9," in Carroll F. Terrell, ed., *Louis Zukofsky: Man and Poet* [Orono, Maine: National Poetry Foundation, 1979], p. 206, fn. 8.) Cf. Abbot Suger's comment on the music of architecture: "what seems mutually to conflict by inferiority of origin and contrariety of nature is conjoined by the single, delightful concordance of one superior, well-tempered harmony" (quoted in Gellrich, *Idea of the Book*, p. 79, from the *De consecratione ecclesiae sancti Dionysii*).

WORKS CITED

Aarsleff, Hans. *From Locke to Saussure*. Minneapolis: Univ. of Minnesota Press, 1982.

Alpers, Svetlana. *The Art of Describing: Dutch Art in the Seventeenth Century*. Chicago: Univ. of Chicago Press, 1983.

Andrewes, Lancelot. *Sermons on the Nativity*. Grand Rapids: Baker Book House, 1955.

Atherton, James S. *The Books at the Wake*. London: Faber, 1959.

Auerbach, Erich. "Figura." Trans. Ralph Manheim. In *Scenes from the Drama of European Literature*, 2d ed. Minneapolis: Univ. of Minnesota Press, 1984.

Augustine, Saint. *Confessions*. Trans. R. S. Pine-Coffin. Baltimore: Penguin Books, 1961.

———. *De Musica*. Ed. W. F. Jackson Knight. Cambridge: R. I. Severs, 1942.

———. *On Christian Doctrine*. Trans. D. W. Robertson, Jr. New York: Liberal Arts Press, 1958.

Austin, J. L. "Performative-Constative." In *Philosophy and Ordinary Language*, ed. Charles E. Caton, pp. 22–35. Urbana: Univ. of Illinois Press, 1963.

Bakhtin, M. M. *The Dialogic Imagination*. Ed. Michael Holquist. Trans. Caryl Emerson and Michael Holquist. Austin: Univ. of Texas Press, 1982.

Balthasar, Hans Urs von. *Man in History*. New York: Sheed and Ward, 1968.

Barkan, Leonard. *Nature's Work of Art*. New Haven: Yale Univ. Press, 1975.

Baron, G. *Marcel Jousse: Introduction à sa vie et à son oeuvre*. Paris: Casterman, 1965.

Barthes, Roland. *Sade/Fourier/Loyola*. Trans. Richard Miller. New York: Hill and Wang, 1976.

Beaujour, Michel. *Miroirs d'encre: Rhetorique de l'autoportrait*. Paris: Seuil, 1980.

Beckett, Samuel. "Dante . . . Bruno. Vico . . Joyce." Trans. Robert Sage. In Samuel Beckett et al., *Our Exagmination Round His Factification for Incamination of Work in Progress*, pp. 1–33. London: Faber, 1929.

Benstock, Shari. "At the Margin of Discourse: Footnotes in the Fictional Text." *PMLA* 98 (1983), pp. 204–225.

Benveniste, Emile. *Problèmes de linguistique générale*. Paris: Gallimard, 1966.

———. *Problems in General Linguistics*. Trans. Mary Elizabeth Meek. Coral Gables: Univ. of Miami Press, 1971.

Berio, Luciano. *Two Interviews*. Trans. and ed. David Osmond-Smith. New York: Marion Boyars, 1985.

Berlin, Isaiah. *Vico and Herder: Two Studies in the History of Ideas*. London: Hogarth Press, 1976.

Bishop, John. *Joyce's Book of the Dark*. Madison: Univ. of Wisconsin Press, 1986.

Blake, William. *The Complete Writings of William Blake*. Ed. Geoffrey Keynes. Oxford: Oxford Univ. Press, 1966.

Bloom, Harold. *The Anxiety of Influence*. New York: Oxford Univ. Press, 1973.

Bohm, David. *Wholeness and the Implicate Order*. London: Routledge and Kegan Paul, 1980.

Bony, Jean. *French Gothic Architecture of the Twelfth and Thirteenth Centuries*. Berkeley: Univ. of California Press, 1983.

Booth, Marcella. *A Catalogue of the Louis Zukofsky Manuscript Collection.* Austin: Humanities Research Center, Univ. of Texas, 1975.

Borges, Jorge Luis. *Labyrinths: Selected Stories and Other Writings*. Harmondsworth: Penguin Books, 1970.

Boyd, Elizabeth F. "Joyce's Hell-Fire Sermons." *Modern Language Notes* LXXV:7 (Nov. 1960), pp. 561–71.

Bradley, Bruce, S. J. *James Joyce's Schooldays*. Dublin: Gill and Macmillan, 1982.

Browne, Sir Thomas. *Religio Medici*. Ed. Jean-Jacques Denonain. Cambridge: Cambridge Univ. Press, 1953.

Budgen, Frank. *Myselves When Young*. London: Oxford Univ. Press, 1970.

Bultmann, Rudolf. *Kerygma and Myth: A Theological Debate*. 2d ed. Ed. Hans Werner Bartsch. Trans. Reginald A. Fuller. London: S.P.C.K., 1964.

Burkes, Kenneth. *Attitudes toward History*. 3d ed. Berkeley: Univ. of California Press, 1984.

———. "Biology, Psychology, Words." In *Dramatism and Development*. Barre, Mass.: Clark Univ. Press, 1972.

———. "Fact, Inference, and Proof in the Analysis of Literary Symbolism." In *Terms for Order*, ed. Stanley Edgar Hyman and Barbara Karmiller, pp. 145–72. Bloomington: Indiana Univ. Press, 1964.

———. *A Grammar of Motives*. Berkeley: Univ. of California Press, 1969.

———. *Language as Symbolic Action*. Berkeley: Univ. of California Press, 1966.

———. *The Philosophy of Literary Form*. 3d ed. Berkeley: Univ. of California Press, 1973.

———. *The Rhetoric of Religion*. Berkeley: Univ. of California Press, 1970.

Cantelli, Gianfranco. "Myth and Language in Vico." In *Giambattista Vico's Science of Humanity*, pp. 47–63. Baltimore: Johns Hopkins Univ. Press, 1976.

A Catechism of Catholic Doctrine. Dublin: M. H. Gill, 1951.

Changeux, Jean-Pierre. *Neuronal Man: The Biology of Mind*. Trans. Laurence Garey. New York: Oxford Univ. Press, 1985.

Churchland, Patricia Smith. *Neurophilosophy: Toward a Unified Science of the Mind-Brain*. Cambridge, Mass.: Bradford Books, 1986.

Clark, Hilary A. "The Idea of a Fictional Encyclopedia: *Finnegans Wake*, *Paradis*, the *Cantos*." Ph.D. diss., Univ. of British Columbia, 1985.

Clark, Kenneth. *The Nude*. London: John Murray, 1956.

Coleridge, S. T. *Biographia Literaria*. London: J. M. Dent, 1906.

Corti, Maria. *Introduction to Literary Semiotics*. Trans. Margherita Bogat and Allen Mandelbaum. Bloomington: Indiana Univ. Press, 1978.

Curtius, E. R. *European Literature and the Latin Middle Ages*. Trans. Willard R. Trask. Bollingen Series XXXVI. Princeton: Princeton Univ. Press, 1973.

Cusa, Nicholas of. *Of Learned Ignorance*. Trans. Germain Heron. London: Routledge and Kegan Paul, 1954.

Dante Alighieri. *The Divine Comedy: Purgatorio*. Trans. Charles S. Singleton. Bollingen Series LXXX. Princeton: Princeton Univ. Press, 1973.

Davenport, Guy. "Au Tombeau de Charles Fourier." In *Da Vinci's Bicycle*, pp. 59–106. Baltimore: Johns Hopkins Univ. Press, 1979.

Deely, John. *Introducing Semiotic*. Bloomington: Indiana Univ. Press, 1982.

Deming, Robert H., ed. *James Joyce: The Critical Heritage*. Vol. 2. London: Routledge and Kegan Paul, 1970.

Derrida, Jacques. *Dissemination*. Trans. Barbara Johnson. Chicago: Univ. of Chicago Press, 1981.

———. *Glas*. Trans. John P. Leavey, Jr., and Richard Rand. Lincoln: Univ. of Nebraska Press, 1986.

———. *Margins of Philosophy*. Trans. Alan Bass. Chicago: Univ. of Chicago Press, 1982.

———. *Memoires: For Paul De Man*. Trans. Cecile Lindsay, Jonathan Culler and Eduardo Cadava. New York: Columbia Univ. Press, 1986.

———. *Of Grammatology*. Trans. Gayatri Chakravorty Spivak. Baltimore: Johns Hopkins Univ. Press, 1976.

———. "Scribble (writing power)." In *Yale French Studies* 58 (1979), pp. 117–47.

———. "Two Words for Joyce." Trans. Geoff Bennington. In *Poststructuralist Joyce*, ed. Derek Attridge and Daniel Ferrer, pp. 145–58. Cambridge: Cambridge Univ. Press, 1984.

———. *Writing and Difference*. Trans. Alan Bass. Chicago: Univ. of Chicago Press, 1978.

Descombes, Vincent. "Variations on the Subject of the Encyclopaedic Book." *Oxford Literary Review* 3:2 (1978), pp. 54–60.

Doherty, James. "Joyce and *Hell Opened to Christians*: The Edition He Used for His Sermons." *Modern Philology* 61 (1963), pp. 110–19.

Dürer, Albrecht. *Dürers Schriftlicher Nachlass*. Ed. K. Lange and F. Fuhse. Halle a.S., 1893.

Eco, Umberto. *The Role of the Reader*. Bloomington: Indiana Univ. Press, 1979.

———. *Semiotics and the Philosophy of Language*. Bloomington: Indiana Univ. Press, 1984.

———. "Semiotics of Theatrical Performance." *Drama Review* 21:1 (March 1977), pp. 107–117.

———. *A Theory of Semiotics*. Bloomington: Indiana Univ. Press, 1976.

———. *Travels In Hyperreality*. Trans. William Weaver. San Diego: Harcourt Brace Jovanovich, 1986.

Eliot, T. S. "Burnt Norton." In *The Complete Poems and Plays of T. S. Eliot*. London: Faber, 1969.

Ellmann, Richard. *The Consciousness of Joyce*. London: Faber, 1977.

———. *James Joyce*. Rev. ed. New York: Oxford Univ. Press, 1982.

———. *Ulysses on the Liffey*. New York: Oxford Univ. Press, 1972.

Ferrer, Daniel. "Echo or Narcissus?" In *James Joyce: The Centennial Symposium*, ed. Morris Beja, Phillip Herring, Maurice Harmon, and David Norris, pp. 70–75. Urbana: Univ. of Illinois Press, 1986.

Fish, Stanley E. *Self-consuming Artifacts: The Experience of Seventeenth-Century Literature*. Berkeley: Univ. of California Press, 1972.

Fletcher, Angus. *Allegory: The Theory of a Symbolic Mode*. Ithaca: Cornell Univ. Press, 1964.

Foucault, Michel. *The Archeology of Knowledge*. Trans. M. M. Sheridan Smith. New York: Harper and Row, 1976.

———. *The Order of Things: An Archeology of the Human Sciences*. Trans. anon. London: Tavistock, 1970.

Frank, Joseph. "Spatial Form: An Answer to the Critics." *Critical Inquiry* 4:2 (Winter 1977), pp. 231–52.

———. "Spatial Form: Thirty Years After." In *Spatial Form in Narrative*, ed. Jeffrey R. Smitten and Ann Daghistany, pp. 202–243. Ithaca: Cornell Univ. Press, 1981.

———. "Spatial Form in Modern Literature." In *The Widening Gyre*, pp. 3–62. Bloomington: Indiana Univ. Press, 1968.

Frankel, Margherita. "The 'Dipintura' and the Structure of Vico's *New Science* as a Mirror of the World." In *Vico: Past and Present*, ed. Giorgio Tagliacozzo, pp. 43–51. Atlantic Highlands, N.J.: Humanities Press, 1981.

Freccero, John. *Dante: The Poetics of Conversion*. Cambridge, Mass.: Harvard Univ. Press, 1986.

———. "Logology: Burke on St. Augustine." In *Representing Kenneth Burke*, ed. Hayden White and Margaret Brose, pp. 52–67. Baltimore: Johns Hopkins Univ. Press, 1982.

Gabler, Hans Walter. "The Seven Lost Years of *A Portrait of the Artist as a Young Man*." In *Approaches to Joyce's "Portrait*," ed. Thomas F. Staley and Bernard Benstock, pp. 25–60. Pittsburgh: Univ. of Pittsburgh Press, 1976.

Gellrich, Jesse. *The Idea of the Book in the Middle Ages*. Ithaca: Cornell Univ. Press, 1985.

Genette, Gérard. *Figures II*. Paris: Seuil, 1969.

———. *Introduction à l'architexte*. Paris: Seuil, 1979.

———. *Mimologiques: Voyages en Cratylie*. Paris: Seuil, 1976.

———. *Narrative Discourse: An Essay in Method*. Trans. Jane E. Lewin. Ithaca: Cornell Univ. Press, 1980.

Gilson, Etienne. *The Christian Philosophy of St. Thomas Aquinas*. Trans. L. K. Shook, C.S.B. New York: Random House, 1956.

Goldberg, S. L. *The Classical Temper*. London: Chatto and Windus, 1961.

Gombrich, E. H. *The Sense of Order*. Oxford: Phaidon Press, 1979.

Greimas, A. J. *Structural Semantics*. Trans. D. McDowell, R. Schlcifer and A. Velie. Lincoln: Univ. of Nebraska Press, 1983.

Grice, H. P. "Logic and Conversation." In *Syntax and Semantics*, vol. 3: *Speech Acts*, ed. Peter Cole and Jerry L. Morgan, pp. 41–58. New York: Academic Press, 1975.

Groden, Michael et al., eds. *The James Joyce Archive*. New York: Garland Publishing, 1978.

Handelman, Susan A. "Jacques Derrida and the Heretic Hermeneutic." *Diacritics* IV (1983), pp. 98–129.

———. *The Slayers of Moses: The Emergence of Rabbinic Interpretation in Modern Literary Theory*. Albany: State Univ. of New York Press, 1982.

Hardison, O. B., Jr. *Christian Rite and Christian Drama in the Middle Ages*. Baltimore: Johns Hopkins Univ. Press, 1965.

Hart, Clive. *Structure and Motif in "Finnegans Wake."* London: Faber, 1962.

Haugeland, John. *Artificial Intelligence: The Very Idea*. Cambridge, Mass.: MIT Press, Bradford Books, 1985.

Havelock, Eric A. *Preface to Plato*. Cambridge, Mass.: Belknap Press of Harvard Univ. Press, 1963.

Hayman, David. "The Joycean Inset." *James Joyce Quarterly* 23:2 (Winter 1986), pp. 137–55.

———. "Nodality and the Infra-structure of *Finnegans Wake*." *James Joyce Quarterly* 16:1–2 (Fall 1978/Winter 1979), pp. 135–49.

———. "Stephen on the Rocks." *James Joyce Quarterly* 15:1 (Fall 1977), pp. 5–17.

Heidegger, Martin. "The Origin of the Work of Art." In *Poetry, Language, Thought*, trans. Albert Hofstadter, pp. 15–87. New York: Harper Colophon Books, 1975.

Herr, Cheryl. *Joyce's Anatomy of Culture*. Urbana: Univ. of Illinois Press, 1986.

Hieatt, Constance. *The Realism of Dream Visions*. The Hague: Mouton de Gruyter, 1967.

Hofstadter, Douglas R. *Gödel, Escher, Bach: An Eternal Golden Braid*. New York: Vintage, 1980.

Hollander, John. *The Untuning of the Sky: Ideas of Music in English Poetry, 1500–1700*. New York: Norton, 1970.

Hopper, Vincent Foster. *Medieval Number Symbolism*. New York: Columbia Univ. Press, 1938.

Husserl, Edmund. *Ideas: General Introduction to Pure Phenomenology*. Trans. W. R. Boyce Gibson. London: Collier, 1962.

Huyssen, Andreas. *After the Great Divide: Modernism, Mass Culture, Postmodernism*. Bloomington: Indiana Univ. Press, 1986.

Innis, Robert E. *Karl Bühler: Semiotic Foundations of Language Theory*. New York: Plenum, 1982.

Iser, Wolfgang. *The Act of Reading*. Baltimore: Johns Hopkins Univ. Press, 1978.

———. *The Implied Reader*. Baltimore: Johns Hopkins Univ. Press, 1974.

Jameson, Fredric. "*Ulysses* in History." In *James Joyce and Modern Literature*, ed. W. J. McCormack and Alistair Stead, pp. 126–41. London: Routledge and Kegan Paul, 1982.

Jauss, Hans Robert. "The Alterity and Modernity of Medieval Literature." *New Literary History* X:2 (Winter 1979), pp. 181–227.

Johnson, Barbara. *The Critical Difference: Essays in the Contemporary Rhetoric of Reading*. Baltimore: Johns Hopkins Univ. Press, 1980.

Jousse, Marcel. *L'Anthropologie du geste*. Paris: Resma, 1969.

———. *La Manducation de la Parole*. Paris: Gallimard, 1975.

Joyce, James. *Dubliners: Text, Criticism, and Notes*. Ed. Robert Scholes and A. Walton Litz. New York: Viking Press, 1969.

———. *Exiles*. New York: Viking Press, 1951.

———. *Finnegans Wake*. London: Faber, 1939.

———. *The James Joyce Archive*. Ed. Michael Groden. New York: Garland Publishing, 1978.

———. *A Portrait of the Artist as a Young Man*. Ed. Richard Ellmann. Definitive text corrected from the Dublin holograph by Chester G. Anderson. New York: Viking Press, 1964.

———. *Stephen Hero*. Ed. John J. Slocum and Herbert Cahoon. New York: New Directions, 1963.

———. *Ulysses*. The Corrected Text, ed. Hans Walter Gabler with Wolfhard Steppe and Claus Melchior. New York: Random House, 1986.

Jungmann, Joseph P., S. J. *The Mass of the Roman Rite: Its Origins and Development*. Trans. Francis A. Brunner, C.S.S.R. Rev. Charles K. Riepe. Rev. and abridged ed. London: Burns and Oates, 1959.

Kenner, Hugh. *Ulysses*. London: George Allen and Unwin, 1980.

Kermode, Frank. *The Genesis of Secrecy*. Cambridge, Mass.: Harvard Univ. Press, 1979.

———. "Novel and Narrative." In *The Theory of the Novel: New Essays*, ed. John Halperin, pp. 155–74. New York: Oxford Univ. Press, 1974.

Kestner, Joseph. "Virtual Text/Virtual Reader: The Structural Signature Within, Behind, Beyond, Above." *James Joyce Quarterly* 16:1/2 (Fall/Winter 1979), pp. 27–42.

Kirby, Ernest T. *Ur-Drama: The Origins of Theatre*. New York: New York Univ. Press, 1975.

Krieger, Murray. "The Ekphrastic Principle and the Still Movement of Poetry; or *Laokoön* Revisited." In *The Play and Place of Criticism*, pp. 105–128. Baltimore: Johns Hopkins Univ. Press, 1967.

Kristeva, Julia. *Semeiotikë: Recherches pour une sémanalyse*. Paris: Seuil, 1969.

Land, Stephen K. *From Signs to Propositions: The Concept of Form in Eighteenth-Century Semantic Theory*. London: Longman, 1974.

Langland, William. *Piers Plowman: The B Version*. Ed. George Kane and E. Talbot Davidson. London: Athlone Press, 1975.

Lemoine, Michel. "L'Oeuvre encyclopédique de Vincent de Beauvais." In *La Pensée encyclopédique au moyen âge*, ed. Maurice de Gandillac et al., pp. 77–85. Neuchatel: Editions de la Baconnière, 1966.

Lemon, Lee T. "*A Portrait of the Artist as a Young Man*: Motif as Motivation and Structure." *Modern Fiction Studies* XII (Winter 1966–67), pp. 439–50.

Lippman, Edward A. *Musical Thought in Ancient Greece*. New York: Columbia Univ. Press, 1964.

Litz, A. Walton. "The Genre of *Ulysses*." In *The Theory of the Novel: New Essays*, ed. John Halperin, pp. 109–126. New York: Oxford Univ. Press, 1974.

———. "Vico and Joyce." In *Giambattista Vico: An International Symposium*, ed. Georgio Tagliacozzo, pp. 245–55. Baltimore: Johns Hopkins Univ. Press, 1969.

Lotman, Jurij M. "The Dynamic Model of a Semiotic System." Trans. Ann Shukman. *Semiotica* 21:3/4 (1977), pp. 193–210.

———. *The Structure of the Artistic Text*. Trans. Ronald Vroon. Ann Arbor: Michigan Slavic Contributions no. 7, 1977.

Löwith, Karl. *Meaning in History*. Chicago: Univ. of Chicago Press, 1949.

Luria, A. R. *Cognitive Development: Its Cultural and Social Foundations*. Trans. Martin Lopez-Morillas and Lynn Solotaroff. Ed. Michael Cole. Cambridge, Mass.: Harvard Univ. Press, 1976.

McCarthy, Patrick A. *The Riddles of "Finnegans Wake."* London: Associated Univ. Press, 1980.

———. " 'A Warping Process': Reading *Finnegans Wake*." In *Work in Progress: Joyce Centenary Essays*, ed. Richard F. Peterson, Alan M. Cohn and Edmund L. Epstein, pp. 47–57. Carbondale: Southern Illinois Univ. Press, 1983.

Macherey, Pierre. *A Theory of Literary Production*. Trans. Geoffrey Wall. London: Routledge
and Kegan Paul, 1978.
McHugh, Roland. *The Sigla of "Finnegans Wake."* Austin: Univ. of Texas Press, 1976.
McLuhan, Marshall. *Understanding Media*. Toronto: Signet, 1964.
Macrobius. *Commentary on the Dream of Scipio*. Trans. William Harris Stahl. New York:
Columbia Univ. Press, 1952.
Madtes, Richard E. *The "Ithaca" Chapter of Joyce's "Ulysses."* Ann Arbor: UMI Research
Press, 1983.
Marin, Louis. "Un Chapître dans l'histoire de la théorie sémiotique: la théologie eucharistique
dans 'La Logique de Port-Royal' (1683)." In *History of Semiotics*, vol. 7, ed.
Achim Eschbach and Jürgen Trabant, pp. 127–44. Amsterdam: John Benjamins,
1983.
Mendelson, Edward. "Encyclopedic Narrative: From Dante to Pynchon." *Modern Language
Notes* 91:6 (Dec. 1976), pp. 1267–75.
Merivale, Patricia. "Learning the Hard Way: Gothic Pedagogy in the Modern Romantic
Quest." *Comparative Literature* 36:2 (Spring 1984), pp. 146–61.
Michelet, Jules. *Introduction à l'histoire universelle: Tableau de la France—Préface à l'his-
toire de France*. Paris: Bibliothèque de Cluny, Libraire Armand Colin, 1962.
Minnis, A. J. *Medieval Theory of Authorship: Scholastic Literary Attributes in the Later
Middle Ages*. London: Scolar Press, 1984.
Minsky, Marvin. *The Society of Mind*. New York: Simon and Schuster, 1985.
Moos, Stanislaus von. *Le Corbusier: Elements of a Synthesis*. Cambridge, Mass.: MIT Press,
1979.
Newman, Francis Xavier. "Somnium: Medieval Theories of Dreaming and the Form of
Vision Poetry." Ph.D. diss., Princeton Univ., 1963.
Norris, Margot. *The Decentered Universe of "Finnegans Wake": A Structuralist Analysis*.
Baltimore: Johns Hopkins Univ. Press, 1974.
Ong, Walter J. *Interfaces of the Word: Studies in the Evolution of Consciousness and Culture*.
Ithaca: Cornell Univ. Press, 1977.
———. *Orality and Literacy: The Technologizing of the Word*. London: Methuen, 1982.
———. *Rhetoric, Romance, and Technology*. Ithaca: Cornell Univ. Press, 1971.
Opland, Jeff. *Xhosa Oral Poetry: Aspects of a Black South African Tradition*. Cambridge:
Cambridge Univ. Press, 1983.
Orr, Linda. *Jules Michelet: Nature, History, and Language*. Ithaca: Cornell Univ. Press,
1976.
O'Shea, Michael J. *James Joyce and Heraldry*. Albany: State Univ. of New York Press,
1986.
Oyama, Susan. *The Ontogeny of Information*. Cambridge: Cambridge Univ. Press, 1985.
Panofsky, Erwin. *Gothic Architecture and Scholasticism*. New York: Meridian, 1976.
Pavis, Patrice. *Languages of the Stage: Essays in the Semiotics of Theatre*. New York:
Performing Arts Journal Publications, 1982.
Peabody, Berkley. *The Winged Word*. Albany: State Univ. of New York Press, 1975.
Pompa, Leon. "Imagination in Vico." In *Vico: Past and Present*, ed. Giorgio Tagliacozzo,
pp. 162–70. Atlantic Highlands, N.J.: Humanities Press, 1981.
Poulet, Georges. "Phenomenology of Reading." *New Literary History*, I:1 (Fall 1969), pp.
53–68.
Powers, Joseph M., S.J. *Eucharistic Theology*. New York: Herder and Herder, 1967.
Quartermain, Peter. " 'I am different, let not a gloss embroil you'." *Paideuma* 9:1 (Spring
1980), pp. 203–210.
———. " 'Not at all surprised by science': Louis Zukofsky's First Half of '*A*' — 9." In
Louis Zukofsky: Man and Poet, ed. Carroll F. Terrell, pp. 203–225. Orono:
National Poetry Foundation, 1979.
Quilligan, Maureen. *The Language of Allegory: Defining the Genre*. Ithaca: Cornell Univ.
Press, 1979.

Quinet, Edgar. *Oeuvres complètes*. Paris: Pagnerre, 1857.

Rabaté, Jean-Michel. "Lapsus ex machina." In *Poststructuralist Joyce*, ed. Derek Attridge and Daniel Ferrer, pp. 79–101. Cambridge: Cambridge Univ. Press, 1984.

———. "The Silence of the Sirens." In *James Joyce: The Centennial Symposium*, ed. Morris Beja, Phillip Herring, Maurice Harmon and David Norris, pp. 82–88. Urbana: Univ. of Illinois Press, 1986.

Reynolds, Mary T. *Joyce and Dante: The Shaping Imagination*. Princeton: Princeton Univ. Press, 1981.

Ricoeur, Paul. *Hermeneutics and the Human Sciences*. Trans. and ed. John B. Thompson. Cambridge: Cambridge Univ. Press, 1981.

———. *The Rule of Metaphor*. Trans. Robert Czerny, Kathleen McLaughlin and John Costello, S.J. Toronto: Univ. of Toronto Press, 1977.

Riffaterre, Michael. *Semiotics of Poetry*. Bloomington: Indiana Univ. Press, 1978.

Riquelme, John Paul. *Teller and Tale in Joyce's Fiction: Oscillating Perspectives*. Baltimore: Johns Hopkins Univ. Press, 1983.

Rosen, Charles. *Schoenberg*. London: Marion Boyars, 1976.

Saldívar, Ramón. *Figural Language in the Novel: The Flowers of Speech from Cervantes to Joyce*. Princeton: Princeton Univ. Press, 1984.

Scheub, Harold. "Body and Image in Oral Performance." *New Literary History* 8 (1977), pp. 345–67.

———. "Oral Narrative Process and the Use of Models." *New Literary History* 6 (1974), pp. 353–77.

Schillebeeckx, Edward, O.P. *The Eucharist*. Trans. N. D. Smith. New York: Sheed and Ward, 1968.

Scholes, Robert, and Richard M. Kain, eds. *The Workshop of Dedalus*. Evanston: Northwestern Univ. Press, 1965.

Searle, John R. *Expression and Meaning*. Cambridge: Cambridge Univ. Press, 1979.

Seay, Albert. *Music in the Medieval World*. 2d ed. Englewood Cliffs, N.J.: Prentice-Hall, 1975.

Silverman, Kaja. *The Subject of Semiotics*. New York: Oxford Univ. Press, 1983.

Simson, Otto von. *The Gothic Cathedral*. New York: Pantheon, 1956.

Smith, John B. *Imagery and the Mind of Stephen Dedalus: A Computer-Assisted Study of Joyce's "A Portrait of the Artist as a Young Man."* Lewisburg: Bucknell Univ. Press, 1980.

Spearing, A. C. *Medieval Dream-Poetry*. Cambridge: Cambridge Univ. Press, 1976.

Sperry, R. W. "Orderly Function with Disordered Structure." In *Principles of Self-Organization*, ed. Heinz von Foerster and George W. Zopf, Jr., pp. 279–89. New York: Pergamon Press, 1962.

Steiner, Peter. "The Conceptual Basis of Prague Structuralism." In *Sound, Sign and Meaning: Quinquagenary of the Prague Linguistic Circle*, ed. Ladislaw Matejka, pp. 372–77. Ann Arbor: Michigan Slavic Contributions no. 6, 1976.

Steiner, Wendy. *The Colors of Rhetoric: Problems in the Relation between Modern Literature and Painting*. Chicago: Univ. of Chicago Press, 1982.

Stevens, John. *Words and Music in the Middle Ages: Song, Narrative, Dance and Drama, 1050–1350*. Cambridge: Cambridge Univ. Press, 1985.

Stoïanova, Ivanka. *Geste-texte-musique*. Paris: Inédit, 1978.

Stravinsky, Igor. *Poetics of Music in the Form of Six Lessons*. Trans. Arthur Knodel and Ingolf Dahl. Cambridge: Cambridge Univ. Press, 1970.

Strunk, Oliver, ed. *Source Readings in Music History*. New York: Norton, 1950.

Sullivan, Kevin. *Joyce among the Jesuits*. New York: Columbia Univ. Press, 1958.

Tagliacozzo, Giorgio. "Epilogue." In *Giambattista Vico: An International Symposium*, ed. Giorgio Tagliacozzo and Hayden White, pp. 610–13. Baltimore: Johns Hopkins Univ. Press, 1969.

———, and Margherita Frankel. "Progress in Art? A Vichian Answer." In *Vico: Past and*

Present, ed. Giorgio Tagliacozzo, pp. 238–51. Atlantic Highlands, N. J.: Humanities Press, 1981.

Thom, René. *Structural Stability and Morphogenesis*. Trans. D. H. Fowler. Reading, Mass.: W. A. Benjamin, 1975.

Thrane, James R. "Joyce's Sermon on Hell: Its Sources and Backgrounds." *Modern Philology* 57 (1960), pp. 177–98.

Ulmer, Gregory L. *Applied Grammatology: Post(e)-Pedagogy from Jacques Derrida to Joseph Beuys*. Baltimore: Johns Hopkins Univ. Press, 1985.

Vance, Eugene. "Mervelous Signals: Poetics, Sign Theory, and Politics in Chaucer's *Troilus*." *New Literary History* X:2 (Winter 1979), pp. 293–337.

———. "The modernity of the Middle Ages in the future." *Romanic Review* 64 (1973), pp. 140–51.

———. "Pas de Trois: Narrative, Hermeneutics, and Structure in Medieval Poetics." In *Interpretation of Narrative*, ed. Mario J. Valdés and Owen J. Miller, pp. 118–34. Toronto: Univ. of Toronto Press, 1978.

Verene, Donald Phillip. "The New Art of Narration: Vico and the Muses." *New Vico Studies* (1983), pp. 21–38.

———. "Vico's Philosophical Originality." In *Vico: Past and Present*, ed. Georgio Tagliacozzo, pp. 127–43. Atlantic Highlands, N. J.: Humanities Press, 1981.

———. "Vico's Philosophy of Imagination." In *Vico and Contemporary Thought*, ed. Giorgio Tagliacozzo, Michael Mooney, and Donald Phillip Verene, pp. 20–39. London: Macmillan, 1980.

———. *Vico's Science of Imagination*. Ithaca: Cornell Univ. Press, 1981.

Vico, Giambattista. *The Autobiography of*. Trans. Max Harold Fisch and Thomas Goddard Bergin. Ithaca: Cornell Univ. Press, 1944.

———. *The New Science*. Trans. from the 3d ed. by Thomas Goddard Bergin and Max Harold Fisch. Ithaca: Cornell Univ. Press, 1948.

———. *Selected Writings*. Ed. and trans. Leon Pompa. Cambridge: Cambridge Univ. Press, 1982.

Vinaver, Eugène. *The Rise of Romance*. Oxford: Oxford Univ. Press, 1971.

Walzl, Florence L. "The Liturgy of the Epiphany Season and the Epiphanies of Joyce." *PMLA* LXXX:4 (Sept. 1965), pp. 436–50.

Warburton, William. *The Divine Legation of Moses Demonstrated (1765)*. New York: Garland Publishing, 1978.

Weir, Lorraine. "The Choreography of Gesture: Marcel Jousse and *Finnegans Wake*." *James Joyce Quarterly* 14:3 (Spring 1977), pp. 313–25.

———. "Eyespeech and Object: Joyce's Visual Cycle." Ph.D. diss., University College, Dublin, 1971.

———. "Permutations of Ireland's Eye in *Finnegans Wake*." *Canadian Journal of Irish Studies* 5:2 (1978), pp. 23–30.

———. "Phoenix Park in *Finnegans Wake*." *Irish University Review* 5:2 (Autumn 1975), pp. 230–49.

Wilkins, Peter. "Transformations of the Circle: An Exploration of the Post-Encylopedic Text." M. A. thesis, Univ. of British Columbia, 1985.

Williams, Drid. "The Arms and Hands, with Special Reference to an Anglo-Saxon Sign System." *Semiotica* 21:1/2 (1977), pp. 23–73.

Wittgenstein, Ludwig. *Philosophical Investigations*. Trans. G. E. M. Anscombe. Oxford: Basil Blackwell, 1968.

Worringer, Wilhelm. *Form in Gothic*. Ed. and trans. Herbert Read. Rev. ed. New York: Schocken, 1964.

Yates, Frances. *The Art of Memory*. Harmondsworth: Peregrine Books, 1969.

Zukofsky, Louis. *"A."* Berkeley: Univ. of California Press, 1978.

———. *All*. New York: Norton, 1965.

———. *Bottom: On Shakespeare*. Berkeley: Univ. of California Press, 1987.

————. *It Was*. Kyoto: Origin Press, 1961.

————. *Prepositions*. 2d ed. Berkeley: Univ. of California Press, 1981.

————, and René Taupin. "The Writing of Guillaume Apollinaire: (II)—Le Poète Ressus-
        cite; (III)—& Cie." *Westminster Magazine* XXIII:1 (Spring 1934), pp. 7–46.

Zumthor, Paul. *Langue et techniques poétiques à l'époque romane, XIe-XIIIe siècles*. Paris:
        Klincksieck, 1963.

————. *Speaking of the Middle Ages*. Trans. Sarah White. Lincoln: Univ. of Nebraska Press,
        1986.

INDEX